Improving
Higher Education
Environments for Adults

Nancy K. Schlossberg
Ann Q. Lynch
Arthur W. Chickering

Improving
Higher Education
Environments for Adults

Responsive Programs
and Services
from Entry to Departure

Jossey-Bass Publishers
San Francisco • London • 1989

IMPROVING HIGHER EDUCATION ENVIRONMENTS FOR ADULTS
Responsive Programs and Services from Entry to Departure
by Nancy K. Schlossberg, Ann Q. Lynch, and Arthur W. Chickering

Copyright © 1989 by: Jossey-Bass Inc., Publishers
350 Sansome Street
San Francisco, California 94104
&
Jossey-Bass Limited
28 Banner Street
London EC1Y 8QE

Library of Congress Cataloging-in-Publication Data

Schlossberg, Nancy K., date.
Improving higher education environments for adults.

(The Jossey-Bass higher education series)
Bibliography: p.
Includes index.
1. Universities and colleges—United States—Adminis-
tration. 2. Education, Higher—United States. 3. Adult
education—United States. I. Lynch, Ann Q., date.
II. Chickering, Arthur W., date. III. Title.
IV. Series.
LB2341.S28   1989   378.73   88-32049
ISBN 1-55542-136-9

Manufactured in the United States of America

The paper in this book meets the guidelines for
permanence and durability of the Committee on
Production Guidelines for Book Longevity of the
Council on Library Resources.

JACKET DESIGN BY WILLI BAUM

FIRST EDITION

Code 8909

The Jossey-Bass
Higher Education Series

Consulting Editor
Student Services

Ursula Delworth
University of Iowa

Contents

Preface

"Alterations as usual while business is in progress" reads the new sign posted on campuses all over the country; it will be up for some time to come. After some brief bursts of innovation during the late 1960s and early 1970s, sharp reductions in financial support drove most institutions back toward traditional approaches. According to a popular conception, colleges and universities, like mountains and graveyards, are impervious to outside forces and impossible to change. But now, just as graveyards and mountains succumb to bulldozers and dynamite when throughways must be built, so higher education is undergoing significant changes in the face of irresistible social forces.

One of the most important forces behind these changes is the sharp increase in the number of adults seeking higher education. During the 1970s adult learners accounted for almost half of the enrollment growth. Current projections suggest that by 1990 there will be more people aged twenty-six or over than eighteen- to twenty-five-year-olds pursuing undergraduate education.

Adult life span continues to lengthen. Life expectancy for men who have reached age fifty is now seventy-eight; for women, eighty-three. At present there are thirty thousand people in the United States over one hundred years old, and by 2050 the average life expectancy will actually be one hundred (Siegel and Taeuber, 1986, p. 98). This revolutionary trend forces us to rethink familiar life patterns and expectations about old age. Gunhild Hagestad (1986) suggests that pressuring children to begin preschool earlier, rushing young people through high school and college, and pushing them immediately into graduate school is senseless. Instead, we should be looking for ways to give students a sound preparation over a longer period of time.

Worklife expectancy has also increased sharply, and not only as a result of increased life expectancy. As we have changed from an agrarian and industrial society to an information- and knowledge-based society, injuries and illnesses contracted in the workplace have plummeted. At the turn of the century, men could expect to work until they were forty-eight and women until they were fifty. Now worklife expectancy extends into the sixties, and new retirement legislation legitimizes continued employment until age seventy or beyond. The one life/one career pattern that has prevailed until now is giving way to a pattern of pursuing multiple careers and diverse life-styles.

Post–World War II baby boomers are approaching middle age. There are too many people in that age group for the available jobs. "The baby boom generation is in danger of 'plateauing' in the workplace . . . ," says Anthony Carnevale (1987, p. 4). It is "the generation with the highest expectations for wages, for fulfilment in work, for promotions, and for quality of working life. . . . We are on a collision course with the American economy in terms of its ability to supply those things to us, and that creates both political and economic ramifications. In response, one thing people can do is go to school." So it is not surprising that this population wave is surging toward higher education and will continue to do so.

The implications for educators are enormous. Our society has assigned education, work, and leisure "sequentially to the life stages of youth, adulthood, and old age" (Moody, 1986, p. 191). Our task is to change such newly coined phrases as *lifelong learning, recurring education,* and *blended life pattern* into reality in order to meet the needs of a population that is growing older. Moody writes: "What role can learning play in preparing individuals at every stage of life for a society where most people can expect to live to old age? These challenges will demand a change in the relation between education and the stages of life, a transformation as far-reaching as the 'discovery of childhood' in the nineteenth century" (p. 192).

This demographic revolution will create an educational revolution; in many ways and in many institutions, in fact, it already has. As a consequence, higher education professionals will be forced to revolutionize their work. To deal effectively with the older students will require understanding of their motives, the realities they face, and their orientations toward family, work, and citizenship. It will also require understanding what competence and knowledge they seek and the ways in which they learn.

Unfortunately, much of the relevant information is dispersed throughout a variety of literature not ordinarily accessible to college and university administrators, faculty members, student educational services administrators, and student development professionals. Similarly, although there has been a good bit of experimentation with new alternatives, it has been carried out in an irregular and piecemeal fashion by the nation's two- and four-year institutions.

What we need now in higher education is a comprehensive, integrated approach to create an educational environment responsive to the diverse characteristics, conditions, and needs of the adults trying to use the rich resources that higher education in the United States has to offer. We do recognize that some institutions have special units for adult learners: adult degree programs, returning students programs, minicolleges, or university colleges. But now, sufficient research has been conducted and enough well-tested alternatives are available that a comprehensive approach can be firmly anchored in both theory and practice.

Improving Higher Education Environments for Adults addresses that need. In this book we provide certain key conceptual frameworks for understanding adults as learners and as individuals in transition, each of whom needs to be treated as someone who matters. We assert that educators need to become what Donald Schön (1983) has termed *reflective practitioners*. Vignettes about recent adult learners drawn from our experiences flesh out the conceptual framework. And we make concrete recommendations that can help adults to find their way into our institutions, to make the most of their educational and personal experiences, and to successfully realize their aspirations.

Audience

In this book, we recommend that certain perspectives and concrete steps be taken. For these to succeed, there must be effective collaboration among academic administrators and student educational services administrators, as well as sound day-to-day working relationships among department heads, faculty members, and student development professionals. This book, therefore, is pertinent to the work of all college and university administrators. It also will be useful for those faculty members who recognize the importance of furthering student learning outside the classroom and who take seriously their roles as advisers, mentors, and models. Student development professionals, who carry most direct responsibility for many of the types of programs discussed here, will find a wide range of suggestions for improving the quality of educational activities, not only for adult learners with diverse aims and backgrounds but also for traditional-age students.

Overview of the Contents

Chapter One sets the stage by describing some of the key dilemmas facing adult learners and educational institutions. In this chapter we also set forth the two basic themes that guide our recommendations for change: an emphasis on education as opposed to service and the model of the reflective practitioner as opposed to that of the authority figure.

Chapter Two supplies the key conceptual frameworks, based on pertinent research and theory, that structure our views and recommendations.

In Chapters Three through Eight we address the three major areas of adult learners' experience during their higher education careers: first, moving into the institution, second, moving through learning and personal development experiences at the institution, and third, moving on and building on their experiences. Each of these areas is explored in two chapters: the first (which sets the stage) contains vignettes drawn from real life; the second provides concrete recommendations. The vignettes illustrate some of the major problems experienced by adult learners as they try to explore, use, and build on institutional resources and educational opportunities. The recommendations deal with setting up introductory, supporting, and culminating programs to respond to adult learners' most important needs.

Chapters Nine and Ten describe some of the payoffs these alternative programs can bring to both learners and institutions.

Chapter Eleven offers strategies for institutional change, in particular new ingredients in graduate education to help future higher education professionals provide educational programs responsive to the needs of adult learners.

The reflexes of many administrators, faculty members, and student development professionals have long been conditioned by traditional full-time, resident, eighteen- to twenty-five-year-old undergraduates. Those reflexes and the attitudes associated with them are now becoming increasingly inadequate—often downright dysfunctional—where adult learners are concerned. Surely, though, we can recondition our thinking and expand our repertory of reactions to include more thoughtful alternatives—alternatives responsive to the accelerating societal and demographic changes that higher education must face in the coming decades.

Acknowledgments

Writing this book has been a true collaboration. We have shared enthusiasm, discouragement, and work. And we have come through the process with strengthened caring for each other. The finished book is the result of the efforts of many people. Ursula Delworth, a friend, a colleague, and a Jossey-Bass consulting editor, read every chapter and every revision with the proper balance of support and challenge. Lucy Blanton's ability to turn the work of three authors into a cohesive whole was a relief and joy. We greatly appreciate both Betty Bowers's ability to integrate into one final draft the work of three authors located at three different universities and her commitment to the project and its deadlines. Nancy Matthews provided valuable help in preparing preliminary chapters. Many of the applications for this book were developed through the Higher Education for Adult Mental Health Project (sponsored by the National Institute of Mental Health) and the Higher Learning for Diverse Adults Project (sponsored by the Fund for the Improvement of Postsecondary Education through the Center for the Study of Higher Education, College of Education, Memphis State University). Many interviews were arranged through the Returning Students Program, University of Maryland, College Park, and the Office of Academic Advising, University College, University of Maryland. We thank the many colleagues who provided information and took the time to read our drafts of the manuscript. Most important are the experiences we have had with adult learners, which have confirmed our notion that the best is truly yet to be.

November 1988   Nancy K. Schlossberg
                                          College Park, Maryland

                                          Ann Q. Lynch
                                          Boca Raton, Florida

                                          Arthur W. Chickering
                                          Fairfax, Virginia

The Authors

Nancy K. Schlossberg is professor of counseling and personnel services in the College of Education at the University of Maryland, College Park. She received her B.A. degree (1951) from Barnard College in sociology and her Ed.D. degree (1961) from Teachers College, Columbia University, in counseling. She has served on the faculties of Wayne State University, Howard University, and Pratt Institute. She was the first woman executive at the American Council on Education, where she established the Office of Women in Higher Education.

Schlossberg's major research activities are in the fields of adult development, adult transitions, and career development. Her books include *Counseling Adults in Transition* (1984) and *Perspectives on Counseling Adults* (1978, with L. Troll and Z. Leibowitz).

Schlossberg holds the position of Fellow in two divisions of the American Psychological Association (APA) and in the Gerontological Society of America. In 1983 she was APA G. Stanley Hall Lecturer on Adult Development and was named a Distinguished Scholar at the University of Maryland. In 1987 she received the National Career Development Association's Eminent Career Award.

Ann Q. Lynch is associate professor of counselor education in the Department of Professional and Human Services,

xvii

College of Education, Florida Atlantic University. She received her B.A. degree (1953) from Duke University in mathematics and education and both her M.Ed. degree (1965) in counseling and guidance and her Ed.D. degree (1968) in personnel services from the University of Florida. She served as president of the Association for Psychological Type-Southeast and the Florida Association of Women Deans, Administrators and Counselors, and she was nominated to *Who's Who in American Women.*

Lynch's main subjects of research have been in higher education, counseling, preventive mental health, psychological type, and adult learners. Her experience with adult learners has included serving as executive director of the Higher Education for Adult Mental Health Project, sponsored by the National Institute of Mental Health through the Center for the Study of Higher Education, College of Education, Memphis State University. Her publications include several chapters and articles: "Comprehensive Counseling and Support Programs for Adult Learners" in *New Perspectives on Counseling Adults* (1984, with A. W. Chickering); "Model Programs to Serve Adult Learners" in *Phi Delta Kappan* (1985, with R. Doyle and A. W. Chickering); "Type Development and Student Development" in *Applications of the Myers-Briggs Type Indicator in Higher Education* (1987); and "Individual Enhancement as the Personal Purpose of Education" in *Social Goals and Educational Reform* (1988, with A. W. Chickering).

Lynch has also served as associate professor of counseling and personnel services at Memphis State University and as university counseling psychologist at the University of Florida.

Arthur W. Chickering is a professor in the Department of Educational Leadership and Human Development, College of Education and Human Services, George Mason University. He received his B.A. degree (1950) in modern comparative literature from Wesleyan University, his M.A. degree (1951) in teaching English from the Graduate School of Education, Harvard University, and his Ph.D. degree (1959) in school psychology from Teachers College, Columbia University.

Chickering began his career in higher education as psychology teacher and coordinator of evaluation at Goddard College from 1959 to 1965. From 1965 to 1969 he directed the Project on Student Development in Small Colleges, a four-year action research project on interactions between educational practices, college environments, and student development. During 1969–70 he was a Visiting Scholar at the American Council on Education; and from 1970 to 1977, as the founding vice-president for academic affairs, he played a major role in creating Empire State College. From 1977 to 1988 he was distinguished professor and director of the Center for the Study of Higher Education in the College of Education, Memphis State University.

Chickering is the author of many publications, including *Education and Identity, Commuting Versus Resident Students*, and *The Modern American College*. He has received the E. F. Lindquist Award from the American Educational Research Association for his studies of college impacts on student development, the Outstanding Service Award from the National Association of Student Personnel Administrators, and the Distinguished Contribution to Knowledge Award from the American College Personnel Association. He has chaired the boards and been a board member of the American Association for Higher Education, the Association for the Study of Higher Education, and the Council for Adult and Experiential Learning. He has received an honorary degree in humane letters from the University of New Hampshire and the E. F. Newman Award from Lourdes College, and he has served on the editorial boards of the *Journal of Higher Education* and the *Journal of Higher Education Administration.*

Improving
Higher Education
Environments for Adults

Applying New Perspectives
to Educating Adults

Adults learn everywhere—at supermarkets, in front of television, at church, work, home, and school. Aslanian and Brickell (1980) point to the increasing number of adults whose engagement in new learnings is triggered by transitions; Cross (1981) outlines the many settings in which adults learn, with details about the motivators and barriers to such learnings; Barton (1982) describes the problems and possibilities of connecting adult learners with learning opportunities; and Hodgkinson (1983) points out that 75 percent of adults involved in formal education participate in a "second system of postsecondary education" that takes place in industry, the military, government, and voluntary agencies. Clearly adults are engaged in learning, yet for many adult learners, higher education is not the setting of choice. Why?

We believe that the character of the adult experience and the character of educational institutions are out of synchrony. A dilemma exists: Adults are heterogeneous, and as they age, their life patterns become more divergent; meanwhile, bureaucracies tend to be rigid and hierarchical, in many cases encouraging dependency rather than autonomy.

Adults as Learners

Is the adult learner someone who has been out of school for several years and has decided to return? Is the adult learner a person who decides to change direction, to study law, for example? Is this individual aged fifty or thirty, experienced or inexperienced? Is there a distinct way in which adults learn? In other words, is an adult learner a definable entity?

The answer is both yes and no. Yes—adult learners have special needs and capacities that distinguish them from traditional-age students, as evidenced by the growing number of articles and books on the subject. No—adult learners are a heterogeneous group, just as younger learners are.

Either answer gives rise to difficulties. To say the adult learner is a distinctive category makes age the central variable, so that one might disregard other important characteristics of the adult learner or, worse, conclude that some people are simply too old to learn, which feeds the ageism of our society. But denying the existence of adult learners as a distinct category may well lead to overlooking some of the special needs of that population, needs that should be addressed by educators and policy makers.

Adult learners differ. We know that some are bright, others dull; some are knowledgeable, others ignorant; some are energetic, others apathetic; some are anxious, others self-confident; some process information in a rigid manner, others are able to handle and digest complex, ambiguous material. They vary in age, and place in the life span, and social class. We can use three categories of all this variability—age, role, and learning capacity—to begin to describe the character of the adult experience, of adult learners.

Age. To what degree can we differentiate people by age? Some theorists see chronological age itself as the defining variable. For example, according to Levinson and others (1978), the issues of a twenty-year-old are not the same as those of a forty-year-old. Levinson links adult behavior to age and describes six distinct phases or stages that emphasize sequentiality and similarity in the adult experience. This stage approach has been widely noted in both the scholarly and popular press. Opposing the stage theorists are such scholars as Bernice Neugarten who analyze the complexities, varieties, and heterogeneities of adulthood, look at continuity and change across the course of life, and are more concerned with lack of predictability, with the surprises or unexpected things that can happen at any age to anyone. Neugarten concludes that people grow old differently, and that the range of their differences becomes greater, not narrower (Neugarten and Neugarten, 1982).

We cannot assume that adult lives follow an orderly, linear process. The process, in actuality, is circular: Careers are interrupted and started, and individuals make loops as their lives unfold. Examples of such loops are the woman who becomes a college freshman at age forty-five or the man who starts a new family at age fifty. People engage in renewal activities all through adulthood; for example, in a given class we might find three grandmothers ranging in age from fifty to eighty. We are witnessing a demographic change in which four- and five-generation families may become the norm, in which one can be both a grandmother and a granddaughter simultaneously. The fact that one is a grandmother, mother, or wife should not be the end of inquiry; it says nothing about whether a person is ending or beginning a career. Furthermore, by sight, one cannot always tell the difference between people who are thirty or fifty—dress is not so very different, nor are hairstyles. Fifty- and sixty-year-olds now wear jeans to class.

It is tempting, but wrong, to assume that appearance or age can provide an understanding of what people think or feel or how they behave. Many educators talk and think about the adult learner as if there were such a recognizable entity with a set way of learning, for whom there is a set way of teaching. There is, instead, a fluid life course, what Patricia Cross (1981) calls the blended life pattern, in which a person's life does not necessarily follow a prescribed course—meaning it is not assumed that one will go to school, work, marry, and have children in that order. The facts about adult students that count are really quite different from many widely held assumptions. People of all ages are heterogeneous and diverse, but as people age, their idiosyncratic life experiences and different commitments produce much more variability, not less.

Role. Attention needs to be given to the particular adult learner's involvement in other roles (functions) and activities as we try to understand his or her attitude toward and response to education. One useful way of looking at role involvement is through the classification scheme proposed by Lowenthal [now Fiske], Thurnher, and Chiriboga (1975).

In the first phase of their longitudinal study of 216 middle-class and lower-middle-class men and women living in the San Francisco area, they computed social role involvement scores. Subjects were divided into high school seniors, newlyweds, middle-aged parents, and preretirement couples, groups that face major life transition. The score was based on the number of roles in which the individual was engaged (spouse, child, parent, grandparent, sibling, friend, organization member), weighted by the frequency of participation in that role (number of activities carried out jointly with spouse). From these scores emerged four life-styles: *simplistic*—few roles and a limited range of activities; *diffuse*—few roles but a varied activity pattern; *focused*—many roles but a narrow range of activities; and *complex*—many roles and a variety of activities.

Clear sex differences emerged at some stages. The life-style of high school girls tended to be diffuse, whereas that of high school boys tended to be complex. Both men and women at the newlywed stage exhibited a complex life-style. The majority of midlife men had a focused life-style, "reflecting no doubt their preoccupation with establishing maximum financial security (and, for some, occupational status) before retirement" (pp. 13–15). The life-style of midlife women, however, tended to be simplistic. The authors' explanation is worth noting: "Perhaps these women had withdrawn to retool for the next, post-parental stage" (p. 15). At the preretirement stage, the number of men with a focused life-style decreased, and the number with a simplistic or complex life-style increased; the number of women with a simplistic life-style decreased, and the number with a diffused or focused life-style increased. The life-styles of the sexes tended to converge at the preretirement stage. It should be emphasized, however, that role involvement is not dependent on sex or age. Men and women at any stage can exhibit any of the four life-styles.

A second useful way of looking at role involvement is through a typology proposed by Campbell, Wilson, and Hanson

(1980). The typology, directly related to adult learners, was developed in a study of undergraduates aged twenty-five and over at the University of Texas in 1979. On the basis of time spent in various activities (such as working at a paying job, doing schoolwork, doing things with the family), these adult learners were classified into five types:

> *Type 1*—Full-time students who were not employed, spent more than forty hours a week with their families, and had little free time.
>
> *Type 2*—Full-time students who were not employed, had few family responsibilities, and had a considerable amount of free time. Over half of this group were single or divorced.
>
> *Type 3*—Part-time students who were employed full time, spent little time with their families, and had considerable free time.
>
> *Type 4*—Full-time students who were not employed, spent little time in family, social, or recreational activities (despite their family ties), spent a great deal of time (an average of over sixty hours a week) on schoolwork, and had little free time. About a third had at least one child at home.
>
> *Type 5*—Part-time students who were employed full time, had signed up for one or two courses, spent a great deal of time in family activities, and had very little free time.

Campbell and his associates found that the five types of adult learners differed "on the degree of difficulty they had in deciding to return to school, and on the kind of problems they had after enrollment" (p. 85).

In a recent study of women's decisions to enroll in college, most women attributed lessening role demands—"children old enough, empty nest, adequate child care, breathing space, workload down, lost job"—as those factors enabling them to return to or enter school (Mohney and Anderson, 1988, p. 273).

Thus, for adult learners, role involvements influence decisions to pursue education, to what degree, and in what manner.

Learning Capacity. Adults fear that as they age their learning capacity will diminish. We need to spread the word that the laboratory differences in intelligence between young and old persons have little relevance as an explanation of how people function in everyday life (Baltes and Reese, 1984). A nineteen-year-old boy might remember a list of names more accurately and faster than his sixty-year-old father; however, the father is more likely to successfully arrange for a competent plumber whose rates are reasonable to come to the house at a convenient time in the immediate future.

Even more encouraging is the work of Baltes and Willis (1982), which examines situations or environmental conditions in which older people's intellectual functioning can be modified through training. In one study, they develop an intervention designed to improve problem-solving abilities; in another, they train older adults to change their performance on a test. Both studies provide "evidence for intra-individual plasticity." They conclude that "older individuals generally live in a context of cognitive deprivation" and that "relatively short-term behavioral interventions result in significant improvement" (p. 535).

Similarly, Kohn (1980) demonstrates that learning capacity may increase, rather than decrease, over time in certain contexts. Kohn asserts that substantive complexity is a central structural characteristic of the work experience. He writes, "If two men of equivalent intellectual flexibility were to start their careers in jobs different in substantive complexity, the man in the more complex job would be likely to outstrip the other in further intellectual growth. This, in time, might lead to his attaining jobs of greater complexity, further affecting his intellectual growth. Meantime, the man in the less complex job would develop intellectually at a slower pace, perhaps not at all, and in the extreme case might even decline in his intellectual functioning. As a result, small differences might lead to increasing differences in intellectual development" (p. 203). Adult learners add a new complex environment and set of challenges to their lives when they go to college. Kohn's work helps us understand the dramatic increases in learning capacity they often experience.

Stephen Brookfield (1986) suggests that we are barraged

by myths and assumptions about how adults learn. He recognizes the temptation to develop principles about adult learning that are based on folklore, such as "All adults prefer self-planned, self-paced projects." What Brookfield's research shows, however, is that the distinguishing feature of adult learning is the adult's capacity for critical reflection—the ability to identify one's underlying assumptions and consider alternative ways of behaving and living.

Institutions as Bureaucracies

During lunch with an adult learner who is a mature woman, we asked her, "What does it feel like to be an adult student?" After a moment's hesitation, she answered, "I'm a bag lady. I shuffle around the school in winter with two bags—one for books and one for boots. I have no place to go to sit, to receive messages, to make phone calls. I am dependent upon professors letting me come into their offices. I have no way to hear if my child is ill. I have no dignity."

Three major ingredients of current higher education emerge from her story: the dependent status of adult learners, their marginality, and the bureaucratic structure of colleges and universities. Students, traditionally thought of as children and young adults, are assumed to be dependent on authorities and in need of expert guidance from scholars and bureaucrats. Adults, traditionally thought of as in charge of their own and others' lives, are assumed to be trying to maintain control over their lives, to preserve their independence. Thus, when we put the terms *adult* and *student* together, we sense a paradox—and educational institutions tend to neglect *adult* and emphasize *student*.

A study of male professionals in work organizations is relevant. Dalton, Thompson, and Price (1977) identified the potential career progression for professional men. At the start of their careers, professional men serve in apprentice-like roles and are psychologically dependent. As they move up the ladder, they become colleagues and psychologically independent. Next, they are seen as mentors, responding to the psychological dependency of others. In the final career step, they are sponsors and are psychologically involved with issues of power.

The educational bureaucracy originally served only young adults who were in apprentice-like roles dealing with dependency issues. Older adults who begin school or return to school are usually colleagues, mentors, or sponsors in their families, jobs, and communities. Suddenly these adults are Bill, Joe, and Anna, and those in charge, sometimes younger and with less experience, are "Professor" and "Doctor." No wonder many adult learners find it difficult to regress from an independent and more powerful status to become apprentices again, dependent on faculty and administrators. In addition, educational institutions often subject students to an authoritarian, hierarchical bureaucracy operated by faculty and administrators. Curriculum content, course schedules and structures, grading, and policies on attendance, discipline, and financial aid are generally set with little or no participation by students—old or young. Merton (1957a), in his chapter titled "Bureaucratic Structure and Personality," discusses the hierarchical nature of bureaucracy. The structure that makes bureaucracy work, with specified obligations and privileges that are defined in very specific ways, also contains its "dysfunctions." And the main one is a bureaucracy's inability to adapt to new conditions, in this case, the changing learner population.

The needs of adults and the character of colleges diverge: Adults want to feel central, not marginal; competent, not childish; independent, not dependent; colleges and universities rely on rigid rules, regulations, and policies. As a consequence, adults and educational institutions are out of sync.

Perspective Shifts

If the adult learners in our institutions are to flourish and take charge of their own existences, create their own futures, become powerfully effective workers, parents, and citizens, fundamental shifts in perspective are needed: from a services approach to an educational one, and from a treatment orientation to a preventive mental health one. We argue, too, for numerous modifications and additions to the typical entering, supporting, and culminating programs for students at most colleges and universities. But neither the basic shifts in orientation nor more detailed changes can be created, nurtured, sustained, and improved without a posture toward ourselves as professionals and toward our own practices that is consistent with the orientation we suggest.

Better than anyone else to date, Donald Schön, in *The Reflective Practitioner* (1983), exemplifies the professional attitudes required to create and re-create an educational institution in which adult learners will be well educated. Schön's seminal perspectives on professional practice are highly consistent with our orientation toward educational services; they are also consistent with the conceptual frameworks we espouse concerning assessment, institutional changes, and continued professional development.

Schön (who uses *he, him,* and *his* as inclusive pronouns) frames the issue like this:

> Within the dominant tradition which has grown up over the past 400 years, the professional's claim to extraordinary knowledge is rooted in techniques and theories derived from scientific research undertaken for the most part in institutions of higher learning. The status of professional experts, their claims to social mandate, autonomy, and license, are based on the powerful ideas of Technical Rationality and the technological programs. There is no more vivid sign of the persistence of these ideas than the hunger for technique which is so characteristic of students of the professions in this decade.
>
> In the traditional professional-client contract, the professional acts as though he agreed to deliver his services to the client to the limits of his special competence, to respect the confidences granted to him, and not to misuse for his own benefit the special powers given him within the boundaries of the

relationship. The client acts as though he agreed, in turn, to accept the professional's authority in his special field, to submit to the professional's ministrations, and to pay for services rendered. In a familiar psychological extension of the informal contract, the client agrees to show deference to the professional. He agrees not to challenge the professional's judgment or to demand explanations beyond the professional's willingness to give them. In short, he agrees to behave as though he respected the professional's autonomy as an expert [pp. 288, 292].

Ivan Illich and others articulate a radical critique of this tradition. This critique says that professionals maintain a mystique of expertise as a vehicle for social control of the poor, the oppressed, minorities, and the like. This critique typically goes on to assert that when professional expertise is demystified, the realities fall far short of the claims. These critics advocate what Schön calls "a new breed of citizen-practitioners" who can take over professional turf. Schön does not agree with this critique. He responds by saying, "Unreflective practitioners are equally limited and destructive whether they label themselves as professionals or counterprofessionals" (p. 290).

Schön describes the reflective practitioner thus:

Just as reflective practice takes the form of a reflective conversation with the situation, so the reflective practitioner's relation with his client takes the form of a literally reflective conversation. Here the professional recognizes that his technical expertise is embedded in a context of meanings. He attributes to his clients, as well as to himself, a capacity to mean, know, and plan. He recognizes that his actions may have different meanings for his client, which means that he needs often to reflect anew on what he knows. . . . There is the recognition that one's expertise is a way of looking at something which was once constructed and may be reconstructed; and there is both readiness and competence to explore its meaning in the experience of the client. The reflective practitioner tries to discover the limits of his expertise through reflective conversation with the client [pp. 295–296].

This perspective on professional practice has fundamental consequences for the formal and informal contracts established between practitioners and clients. The client is not expected to believe in or to accept the professional's authority and expertise; suspension of disbelief is the only requirement. But the client does agree to look at the situation, try to understand it, let the professional know when it is not being understood, and give accurate reports as to what seems effective and what does not. The professional agrees to perform as competently as possible, to help the client understand the advice being rendered and the rationale, evidence, or prior experiences behind it. In addition, the professional agrees to make confrontation by the client easy and to try to learn the meanings specific actions have for the client.

Schön's thinking has profound implications, not only for professional practice but, more important, for our attitudes toward ourselves as professionals and toward our own continued professional growth and personal development. His perspective implies that we must view ourselves as effective agents for our own development and learning. It implies an active interest in self-assessment and an openness to change. It implies a capacity to question existing assumptions, conventions, norms—to call attention to the emperor's rosy skin when others may turn a blind eye, to make a noise when there is a conspiracy of silence, to speak truth to power. When Einstein was asked how he got started on his theory of relativity, he replied, "I questioned an axiom." That's the spirit!

Daniel Boorstin (1987), when retiring as the director of the Library of Congress, said, "The great obstacle to progress is not ignorance but the illusion of knowledge." We professionals in higher education need to take that message to heart.

Traditional socialization, and much of graduate preparation, runs sharply contrary to the fundamental orientation that underlies our recommendations. This socialization is expressed by the historical pervasiveness of the term *student personnel services*, with the emphasis on *services*. We suggest shifting the emphasis to a point where we see ourselves as educators who make fundamentally useful educational contributions pertinent to the educational objectives of our institutions. Such a shift calls for a very different way of thinking about our professional roles, the criteria for program evaluation, the kinds of professional preparation and ongoing professional development required, and the nature of our interactions with students, faculty, and administration. It also means that we must actively work to shift the way our faculty and administrative colleagues see us. But the change must begin at home, with us. The language, self-perceptions, and behaviors of "service" point us in the wrong direction. Until we adopt the language of "education," we will be perpetually peripheral. As an expression of this shift, we recommend a change in terminology, replacing *student personnel services* with *student educational services* and replacing *student personnel professionals* with *student development professionals*. This terminology change already has occurred in some institutions. We recommend its universal adoption.

These perspective shifts, viewing ourselves as reflective practitioners and educators rather than as professionals providing treatment or service, rest on the conceptual orientation that views adults as learners and institutions as educators, where all are involved in learning and living, and all feel they matter.

In Conclusion

In this chapter, we have set the stage for discussion that follows. We make the case that adult learners are heterogeneous and cannot be easily categorized, and that with few exceptions, educational institutions are inflexible bureaucracies. To meet the needs of adult learners, educators in general, and student development professionals in particular, need to change their basic perspective as they view adult learners and educational environments.

Understanding Adults' Life and Learning Transitions

Human development takes place in a social context. Because we are discussing adult learners in educational institutions, our conceptual framework is anchored in two major areas: adult learners and educational environments.

Conceptualizing Adult Learners

Tempting though it is to categorize adult learners just by age, stage, role complexity, cognitive capacity, or learning styles, we subscribe to Neugarten's emphasis on variability, or what she calls "individual fanning out." Neugarten makes the point that individuals in a group of sixty-year-olds are less similar to each other than those in a group of six-year-olds: "As lives grow longer, as the successive choices and commitments accumulate, lives grow different from each other" (1979, p. 891).

What might this diverse and heterogeneous group labeled adult learners have in common? We found that transition theory can be applied to learners young or old, male or female, minority or majority, urban or rural. When an adult thinks about returning to school, does so, and then leaves, he or she is in transition. Most adults returning to school are in either a career or a family transition. Aslanian and Brickell (1980) note that for women, family transitions are the foremost trigger for return-

13

ing to school, with career transitions coming in second. For men it is just the opposite: Career transitions come first and family second. Transitions that prompt a return to school join transitions inherent in the educational process itself. The transitions within education are our focus; these we can understand and, to some extent, guide.

The Transition Framework. Using the transition framework we can conceptualize a group as variable as adult learners. Whether learners are young or old, bright or dull, energetic or apathetic, anxious or self-confident, we can use the framework to assess where they are in their learning experience and what their resources are for coping with it. The framework helps determine a learner's position in the transition process: Is the learner moving into a new situation, moving through it, or moving on? We can also identify each individual's potential strengths and weaknesses for coping with the learning situation or environment.

What are transitions and what is the transition process? Adults returning to school are changing their way of seeing themselves. They are altering their roles, routines, and relationships at home, in the community at large, and in the educational setting. A transition is thus an event (such as returning to school after working for many years) or a nonevent (staying in school over an unusually long period of time without completing a degree) that alters one's roles, relationships, routines, and assumptions (Schlossberg, 1984).

The transition experienced by twenty men and women who return to school after fifteen years will be different for each. What looks like the same transition on the outside will actually vary, depending on the way it alters the individual's life. For one person, returning to school can be a part-time activity in which no other roles are changed. Joe has returned to school but he is still a worker, parent, and church-goer. He has taken on one new role, changed a few assumptions, and changed a few routines. Bill, by contrast, had a full-time professional job and decided to return to school full time, giving up job and salary. In his case, his wife returned to work, and they placed their children in day care—leading to profound changes in roles for all the family. The change in roles, relationships, routines, and assumptions has been much greater for Bill than for Joe.

In spite of enormous individual differences, all adult learners experience transitions in education as a process over time. The transition process extends from the first moment one contemplates returning to school to the time when the experience is complete and integrated into one's life. To understand the transition process in the lives of adult learners, we must break it down into three main parts: *moving into* the learning environment, *moving through* it, and preparing to leave, or *moving on.* Bridges (1980) discusses the transition process as having three phases: endings, neutral zones, and beginnings. We can thus view the task of moving in as ending something else and the task of leaving as an opportunity for a new beginning.

A transition is like a trip. Preparation for the trip, the actual trip, and its aftermath all elicit feelings and reactions. But feelings at the start of a trip differ from reactions to it later. In the same way, reactions to a transition continue to change as the transition is integrated into one's life.

In any transition, the first stage is moving in. People who move into a new situation, whether a new marriage, the Peace Corps, or an educational environment, have some common agendas and needs. They need to become familiar with the rules, regulations, norms, and expectations of the new system. Many institutions devote a great deal of time to orientation, a process designed to help individuals know what is expected of them. In a theoretical discussion of employees moving into organizations, Louis (1980) proposes that employees should have clear expectations about what is in store and be socialized into the explicit and implicit norms, roles, and culture of the organization. Previous research focusing on "recruit turnover" and "organizational socialization" (p. 226) suggests to Louis that to minimize employee turnover, more systematic attention is necessary when employees enter an organization. By substituting learners for workers, we can extrapolate from Louis's work: "Turnover" occurs because of unrealistic, inflated, or unmet expectations that are not addressed at the beginning of a transition.

Once in, adult learners confront such issues as how to balance their academic activities with other parts of their lives and how to feel supported and challenged during their learning journey. This moving-through period begins once learners know the ropes. Because it can be a long transition, learners may need help sustaining their energy and commitment. For some, this in-between time can evoke new questions about the transition: "Did I do the right thing?" "Why am I bored?" "Can I commit to this transition?" Many jokes about the "seven-year itch" stem from this middle period when reevaluation takes place.

Learners' moving out can be seen as ending one series of transitions and beginning to ask what comes next. Grieving can be used as a model to explain this phase in the structured learning process. As Marris (1974) points out, people feel grief in many situations of loss other than those most commonly recognized as bereavement. In leaving familiar surroundings and people or the ways of functioning and interacting to which one has become accustomed, one experiences disequilibrium. Changing jobs, moving, or returning to school are transitions in which adults mourn the loss of goals, friends, and structure.

Bridges (1980, p. 90) writes, "Considering that we have to deal with endings all our lives, most of us handle them very badly. This is in part because we misunderstand them and take them either too seriously or not seriously enough." Louis (1980) also points out that organizations have not paid the same attention to helping employees move out as they have to helping them move in, nor has anyone really developed a detailed conceptualization of what is needed to help people leave, let go, and reinvest.

The only certainty in the transition process is that people's reactions to an event or nonevent, such as returning to school or not returning to school, will change over time for better or worse. When we interviewed a woman as she prepared to take the learning plunge, she was full of excitement and expectations that getting a degree would be fun, would be her ticket to independence. When we interviewed her three months after she began her program of study, she was discouraged. She felt old and displaced. In contrast, we interviewed another woman who had been afraid to return to school, but once she began participating, she was thrilled with the process. Of course, the way a person feels at the beginning of a transition may not necessarily be reversed, but over time, reactions to the transition will certainly change. People in our studies have told us they do not believe their reactions will change—if school is stressful now, they believe it will always be so. Part of our job is to help change such attitudes.

Another important point is that the larger the transition—either good or bad—the more it will pervade an individual's life. At first, one is a beginning student, new widow, or new parent. A period of disruption follows, in which old roles, relationships, assumptions, and routines change and new ones evolve. Then finally, gradually, the sharp awareness of having graduated or having become a parent becomes only one of the many dimensions of living—the transition has been integrated. The extent to which a transition pervades daily life affects the degree to which one must adjust.

Studies of change—whether moving, losing a job, returning to school, caring for aging parents, or retiring—have shown that people in transition have both strengths and weaknesses. We have clustered these potential resources or deficits for coping with change into four major categories, the four S's: situation, self, supports, and strategies (Schlossberg, 1987). By looking at the balance of resources and deficits in each of these categories, it is possible to predict how a person will cope.

> *Situation:* Does the person see the transition as positive, negative, expected, unexpected, desired, or dreaded? Did the transition come at the worst or best possible time? Is it "on time" or "off time"? Is it surrounded by other stresses? Is it voluntary or imposed? At what point is the transition—beginning, middle, or near the end? Is this a personal transition or a reaction to someone else's?
>
> *Self:* What is the person's previous experience in making a similar transition? Does the person believe there are options? Is the person basically optimistic and able to

deal with ambiguity? If so, he or she will bring to the transition the greatest resource of all: a strong sense of self.

Supports: External supports and options include both financial assets and potential emotional support from family, close friends, and co-workers. Dealing with transitions successfully requires that those close to us offer more support than sabotage. Which way does the person feel—supported? Sabotaged?

Strategies: Understanding the nature of transitions can help us find ways to cope with them. Sociologist Leonard Pearlin (1982) points out that there is no "magic bullet" coping strategy. Instead, the creative coper uses a number of strategies, including those that change the situation (negotiating for help at home), change the meaning of the situation (not feeling devastated over a grade of C; approaching some tasks with humor), and help the person manage stress (running, swimming, meditating, relaxing).

Learner Agendas. Agendas vary for adults returning to education. Some return because the boss says they must; others return out of a desire to move up and out. The learners we interviewed came for career, family, and personal reasons. Their agendas centered on identity, achievement, change, generativity, and competency. These findings overlap with those of Chickering's (1969) study of young adults, whose major tasks were to develop competence, manage emotions, develop autonomy, establish identity, free interpersonal relationships, develop purpose, and establish integrity. Chickering calls these seven tasks *vectors of development* because they have direction and magnitude, which together create a force for human development and change. The vectors apply to older adults returning to education, who find themselves confronted with these issues at a new level, as well as to adolescents and young adults entering higher education for the first time. In general, the vectors are developmentally sequential.

The first vector is an overarching, general sense of competence, or confidence in being able to cope and achieve whatever happens. Within this vector, learners of all ages develop an intellectual competence that influences their professional and vocational choices; a physical and manual competence that relates to the stamina needed for conducting life activities and for athletics and dexterity; and an interpersonal competence that involves the ability to work cooperatively with others so that life tasks may be achieved.

Managing emotions, the second vector, focuses on self-control and expressing oneself appropriately to circumstances. The third vector, developing autonomy (which Chickering now prefers to call interdependence) comprises emotional independence (freedom from the need for constant reassurance, affection, and approval from parents, peers, and others), instrumental independence (ability to act and cope without seeking help), and, importantly, a culminating recognition and acceptance of interdependence.

Establishing identity, the fourth vector, builds on developments in competence, managing emotions, and autonomy. It involves clarifying ideas of physical needs and characteristics, personal appearance, sexual identification, gender roles, and behavior. Establishing identity also includes acquiring confidence that one's ability to remain the same over time is mirrored by others' perceptions. With a solid sense of identity, individuals are better positioned to develop in the three remaining vectors.

Freeing interpersonal relationships, the fifth vector, means increasing one's tolerance and the capacity to respond to others as individuals (as opposed to stereotypes). A shift occurs toward greater trust, independence, individuality, and intimacy in friendship and love relationships. In the sixth vector, developing purpose, clear answers are sought to such questions as "Who am I going to be?" and "Where am I going?" Individuals integrate vocational plans, avocational interests, and life-style considerations; they plan and prioritize, and give direction and meaning to their lives.

In establishing integrity, the final vector, internally consistent sets of belief are formed that give guidance for behavior. Values are humanized (become less absolute, more relative), personalized (values of others, such as parents, are internalized), and made congruent (behavior becomes consistent with personal values).

The continuing applicability of vectors to the agendas of both adult learners and traditional-age students is clear from a recent reexamination by Chickering (Thomas and Chickering, 1984). Of course, the major qualities that differentiate adult learners from traditional-age students and affect their agendas are just as clear. Lynch and Chickering (1984, p. 49) summarize the ways adult learners are different as follows:

- A wider range of individual differences, more sharply etched
- Multiple demands and responsibilities in terms of time, energy, emotions, and roles
- More—and more varied—past experiences
- A rich array of ongoing experiences and responsibilities
- More concern for practical application, less patience with pure theory, less trust in abstractions
- Greater self-determination and acceptance of responsibility
- Greater need to cope with transitions and with existential issues of competence, emotions, autonomy, identity, relationships, purpose, and integrity

Brookfield (1986) would add that the capacity to be critically reflective is what differentiates learning by adults from that by adolescents and children.

These differentiating qualities, and the way in which learner agendas (centering on identity, achievement, change, generativity, and competence) overlap with the seven vectors, suggest the recurrence of underlying themes throughout life. We are able to see both tremendous variation in each individual story and continuity across the course of life.

The Need to Matter

Another critical dimension for adult learners is their need to matter. Whether they are moving in, moving through, or moving on, they need to feel appreciated and noticed.

A faculty member was forced to cancel a class lecture because of the flu. The class was large, with students from many departments and neighboring institutions. The faculty person, with the help of a secretary, called every student in the class. The following week, students remarked that never in their experience as students had a faculty member had the consideration to call them; in fact, they had never received a phone call from either a faculty member or an administrator. They were amazed, touched, and grateful. This anecdote saddened us. Why should this be so unusual? Why should consideration of students be so startling?

Mattering refers to the beliefs people have, whether right or wrong, that they matter to someone else, that they are the object of someone else's attention, and that others care about them and appreciate them. Mattering was originally labeled by Morris Rosenberg, a sociologist, as "a motive: the feeling that others depend on us, are interested in us, are concerned with our fate, or experience us as an ego-extension" (Rosenberg and McCullough, 1981, p. 165). His research showed that adolescents who feel they matter to others will be less likely to commit delinquent acts. He also suggested that people in retirement who no longer feel they matter—that others no longer depend on them—will have difficulty adjusting to their new status.

Recently, adult learners were studied who had participated in some of the nontraditional educational options designed and promoted by the Council for the Advancement of Experiential Learning (Schlossberg and Warren, 1985). Over and over adult learners said they felt they mattered to an adviser, to an institution. This feeling of mattering actually kept them engaged in learning. Schlossberg, Lassalle, and Golec (1988) are developing a mattering scale to be used by adult learners in institutions of higher education to answer this question: Are the policies, practices, and classroom activities geared to making people feel they matter? They took the five dimensions of mattering identified by Rosenberg and other researchers and generated items pertinent to those dimensions for adult learners. For example:

> *Attention:* "The most elementary form of mattering is the feeling that one commands interest or notice of another person" (Rosenberg and McCullough, 1981, p. 164).
> - I have a place on campus to put my things, get mail and messages.
> - People in classes know my name.
> - I get thoughtful comments on my papers.
>
> *Importance:* We are the object of a person's concern and believe that a person cares about what we want, think, and do.
> - My adviser has office hours at times I can be on campus.
> - Someone notices if I miss a class.
> - I have been able to get financial aid.
>
> *Dependence:* All of us depend on others, but what is special about mattering is that it focuses on others' dependence on us.
> - My professors depend on my participation in class.
> - My classmates call me at home if I am absent.
>
> *Ego-extension:* We feel that others will be proud of our accomplishments and disappointed with our failures.
> - My professors are interested in my progress, even after I leave school.
>
> *Appreciation:* We feel that others are thankful for what we are and what we do.
> - I have been able to get credit for learning from my life experiences.
> - The administration seems to consider adult learner priorities as important as traditional-age student priorities.

In setting the stage for adult learners to feel as if they matter—by providing desk space, messages, convenient office hours, appropriately designed courses—educational institutions also set the stage for adult learners to connect to and keep successfully involved with our institutions. We believe that what Rosenberg suggests and what we are testing is true and that educators need to pay more attention to programs, practices, and policies in relation to the five dimensions of mattering for all students.

Conceptualizing Educational Environments

In Chapter One, we recognized the lack of synchrony between the variability of adults (in terms of roles, age, and capacity) and the rigidities of the educational bureaucracy. We further called for a shift in perspective to one that envisions institutions as educators, in which all participants are involved in learning and living. To make this shift to an educational orientation from a services orientation, we need to approach educational environments from an ecological perspective, to see our institutions as environments that have the potential for facilitating or hindering adult learning. Ecology, a term borrowed from biology, deals with the interaction between an organism and its environment. (An animal or plant may flourish in one setting yet fail in another.) Thus, to understand human development, we must be aware that although behavior is determined in part by the chance of the individual's birth, certain evidence exists to illustrate that when the environment is altered, behavior and performance will also alter. To talk about normal growth and development is all very well, but for those whose development does not follow the normal sequence, such questions arise as: What's wrong with me? What's wrong with the environment? Ecological questions instead ask: Why does one person fail in one setting but achieve in another? Why does one social class have differing degrees and kinds of mental illness? The essence of the ecological perspective is that the onus cannot be placed on either the individual or the environment; rather human behavior is a continuous interaction between the two.

Learner-Environment Fit. Rudolph Moos (1979) and his colleagues at the Stanford Social Ecology Laboratory have developed ways of assessing any environment, whether a school, nursing home, prison, family, or residence hall. Their assessment focuses on three major dimensions of any environment: the relationship dimension, the personal growth dimension, and the clarity of expectations.

The first domain, the relationship dimension, assesses "the extent to which people are involved in a setting, the extent to which they support and help one another, and the extent to which they express themselves freely and openly." The second, personal growth or goal orientation, measures "the basic goals of the setting, i.e., the areas in which personal development and self-enhancement tend to occur." The third domain, clarity of expectations or system maintenance, "measures the extent to which the environment is orderly and clear in its expectations, maintains control and response to change" (pp. 15–16).

In an accumulating body of literature, researchers are beginning to explain behavior by analyzing the social context in which it occurs and asking: Is it supportive? Does this environment enhance or stimulate adult learning?

Campbell, Wilson, and Hanson (1980) studied the adjustment process for adults (twenty-five years and older) who returned to school as undergraduates at the University of Texas. By taking an ecological approach to assessing the educational experience, they focused on the "degree of fit between the characteristics of the individual student and the properties of the student's environment" (p. 1). They conceived psychological adjustment in terms of "person-environment fit" during four stages in the return to school:

> *Balance* The person is in a state of equilibrium, "neither enrolled in school nor actively considering a return to school," but employed full time, taking care of the home and raising children, or whatever. "The overall degree of person-environment fit may range, however, from very good to poor" (p. 4).
>
> *Conflict* The equilibrium is threatened, and the person

actively contemplates returning to school. The motivating forces may be personal (for example, need for intellectual stimulation or environmental job requirements, need for a second income in the family). Other forces act as barriers to the return (for example, lack of confidence in academic ability, financial constraints, or family opposition). "Thus, individuals considering re-enrollment are typically in a state of conflict" (p. 4).

Transition The person makes a commitment to enroll in school, "a major decision having impact on all realms of the person's life and . . . therefore, potentially a highly stressful period" (p. 5).

Outcome The person achieves a new state of equilibrium incorporating the return to school. Again, the person-environment fit may range from very good to poor.

To assess the person-environment fit in both the balance and the outcome stages, the researchers used an Index of Well-Being (Campbell, Converse, and Rodgers, 1976), an instrument predicated on the assumption that "the optimum 'fit' occurs . . . when (1) the particular combination of social settings provides multiple opportunities for fulfilling a wide range of personal needs; (2) the person is accommodating to the demands of each social setting; (3) in negotiating the environment to meet these needs and social demands, the individual is experiencing a degree of challenge that stimulated personal growth but is not overwhelming; and (4) in addition to satisfying personal needs, the person is progressing toward fulfillment of higher-order needs" (Campbell, Wilson, and Hanson, 1980, p. 134).

Some of the major findings to emerge from this particular study provide a useful summary for understanding adults in the midst of returning to learning: (1) Most adult learners found that their life-style was disrupted considerably by returning to school. (2) Adjustment was most difficult for those coping with other major life changes (such as divorce or job change), those who had been anxious about the return, those whose life-styles were changed most drastically, and those (such as single parents) with heavy family responsibilities. (3) Of the adult learners who said they needed campus services, those who experienced the greatest adjustment difficulty were least likely to make use of such services.

This study builds on a tradition that equates "adjustment" with the interaction of an individual in a particular environment. As the many studies of Moos confirm, an environment high on order will fit with certain learners but not with others. We suggest that by assessing individual learners and learning environments, it is possible to better predict adult learner involvement, retention, and satisfaction.

Prevention Orientation. In addition to the shift from a services orientation to an educational orientation for our institutions, we have also called for a shift in orientation from treatment to prevention. This shift has been seeping into the literature more and more; it urges the counselor to be an environmentalist (as opposed to an individual therapist), the student development professional to be involved in prevention rather than remediation, and all administrators and educators to be proactive rather than merely reactive.

The Task Panel on Prevention, of the President's Commission on Mental Health (1978), defined the essential characteristics of prevention in mental health as a network of strategies qualitatively different from the field's dominant approach:

1. Prevention is proactive, building adaptive strengths, coping resources, and health.
2. Prevention is concerned about total populations, especially groups at high risk.
3. Prevention's main tools and models are those of education and social engineering.
4. Prevention assumes that equipping people with personal and environmental resources for coping is the best way to ward off maladaptive behavior.

Student development professionals are in a position to identify environmental circumstances causing stress and then to collaborate with other educators in the institution to eliminate or ameliorate that stress.

One effective problem-solving strategy comes from the business community. Ralph Barra (1983) of Westinghouse writes that all organizations experience problems. Some can be solved by individual effort, but environmental problems, for example, may require the help of others. Barra suggests the use of quality circles. These are opportunities for employees and managers to collaborate on identifying a problem, to investigate its cause, and to design specific strategies for solving it.

We know of no attempt as yet to include adult or other learners in quality circles, but Steele, Rue, Clement, and Zamostry (1987) report on using them in an admissions office. Groups composed of clerical workers, admissions counselors, and administrators developed different strategies for problem solving. Several new programs were generated, one of which improved office procedures. However, these researchers warn that quality circles are expensive and time consuming.

The basic principle for a quality circle is to gather in a particular setting all those affected by a problem. This suggests that student development professionals could take the lead in gathering together adult learners, administrators, faculty, and counselors. Together they could identify problems, such as classroom atmospheres in which adult learners feel put down, the general atmosphere that treats adult learners like bag people, student fees used for the activities of traditional-age students, or inconvenient bookstore hours and faculty office hours. Eventually, the group could focus on a particular problem, work together in looking beyond the surface, dig into causes and ramifications, then work together to establish a goal and develop specific strategies to use in reaching the goal.

Of course, those in business point out that quality circles are effective only if they become part of a more general quality of worklife. Thus, initiating quality circles could lead to a larger question: Is the overall campus a place where one feels part of a community, experiences a sense of belonging, and feels that one matters?

What we are suggesting is that institutions study themselves and assess the degree to which they are attuned to adult learners, whether it is to their diverse learning styles (Kolb,

1981), their diverse ways of processing intellectual information (Perry, 1968), or their varied age, roles, or capacity. We have the measurement tools to do this, and we have strategies to make it work. Do we have the will to do it?

Learners and Environments

When Cross (1981) identified those factors that act as barriers to moving in, she took account of both learner and environmental factors. She groups these barriers into three main categories: dispositional factors, situational factors, and institutional factors.

For adult learners, dispositional barriers flow from prior experiences and self-perceptions: "I'm too old to try to learn new things." "I may not have the energy or stamina to take on that extra work and stick with it." "I am not sure I really will enjoy studying." I'm tired of school as a way to learn." "My goals aren't clear." "I don't want to seem too ambitious to my friends or relatives." Such barriers deter adult learners in different ways and keep them from achieving their goals.

Situational barriers arise from real-life conditions—lack of money and time, home and job responsibilities, needs for child care or elder care, inadequate transportation, lack of an adequate place to study. These situations are not a permanent part of a particular adult learner's life, but they may be part of so many adult learners' lives that institutions need to build in solutions, such as a family care facility, computer matching for transportation, or lounges for study and socializing.

Institutional barriers arise from typical administrative, organizational, and educational practices—restricted class schedules, inadequate laboratories, too few hours for the library, procedural red tape, inappropriate entry requirements, unavailability of advisers. The solution to such problems rests on the shoulders of the administrators and in changing the environment to be more conducive to adult learner participation.

Like Cross, we suggest that ways to facilitate learning must focus on both individuals and institutions. Mattering focuses on both and can be a means for removing barriers. Those who are committed to providing environments that make people feel they matter must ask: How do individuals in our setting perceive the institution? Do they feel they matter? What is the institution doing in terms of classrooms, policies, resources, and administration to produce an environment in which more people feel they matter? We hypothesize, but leave it for others to test, that adults who score high in mattering—that is, who feel noticed, appreciated, and depended upon by their institutions—will become and remain more involved in higher education.

Astin (1984) suggests a theory of student involvement, based on more than twenty years of research, for predicting retention of traditional-age college and university students. *Student involvement* refers to the amount of physical and psychological energy a student devotes to the academic experience. Adult learners cannot be involved in the same way as their younger counterparts; however, Astin suggests that involvement contains a psychological as well as an activity dimension. Therefore, even though one is not physically involved in a setting full time, one can feel committed to the learning process.

By definition, a highly involved student is one who devotes considerable energy to studying, spends much time on campus, participates actively in student organizations, and interacts frequently with faculty members and other students. The behavioral aspects are critical: what the individual does, how he or she behaves, defines or identifies involvement.

Student involvement theory, according to Astin (p. 298), has five basic postulates:

1. Involvement refers to the investment of physical and psychological energy in various objects, either highly generalized (the student experience) or highly specific (preparing for a chemistry exam).
2. Involvement occurs along a continuum. Different students share different degrees of involvement in the same object, and the same student shows different degrees of involvement in different objects at different times.

3. Involvement has both quantitative and qualitative features. Involvement can be measured by how many hours a student spends studying (quantitative) and by whether the student reviews and comprehends the assignment or stares at the book and daydreams (qualitative).
4. The amount of student learning and personal development associated with any educational program is directly proportional to the quality and quantity of student involvement in that program.
5. The effectiveness of any educational policy or practice is directly related to the capacity of that policy or practice to increase student involvement.

The last two items are key educational postulates. They provide clues to designing more effective educational programs for learners and are subject to empirical proof.

The theory of student involvement encourages us, as educators, to focus less on our own concerns and more on our students—how motivated they are and how much time and energy they devote to the learning process. This theory is more concerned with the behavioral mechanisms or processes that facilitate student development (the *how* of student development) than with theories of developmental outcomes (the *what* of student development). Student involvement theory suggests that the most precious institutional resource may be *student time.* The extent to which students can achieve particular developmental goals is a direct function of the time and effort they devote to activities designed to produce these gains. We compete with other forces in the student's life for a share of their time and energy. Every institutional policy and practice has implications for how students must spend valuable time (class schedules, orientation, advising, faculty office hours, on-campus jobs, parking, off-campus locations, child care).

Over his years of research, Astin (1984) has identified the following factors in the college and university environment that significantly affect students' persistence in higher education:

- Living in a campus residence
- Participating in extracurricular activities or honors programs or professors' undergraduate research projects
- Holding a part-time job on campus
- Attending a four-year college (rather than a two-year college)
- Identifying with the college or university environment through similarity of race, religious background, or size of institution compared to hometown
- Interacting frequently with faculty

Astin's study also found that men were more likely to give boredom with courses as a reason for dropping out of college, whereas women gave marriage, pregnancy, or other responsibilities as their reasons.

Much of Astin's (1977) research is based on the traditional-age student population—can we apply his student involvement theory to adult learners? Some factors related to persistence, such as living on campus, holding a part-time job on campus, and participating in extracurricular activities, are clearly less applicable to adult learners. Adult learners are generally more highly motivated, more involved in learning and studying and in interaction with faculty and staff than traditional-age students are; yet adult learners are generally commuter students and live off campus, many hold full-time jobs off campus, more attend two-year institutions than four-year institutions, and few participate in extracurricular activities. In addition, adult learners are often part-time students and frequently interrupt course work for job and family reasons; their degrees may take five or six years to complete.

We have some hunches about why adult learners appear highly motivated and are perceived as more involved by faculty, although despite at least half of Astin's factors do not apply to them. For one thing, adult learners may spend *proportionately* more discretionary time (that is, time available for studying after classes, work, eating, and household and family responsibilities are over) studying than traditional-age students do. A second hunch is that developmentally, most adult learners are more likely to be anchored in clearly defined work and family roles and relationships, and they may have less need to be searching for peer relationships than are traditional-age students, who are forming their early identities. Third, the amount and quality of interaction with faculty may be greater for adult learners than for traditional-age students. Adult learners may feel more comfortable asking questions and relating to faculty as age peers than are younger students, who may see faculty as authority figures to be avoided. These hunches are, of course, highly speculative; the question of how student involvement theory applies to adult learners is wide open for research.

In Conclusion

To restate our argument, the needs of adult learners differ depending on whether they are moving in, moving through, or moving on. Environmental responses need to provide differential opportunities for involving adult learners—that is, for those entering to learn the ropes, for those moving through to hang in there, and for those moving on to disengage and reinvest.

As educators—faculty, administrators, student development professionals—developing differentiated responses to learners in transition, we need to provide the appropriate mix of support and challenge. Daloz (1986) suggests concrete activities that lead to support and challenge. To give support, one needs to listen, provide structure and clear expectations, name what the learner is feeling, and serve as the learner's advocate. As demonstrated in Chapters Three, Five, and Seven, which relate adult learners' experiences, we try to listen carefully to their agendas, take account of their resources, and serve as their advocates.

Daloz suggests that challenge is best offered by providing "new frames of meaning" or suggesting "constructive hypotheses" about what one is doing. In Chapters Four, Six, and Eight, which look at environmental responses to learner needs, we try to suggest some new ways of offering support and challenge for learners.

And further, Daloz suggests that support and challenge lead to a vision of what can be, to a map of the future. And that is what we try to do in this book—provide a map of a future in which adults will feel they matter each time they move in, move through, and move on from a particular learning experience and in which institutions will be truly educative and responsive to all.

THREE

Moving In: Adults' Needs on Entering Higher Education

Who are the legions of men and women reportedly returning to college? Do they see education as leverage for their future? As a means of self-fulfillment? We read newspaper articles about grandparents and grandchildren marching in the same graduation ceremony. Returning to school is now more than a trend; it is becoming the norm.

We talked with a number of men and women who were considering a return to college, in order to get a deeper sense of what triggers their thinking. What are the barriers to their return? What motivates them? What would they like in the way of student educational services to help them make a wise and considered decision? Their answers gave us clues to their agendas, issues, and concerns. Our findings reflect a general paradox: Each individual has his or her own story that is special, yet underlying universal principles tie all individual adult learners together.

As to our methodology, we puzzled over how many interviews would be needed to obtain a reasonable range of individual diversity. Because the experience of adult learners differs depending on where they are in the learning process, we interviewed adults during one of three periods: as they were considering moving in, as they were moving through, and as they were moving on. Interviews were conducted by telephone or in person. The interviewer asked a set of questions and probed for further information when appropriate. Those interviewed were identified through several sources: the Returning Students' Program of the Counseling Center at the University of Maryland, College Park; Academic Advising of University College at the University of Maryland; and Mini College, University College, and the Adult Student Information Center at Memphis State University. In addition, we met with classes of returning adult learners at both institutions. In the vignettes that follow, names have been changed, and some profiles are composites.

Rather than the results of a carefully crafted research study, our interviews and group meetings are presented as dramatic illustrations of our views on adult learners and student educational services. Had we intended a research study, our sampling would have been broader, and we would have included comparison groups of adults not in school, of adults in nontraditional educational settings, and of adults learning in noncollegiate settings, as well as of adult learners attending community colleges, four-year colleges, and universities for no credit. Our intention is to use the voices of a few adult learners to underscore our conceptualizations and to speak for many adult learners in higher education.

This chapter, concerned with understanding adult learners moving into education, describes four learners and their resources for coping, based on the four S's—situation, self, supports, and strategies—discussed in Chapter Two. We describe the major issue underlying each vignette as well as the implications for each adult learner. These vignettes provide the basis for the last part of the chapter, which intertwines the agendas of the entering adult learners with parts of the conceptual framework described in Chapter Two. The vignettes also demonstrate the need for new educational services for entering adult learners. (Chapter Four gives guidelines for developing entering programs for learners in transition.)

Each learner is unique; nevertheless, we suggest that interviews at random with any four prospective learners will reflect common needs for competence, autonomy, identity, relationships, purposes, integrity, and emotional development, as in Chickering's (1969) vectors of human development. The vignettes in this chapter deal with most of these issues. When combined with interviews in chapters that follow, all of the underlying issues are addressed.

Maggie: "I Need to Find Out Who I Am"

Maggie has two children, nine and twelve years old. She has worked as a travel agent for ten years. "I now want to do something useful," she stated. "I feel a need to pursue something, to have stimulation and contact with women my own age." As we talked, she revealed more complications in her situation than had appeared at first. Her youngest child has a chronic liver disease and cannot attend school full time. This means that Maggie must be at home a great deal and must have a flexible schedule.

Maggie knows how easy it is to become totally involved with her youngest child. She does not want to wallow in the difficulties of her situation; at the same time, she cannot ignore their effect on her life. She feels she must identify something that will be fulfilling, that will help her develop an identity of her own, yet still enable her to meet her first responsibilities to her children.

Maggie's lack of clearly defined goals stands as a major obstacle to returning to college. She is not sure what she wants to study. In addition, her self-esteem is low, and she questions her ability to do college-level work. It is true that her deficits in writing and computational skills will warrant some introductory or developmental courses. Also true is that her child with the chronic liver disease presents a major barrier for Maggie's engagement in almost any activity. Conflict seems certain between Maggie's need for a flexible schedule to meet family requirements and her need to study, take exams, and write papers to meet course requirements. Her determination to develop an identity beyond that of mother and wife provides the motivation to overcome the barriers. She views college as the vehicle to do something for herself, to find out "who I am."

Maggie's supports come from her husband, who wants her to pursue her interests. Yet he also acknowledges the need for her attention to the family. In terms of her strategies, Maggie recalled that she had little guidance in high school. She wants that now. She would like someone to help her identify her interests and put her in touch with different people working in the fields she is considering. She needs to know her options. She needs career counseling. The services she wants are typically available only to enrolled students.

Underlying Issue: The Search for a New Identity. Over and over we hear people express the need to develop and articulate a sense of who they are. Obviously, people do have a sense of self, but it changes as life unfolds. The voices of those considering education are voices of people in transition. They were somebody—a travel agent, a mother of small children, a secretary, a farmer. For many reasons their former identity no longer fits. Now they see education as a vehicle for finding a new identity.

According to Erikson (1959), the crisis of identity occurs in late adolescence; young people must establish a sense of self and find a place as an individual in the adult world. When they fail to achieve identity, they are left with "role diffusion" and cannot develop further. Chickering (1969, p. 80) elaborates: "Identity . . . is that solid sense of self that assumes form as the developmental tasks for competence, emotions, and autonomy are undertaken with some success, and which, as it becomes more firm, provides a framework for interpersonal relationships, purposes, and integrity. . . . Developing this inner feeling is like learning to drive. First, signals and signs must be learned and behaviors must be mastered. In time . . . driving becomes a pleasure, not a chore."

We suggest that the crisis of identity is reawakened whenever an individual experiences a major transition. To give an extreme example: A person whose sense of identity is defined by work role or career will experience severe stress when suffering a career setback. For such a person, retirement from the world of work will cause severe trauma. Similarly, the person whose sense of identity derives from homemaking may find the very foundations of life shaken when children leave home or the spouse dies. Thus, when the major source of self—whether work, family, community, or some combination—is changed or eliminated, a crisis can occur.

Although many theorists look at changes in identity over the life course, Fiske's (1980) work is particularly relevant for adults returning to college. She studied the changing commitments of people over time. Commitments are those activities that give meaning to one's life. A person's commitments reflect his or her identity. As one changes one's view of self—I am a person, not just a parent—one's commitments, as reflected through activities, begin to change.

Using cluster analysis of selected adjectives from a checklist, Fiske and her colleagues identified four clusters of value commitments: interpersonal, altruistic (including ethical, philosophical, and religious allegiances), competence/mastery (autonomy, creativity), and self-protective (including concern for physical, economic, and psychosocial survival and well-being). Any setting, whether work, family, or community, may provide the arena for interpersonal, altruistic, or self-protective intentions as well as those relating to mastery or competence. Indeed, Fiske believes that rigid dichotomies, such as work versus leisure, are more confusing than helpful; few people compartmentalize themselves this way. Assessment of subjects at several points in time revealed that individual commitment changes over time and that considerable variability is present in the patterns of change.

Among the women in Fiske's middle-class and lower-middle-class sample, the occupational setting was less important than the home. Their interpersonal and altruistic commitments tended to be directed toward raising their children. Fiske says that "for such women, a midlife conflict may be triggered by a sense of failure of mission as mother or by the realization that their child-rearing days are over. The subsequent struggle, for many, is between what they may view as a moral imperative to settle for being a good wife, and their growing awareness of a need for new arenas outside the confining sphere of the family," where their emerging commitments and search for competence in the outside world may find expression (p. 247).

In the area of mastery, the sexes at midlife shift in different directions. Many midlife men, having peaked occupationally, turn instead to interpersonal relations and altruism, whereas many midlife women begin to put more emphasis on mastery and less on interpersonal and altruistic commitments. Several researchers have noted this apparent crossover of the sexes. According to Fiske, it results in men and women at midlife being on a collision course.

Implications for the Learner. Maggie is searching for a new identity. Her former identities as wife, mother, and travel agent no longer fit. Although she sees her transition in a positive light, her shaky sense of self-confidence is an obstacle. Her transition appears to be happening "on time" (that is, when she thinks it should), at a time when her children are becoming more independent. The stress of her youngest daughter's illness, however, is ever present.

We have caught Maggie at the beginning of her transition—when she is questioning her changing identity. Her commitments are beginning to shift from interpersonal and self-protective to altruistic and mastery. Thus far, she has devoted herself to serving her family, and now she wants to do something that will have meaning for her. She needs new competencies to achieve her new identity.

Gwen: "I Want to Move Forward, to Accomplish and Achieve"

Men and women motivated to return to school are "gutsy." They often push ahead despite obstacles. Gwen is no different.

After Gwen graduated from high school in 1966, she took a number of low-level jobs and participated in a number of short-term training programs, including a Red Cross nurse's aid program, a business course, and a program in cosmetology. Although she had hated school, as time went on she began to get a "hankering" to return. Her mother and boyfriend, however, discouraged her by telling her she was "too dumb and stupid to go to any college." On the morning of her twenty-fourth birthday, she impulsively decided to go to college, no matter what anyone said. She found that the Community College of Baltimore had an open-door policy. She borrowed the $10 application fee, applied for financial aid, and was admitted.

After five years, Gwen obtained her A.A. degree, a fact that reflects her sense of self, her determination, and her spirit. After graduation, she began working at the University of Maryland as a clerical worker in the geography department. Taking advantage of services available to students and staff, she approached the Returning Students' Program to discuss her secret dream to complete her B.S.N. degree in nursing.

When asked about her barriers, she replied, "I am a single parent with two young children who depend on me entirely for their support. Their father has never given a penny in child support money. And I do have some other barriers. The first is my fears. I am afraid I am too old to go back to school. But then I tell myself that isn't true. But a greater fear is my fear of dependency. I know I will have to give up my job so that I can put all my energy in studying. If I give up my job, I cannot afford to keep my car. Therefore, I will have to totally depend on my boyfriend for rides, for money, for everything. That's so scary. And finally, I have an overriding problem—I don't know how to think of my long-range resources, or even how to balance my checkbook. When I went to get help, all I could get was a list of financial aid resources. What I need is financial planning."

Gwen reported that as she was graduating from high school, the teacher asked the students to raise their hands if they were going to college. Every hand but Gwen's was raised. The teacher said nothing to her. Gwen remembers the pain of being ignored. "Why couldn't that teacher have come over and asked me what she could do to help me go on?"

Despite her fears, Gwen wants to move forward. She wants to accomplish and achieve. "I am black, my family was poor, and I have a need inside me to go up one step. I want to be a nurse." Gwen has a definite goal and a strong need to achieve; now she needs financial planning so she can attend college full time. She also needs the uncritical support of her boyfriend, her mother, and others at the institution.

Underlying Issue: The Need to Achieve. Where does this need for achievement come from? What is it? How can we define it? Spence (1985, pp. 1290–1291) reminds us that the discussion of achievement is culture and gender specific and that "our supposedly universal theories of intrinsic motivation and the achievement motives that flow from them" may not be appropriate for all groups. It is particularly important to look at men's and women's achievement motivation from different perspectives. Gilligan (1982) notes that men and women define achievement differently: Men see autonomy and control of their own lives as indices of achievement. For women, these indices are caring and interdependence. Whether or not this claim is "true" for all men and women is less relevant than Spence's reminder that achievement is not an absolute truth but a reflection of the group in question.

Helmreich and Spence (1983) broaden the discussion of achievement by looking at it in multiple settings—homemaking, amateur sports, child rearing, hobbies, school, community, employment. They identify the components of achievement as mastery, competitiveness, and "personal unconcern" (a lack of concern about others' reactions to one's achievement). In a study comparing women's and men's achievement, as measured by the Work and Family Orientation Questionnaire created by Helmreich and Spence, Griffin-Pierson (1986) found that women's scores on competitiveness are often lower than men's. This provides "evidence for Gilligan's . . . hypothesis that it is the competitive aspect of achievement in which women sense danger. It is not achievement that women fear, but the possible fracture of human relationships caused by competition" (p. 314).

Within the multiple contexts where achievement takes place, each individual achieves somewhat differently. Lipman-Blumen and Leavitt (1976) have developed a model of achievement styles—that is, preferred strategies individuals use to get things done or the characteristic ways they approach tasks or goals. For example, *direct achievers* are characterized by individual direct efforts, whereas *relational achievers* are characterized as team players who contribute to the achievement of others. Relational achievers can also be *vicarious achievers*, meeting their achievement needs through the accomplishments of others. We all know parents who try to meet their own achievement needs through the success of their children.

People can also achieve in an instrumental fashion by transferring achievements in one area to other areas. For example, the football hero uses his status to promote products, which leads to more money, or an individual develops what seems to be a social friendship for ulterior business purposes.

People assume different achievement styles or a combination of styles on different occasions. For example, some returning adults achieve directly at school but achieve vicariously at home through children and spouses.

Empirical support for the view that women can achieve and gain competence comes from a study of the wives of coal miners (Giesen and Datan, 1980). Despite the stereotype of older women as "dependent, passive, incompetent, and generally unable to deal with the problems and crises of life" (p. 57), this study found that most of the women interviewed were evidently able to "interact effectively with the environment" and "cope with and solve problems" (p. 60). Moreover, most felt they had gained in competence and handled life better than they had at a younger age.

Implications for the Learner. Because of her financial dependency on others and her need to support her children, Gwen's transition, her drive to complete her B.S.N. degree, could have come at a better time. However, her need to achieve is a strong motivator. She has the inner strength to cope with the situation. Her supports are weak because her relationship with her boyfriend is not secure and her mother has tried to sabotage her efforts in the past. In addition, the institution does not offer financial aid for someone in her low-middle income bracket, so she would have to quit her job and be dependent to be eligible for a grant.

By understanding her situation and her transition, Gwen can develop coping strategies. By understanding that her achievement is focused on caring and interdependence, rather than on autonomy and control, as it is so often for men, she can appreciate her achievement needs. She senses the danger in the possible fracture of her relationship with her boyfriend, and she is afraid of her own dependency needs. Gwen's direct achievement style is one of the qualities that make others admire her. What she needs now is the support of the institution and strategies for gaining access to the financial aid and financial planning that would allow her to be a full-time student.

Walter: "Do I Have to Start at the Beginning?"

Walter left high school when his father was killed in World War II and his mother needed his help in the family hardware store. Walter took the responsibility well, learning the business and learning how to hire, fire, and manage other people. In the meantime, he married and had three children. Walter completed his General Educational Development (GED) Test through night adult education classes in Memphis. He always wanted to go to college, but the store kept him busy. Over time, he expanded the business by opening three more stores, then branching out into a large building supply company with several franchises.

To Walter, it seemed that he had always been interested in history, particularly World War II and its causes and effects. Whenever he traveled to Europe, he visited battlegrounds and cemeteries. He read extensively about American foreign policy and attended and later led discussion groups on topics related to politics and American policies abroad. He became active in the local Democratic Party and was well respected for his ability to research and advise on proposed legislation.

When his oldest son chose not to attend college, Walter was very disappointed. He hoped to influence his two younger sons to pursue higher education. On his fiftieth birthday, he said to his wife, "Now it is time for me to do something I have always wanted to do—get a college degree." He thought he might influence the younger boys as well: "If they see Dad doing it, maybe they will think they can."

When he called an adviser at University College at Memphis State University, Walter told her he wanted to get his degree as fast as possible. "And do I have to start at the beginning? I have had all these experiences, and I have been learning throughout my life through reading, traveling, discussion groups, and politics. I feel that some of what I have been learning should count and that I should not be required to start at the beginning. I want to get a degree in business administration, but I also want to take courses in history and political science."

Underlying Issues: Role Modeling. Even though he had some questions about his ability to compete with younger students, Walter's desire to influence his sons tipped the balance in favor of his going to college. He based his actions on the assumption that people learn through imitation or role modeling. Originally described by sociologists but now a term in common use, *role modeling* has come to be accepted as one of the ways people learn. Most data on learning by imitation stem from studies of young children; however, Merton's (1957b) landmark studies of adults learning to be doctors indicate that people of all ages can learn new roles and skills.

Learning new roles through modeling and imitation requires both that the environment provide models and that individuals make the choice to imitate (Maccoby and Jacklin, 1974, p. 288).

For institutions of higher education, this implies that they must provide a variety of role models and publicize them. They also need to help prospective adults use these role models for personal growth and development. Knowing that an eighty-year-old man has completed his portfolio for a degree through a credit equivalency program, that a woman in her thirties has just begun college on her way to becoming a prison warden, or that men and women of all ages, races, and ethnic identifications can begin higher education at any age can stimulate a potential adult learner.

Implications for the Learner. Walter's financial situation is secure, and he can afford to send his sons to any school they choose. He is at the beginning of a voluntary transition that for him is a personal venture. His disappointment when his oldest son did not attend college made him aware that his own lack of a college education might have given his sons the impression that he did not value its contribution. Walter has a solid sense of self and has coped with many transitions in the past. He is basically a reflective, yet optimistic, person who can deal with life's ambiguities. He has the support of his wife and sons. Among his colleagues, he feels somewhat embarrassed that he is just now beginning college. However, he realizes that he will serve as a role model for his employees and others in the community, as well as for his children. He imagines them thinking, "If Walter can go to college at fifty, then maybe I can, too." Thus, Walter is choosing to be a role model.

The major obstacle for Walter is that he wants recognition for what he has already learned, and he does not know how to approach the university about this. He has developed a successful business and knows a great deal about management and personnel. His interest in and knowledge of history, foreign policy, and politics makes him admired by his discussion group members and by his political party colleagues. Somehow this learning must count for something. It is a matter of principle for him. He wants to be recognized.

John: "Just Show Me the Way!"

John's story, which came to us from a colleague at another university, is typical of many who must fight the bureaucracy of an institution to be admitted and recognized. After high school, John went to a small college but dropped out after a year to go to work. Then, about five years ago he attended a community college for two semesters. He is thirty-three now and realizes that he will not be able to progress in his career without a college degree. He has a strong sense of self, developed from his success as a computer salesman.

John has the support of his family. His employer also has encouraged him to return to college and will even provide tuition reimbursement. John has learned many strategies in the workplace, and he needs them all, and more besides, to cope with the institutional bureaucratic red tape he has encountered and may continue to face.

John's story began in August: when we interviewed at the

end of November, his tale was not yet complete, not yet resolved. When John first came to the university, he was unsure of a major: "I wanted to try to get some advice on how to best use my previous credits from classes I had taken fifteen years ago. I was unable to get the counseling I thought I needed because I was not a registered student at that time." But he had his transcripts sent to the registrar's office to be evaluated and declared a business major, thinking that would give the evaluator a better chance of letting him know what courses he still needed to get a degree.

Ms. White in the registrar's office evaluated the transcripts and mailed a form asking for several course descriptions. John wrote for them, but worried a little because the descriptions he received were vague, were from a small school, and were for courses taken fifteen years ago. Ms. White accepted the economics and chemistry courses. The first semester of accounting was accepted but not the second, because the description did not differentiate between financial and managerial accounting. She sent John to the business department to get authorization from the chairman, Dr. Smith.

Summer school had just gotten out, and everybody was on vacation. John left his name and number but got no call back. After several weeks, he checked back: Dr. Smith asked him to send a copy of the course description and a letter explaining what he needed. John did. Some days later, Dr. Smith called to say he could not accept the second semester. John at last knew he had to sign up for the second semester of accounting.

The English requirement was another difficulty. He had a grade B for one quarter of English composition at the community college five years ago. But that quarter did not equal one semester at the university, so the requirement was not satisfied. However, the university offered a test that gave credit for English composition. John signed up for the test, assumed he would pass, and registered for English 302, the advanced junior-level composition course. But John didn't pass the test. He was "a little disturbed" and went to the English department to find out why. Harry Jones, the person in charge of the test, was not there, but the secretaries said John could not take 302 until he had satisfied the English 100 requirement. John went back to the registrar's office, dropped 302, found a 100 class open, and made the switch. An hour later he came back to the English office to talk with Harry Jones.

"Jones read some of the comments on my essay," said John. "Then he read it over himself because he said he had not been involved in the actual evaluation. He said that one of the major comments was that I had used too many simple sentences (something that a previous English teacher had told me was proper). I explained my background and what I was trying to do. He suggested that the one-quarter English composition course would satisfy the 100 requirement. Then I could take the 302; to do that I would have to have the approval of the head of my particular department, the business department.

"I went down the hall to the business office. Dr. Smith said he did not have the authority to make that approval, that it would have to go before a faculty board, that it was a long, drawn-out process. He made a countersuggestion: since I had a quarter of English composition from a community college, I could take an additional quarter at the nearby community college and fulfill the 100 requirement while taking 302 here. He would authorize me to take the class, but, of course, I would have to get the authorization from the English department to take 302 simultaneously.

"I went back down the hall to the English department, but Harry Jones had already left for the day. This was the last day prior to the Labor Day weekend, so I had to wait until the following Tuesday to check in again. He was not in on Tuesday. Finally on Wednesday, he did approve this idea. Then I had to go back to the registrar's office, drop the 100 class, and try to get back the 302. At that time 302 was filled up. I went back to Harry Jones in the English department, and he said I would have to go back and continue to check each day to see if I could get in, because people were dropping the class. I stood in line early each morning, and after three days there was an opening and I grabbed it. It was not at a good time for me, but I felt I had no choice. I then signed up at the community college for their first quarter of English composition."

John's teacher at the community college could not understand why he was taking the class, his first paper was so good. John told her his long story. She told John he didn't need to come to class, just to turn in whatever papers he chose to, and she would give him an A. Meanwhile, at the university, John's advanced composition papers were getting A's and complimentary comments from the professor, who was amazed that John had not passed the original test.

John was also working to resolve the issue of what to have for a major, now that he had access to counseling services. He took the Strong-Campbell test and the Myers-Briggs Type Indicator. He went to workshops and conducted research on his own. He decided on mathematics and talked to Dr. Lane, the math department's undergraduate coordinator. Dr. Lane encouraged him and said he would be his adviser. John went to the registrar's office to request a reevaluation of his transcript for the math requirements. John had the impression from both Dr. Lane and Ms. White that because his transcript had already been evaluated, more detailed approvals were not needed. But when the official reevaluation came in the mail, John learned that certain classes had to be authorized in writing by the department of his major. John was confused and checked with Ms. White. She said that there was a particular form the department needed to fill out and submit to the registrar giving authorization for applying John's two semesters of calculus, two semesters of chemistry (previously approved and applied to the business major), and one semester of biology.

John asked Dr. Lane for authorization. Dr. Lane said he could evaluate the math, but not the chemistry or biology. John would have to go to those departments for approval. "That really disappointed me," said John. "All I needed for him to do was to okay them for my major, but he insisted that I get the authorization for the science classes from the individual science departments."

John went back to Ms. White in the registrar's office. She showed John the form that needed to be filled out. John went back to the math department and found that a Dr. Adams, not Dr. Lane, would be the one to authorize the math classes. Dr. Adams gave John a form to fill out and wanted a copy of the syllabus. "But," said John, "this was fifteen or sixteen years ago, and we did not have a syllabus at that time. He also asked me if I could tell him what textbook I used. I said after all these years I couldn't remember what textbook I used or who the author was. I said I would get a course description if he wanted that and he said yes.

"I checked with the biology department, and they also indicated that they wanted a course description. They also asked me if I knew what textbook I had used. I said no, after all these years I couldn't remember. I proceeded to the chemistry department. I already had my course description because that had been asked for previously when they were evaluating the chemistry for the business major. I had to make an appointment with the head of the chemistry department for the next week. I then called the school in Kentucky and asked them to send me more course descriptions from the old catalog for my math classes and the biology class."

John's evaluation indicated he wasn't getting credit for his English literature class. Ms. White said the university was very strict in that area, and she needed a course description for that class, too, before she could accept it.

"I got the course descriptions in the mail just yesterday," John reported. "Today, November 25, I went around to the departments again. I went to the math department, filled out the form, and gave Dr. Adams the course description. He said he would review it and fill out the proper form and send me a copy in the mail. If there was no problem, I would get that notification in a week or two, and if there was a problem, he would give me a call. I went to the biology department and got hold of the head of the department, Dr. Williams, and showed him the course description. He said that it would equal Biology 113 here, which is what I needed. He filled out the form, signed it, and indicated that he would send it to the registrar's office and the dean. As for chemistry, I went back to the chemistry department yesterday for my appointment. The head of the department was short of time and on his way out of the office. He asked me to drop off the information. Then he would look it over, fill out the form if there was no problem, and have it ready for me next week after the holiday."

Not long before, John had found out that a note was in

his file at the registrar's office concerning his taking the class at the community college to satisfy the English composition requirement but that there was no copy of the authorization to do so. Ms. White made a copy of the copy John had received in the mail, so that the authorization was now safely a part of his record.

That experience, said John, "made me realize that I am going to have to follow up on the form that Dr. Williams in the biology department was going to forward. I realized that it doesn't always happen the way it is supposed to, and the burden is on me to follow up, to make sure that it gets into my file at the registrar's office."

John is now waiting to find out whether the chemistry—already evaluated and accepted by the business department from the previously provided course description—and the math will be accepted by the math department. "What seems odd to me," John told us, "is that for a business major the chemistry department and other departments involved did not have to evaluate particular courses. And now for the math major, there are different rules, and other departments have to approve some of these classes, even though I am not majoring in their areas.

"I also don't understand why some classes require specific departmental approval when others do not and can be approved by the registrar's office. It seems to me that it would be quicker and more efficient if the registrar, who is requiring this information, acted as the go-between and did the talking with the different departments, rather than sending the student around campus, knocking on doors, making appointments. The way it is now creates unnecessary anxiety for the student. I know that I am wondering whether or not some of these classes—that I thought were already accepted based on the original evaluation of my transcript and the fact that the university had accepted these courses as being transfer credits—will be accepted by the individual departments.

"I want to add one other thing," said John, "that when I went to consult with Dr. Adams about getting my calculus classes accepted, he told me that, once I got all the information together, he would look it over and see what my problem was.

I did not like his choice of words. I felt like telling him that there was no problem, except for all this red tape. If he would just sign the piece of paper I would have all this resolved. I did not like the idea of him suggesting that there was a problem. Because the last thing I wanted to hear was that I had another problem in dealing with the university."

Underlying Issue: The Importance of Control for Mental Health. Most of us are familiar with Sir Galahad's search for the Holy Grail. Kafka's novel *The Castle* and Menotti's opera *The Consul* are more contemporary descriptions of people in mazes of confusing requirements, shifting expectations, and mixed messages.

Whenever we repeat John's story to other adult learners, they nod in understanding and describe similar experiences. Often, however, the outcome is different. John resisted being labeled as a problem. He was determined to see his odyssey through. Some adult learners fear the loss of control in such a bureaucracy, and some accept themselves as problems.

A growing body of research demonstrates that those who feel they have control over their lives, or who are optimistic about their own efficacy in controlling at least some portions of their lives, experience less depression, achieve more at school or work, and are in better health.

In Seligman's original work on learned helplessness, dogs and people placed in situations in which they felt helpless and hopeless gave up and sometimes died. Seligman's work has been expanded to include explanatory style (Peterson and Seligman, 1984). The revised theory now accounts for the fact that people differ in how they explain and react to uncontrollable bad events—some people do not give up, become depressed, or experience failure.

Although some bad events are truly uncontrollable, in many instances reality is ambiguous. The individual's explanation of events, his or her explanatory style, imposes a reality on the events. An individual's explanatory style has three parts: (1) internal/external ("I caused it" versus "An outside force caused it"); (2) stable/unstable ("It is always true that I am incapable" versus "It is only true in this one instance"); and (3) specific/global ("I always have trouble figuring my balance" versus "I am incapable of doing anything right") (p. 548).

When an individual's explanatory style is characterized as internal, stable, or global, the individual is at risk for depression, low achievement, or poor health.

Seligman has developed the Seligman Attributional Style Questionnaire (ASQ) for identifying explanatory styles. Trotter (1987) describes some of the studies in which the ASQ was used. In one, the grade point averages of University of Pennsylvania freshmen and upperclassmen were compared with their ASQ results, SAT scores, and high school grades. "Students with the best explanatory style (unstable, specific, external) got better grades than the traditional methods predicted" (p. 34). In another study, at an insurance company, salespersons with a positive explanatory style were twice as likely as those with a negative explanatory style to be working for the company a year later. Following up on this study, a special force was hired of 100 insurance salespeople who had failed the insurance industry test but who had positive explanatory styles. The company found that the "optimists are outselling the pessimists among the regularly hired agents . . . and the special force is outselling everybody" (p. 34).

John used a positive explanatory style to explain what was happening to him—*he* was not the problem. Many adult learners might explain such events in a way that shows they feel responsible for them or that they feel they are at least part of the problem. Many adult learners also feel unable to control or change the educational bureaucracy. John's long story illustrates how individual success rests on a person's ability to remain optimistic. Thus, in addition to making institutional bureaucracy more responsive to adult learners, we must develop ways to help people become more optimistic in their thinking.

Implications for the Learner. John's transition is one that he desires and one that he views as positive. He has a strong sense of self, has an optimistic explanatory style, and can cope with change. His determination and his coping strategies have helped him manage the stress imposed on him by a bureaucracy that appeared indifferent. Now, at age thirty-three, John wants a chance to change his life, and the institution should be supportive of his chance. For many adults who have a worse situation, low self-esteem, little support at home, less positive explanatory styles, and fewer strategies for coping, combatting such red tape is difficult, even overwhelming. Institutions must find ways to make entry an integrative educational experience for all learners.

Applying the Transition Model to Adults Moving In

When we look back at some of the formal and informal discussions we have had with adults moving into higher education, we are struck by the uniqueness of each person. Whether these adults have been fleeing urban ghettos or the isolation of the suburbs, overcoming a childhood learning disability or family poverty, or taking out time to develop psychologically or academically, we see evidence of resiliency, of second and third chances, and of the never-ending search for self.

Most of the adults we have interviewed are in transition. To identify and assess their readiness for a learning transition, we can look at the transition framework—situation, self, supports, and strategies—for insights into how they can best cope with change.

Situation. For the four adult learners we have been describing, the transition has been primarily voluntary and viewed in a positive light. The decision to enter or return to college is usually one that has been "cooking" for a while. The triggers can be family, as in Gwen's situation; personal, as for Maggie and Walter; or a career change, as in John's case. Both Maggie and Gwen must cope with multiple other stresses besides school. If we examine it one way, this transition appears to be "off time" for all our learners, because going to college has been thought of as belonging to the late adolescent and early adulthood years. However, if we look at it in another way, the transition appears "on time," because college is viewed as the experience that will help them solve the other concerns of their lives.

All of these learners are at the beginning of their transitions. They must leave behind some of their old roles before they take on the role of adult learner. Maggie must find time to study, yet meet the demands of her family. She must arrange for her daughter's care for those times she is away in class or at the library. Walter will shift some of his responsibilities to his junior partner in order to take night classes in business administration. John will take leave from his computer sales job and become a full-time student to study mathematics and computer programming. Gwen's situation is perhaps the most problematic. She wants to give up her clerical job to become a full-time student if she can get a grant and some help with financial planning. Each of these learners is experiencing a major life transition. For each, entering or returning to college becomes a new life milestone.

Self. What do we know about the self-concept of each of our learners from their brief stories? We know that Maggie has low self-esteem and is searching for a new identity. She doubts her ability to do college-level work. Her rusty skills make her question her choice, yet she feels that college is the way for her to develop a new identity and find a meaningful career. Each of our other learners has a strong sense of self, the asset that will help them most in their transitions. John knows he has been a successful salesperson; now he wants to learn mathematics and computer programming to expand his opportunities with his company. Walter, also a successful businessman, wants to be a role model for his children and to be recognized for his accomplishments through a college degree. Gwen has overcome other obstacles, and her strong determination to achieve will take her far.

Support. Maggie, John, and Walter have the support of their families, and John also has his boss's support and encouragement. Walter has the support of his employees and political colleagues. Maggie has a neighbor willing to help with the care of her daughter. Gwen lacks secure support from her boyfriend and her mother. All of these learners are having trouble getting the support they need from their institutions. John's tale of being run from one end of the campus to the other is typical of that of many students. Walter questions how he can get credit for his prior learning. And Maggie is not sure what the university has to offer her.

Strategies. What coping strategies do our adult learners exhibit? Maggie has learned to ask for help from her husband and her neighbor. John has learned time management strategies in his work that he can apply to his college studies. Although Walter is under considerable stress from the demands of his business, he strongly believes that his choice to enter college will have a positive influence on his younger sons. He thinks about his responsibilities to them, to his colleagues, and to himself in a way that will help him cope with the stress of starting college at age fifty. Recently, he has also started an exercise program. While at the community college, Gwen learned strategies for handling her sabotaging mother; handling her dependency on her boyfriend may be more difficult.

In Conclusion

We have looked at a select group of adult learners moving in. They are in different stages of transition readiness. We are now faced with the question, What can student development professionals do to activate an educational response that will eliminate barriers and provide support and challenge necessary for adults moving in and for adult learning to take place?

Designing
Entering Programs
for Adults

Maggie, Gwen, Walter, and John bring quite different purposes and agendas to higher education. They differ dramatically in prior formal education and in knowledge and competence derived from work and life experiences. Maggie, with her problematic family situation and shaky self-confidence, faces many situational barriers. How can she use the university to "find out who I am" and get the competency she needs to be successful in a career that has meaning for her? Some traditional educators might argue the following: Our business is curricula—content, courses, and classes. We are not a psychiatric agency. If Maggie wants to do something useful and have stimulation and contact with women her own age, why doesn't she become active in her church and do volunteer work at the hospital where her daughter needs to go for treatment? Maybe then, after a while, she will know what she wants to major in and will be ready to enroll.

Gwen's strong need to achieve and her toughness born from a difficult background provide a solid basis for tackling college-level learning. Why then is it "so scary" for Gwen to have to depend on her boyfriend "for rides, for money, for everything"? How negative is he about her going on for more education? Did her A.A. degree and her shift to work at the university create some distance between them? Were he and her mother dismayed to learn that she was not "too dumb and stupid to go to any college" after all? And will they be further dismayed when she successfully earns a B.S.N. degree?

Walter is highly motivated to set a good example for his sons—we suspect he also wants to explore and expand the possibilities for a rich and fulfilling postretirement career and lifestyle. Few dispositional and situational barriers stand in his way, but identifying his talents and choosing among educational options present an important early agenda for him.

John has a great deal of self-determination and support. For him, entering has been a prolonged ordeal. Four months, fourteen appointments (with two registrar's office personnel, five faculty members and department heads, and assorted secretaries), many telephone calls, four futile trips, one test, and one community college course later, this mature, competent, experienced person is still not sure where he stands. He wonders whether other problems may be ahead. The entanglements he reports typify the entering and program-planning hassles endured by many adult learners.

These are all healthy persons who see education as the means to a satisfying future. They view colleges and universities as sources of the wisdom, insight, self-understanding, knowledge, and competence that can help them toward significant transitions and satisfying futures. They represent only a small sample of the diverse adult learners we encounter. How can we help them all find their different ways into our institutions, so that they can build strength and self-confidence, improve competence and coping skills, strengthen sense of purpose and the sense of themselves as active agents for their own development? How do we make our entering services part of the solution, instead of adding further burdens, barriers, and complexities to the problems that may have led them to us in the first place?

A Shift in Perspective

Awareness is the first step toward understanding and action. One way to heighten our awareness is to select adult students at random and listen to their experiences of finding their way into the institution, deciding what program to pursue, finding out what kinds of prior learning will be recognized for credit and actually going ahead in a program. In our interviews, each person's experiences were unique, but we know from other conversations that these adult learners' reports are not that unusual. Surely we can find ways to do better by our students.

And surely we can find ways to do better by ourselves. The dollar value of staff and faculty time consumed by such comings and goings, by the variations in norms and forms, by redundancy and recycling, multiplied by the numbers of students who go through these or similar struggles, would break any self-supporting, fee-for-service organization. Our institutions can ill afford the wasted human talent, time, and energy caused by such fragmentation and incoherence.

Chapter Two covered several key theoretical perspectives pertinent to the journeys of Maggie, Gwen, Walter, and John. People need to feel as though they matter to those who depend on them and to those on whom they must depend. Institutions need to act as though each student matters. We emphasized the importance of an ecological perspective that creates a humanizing rather than dehumanizing environment, where each part of the system works in appropriate coordination with the other parts. Rube Goldberg's cartoons are appealing because, despite the disparate combination of elements, somehow these all function together to accomplish a task. The desired result is achieved, despite ups and downs, diversions, and bouncing around. But we can't continue to bounce adult learners around. We need to stand back and take a clear, comprehensive look at our institutional contraption, to see how its various, slapped-together parts might be reorganized to function more effectively and meet the requirements of its varied units and constituencies. Each faculty member, department head, and student development professional cares about having proper requirements met. But authority is so dispersed that efficient and effective decision making suffers seriously. And the student does most of the suffering.

To improve this contraption, we need to make the perspective shifts suggested in Chapter One and elaborated on in Chapter Two, so that we become part of the solution rather than simply another set of problems for entering adult learners. First, we need to see ourselves as reflective practitioners and as educators. Then we need to shift the way we view adult learners. We need to recognize that, from the adult learner's point of view, finding one's way into college, understanding its diverse environments, learning its routines and resources, and then defining a relationship to it all require a large new set of complex learnings. Therefore, we need to think of ourselves primarily as teachers dealing with students who present unique combinations of prior experiences, purposes, and learning styles. We need to recognize that entering adult learners will arrive at our institutions across the full range of Perry's (1981) stages of intellectual and ethical development and that they will differ among the four life-styles—simplistic, diffuse, focused, complex—described by Lowenthal, Thurnher, and Chiriboga (1975). Our entering services, as educational activities, must take account of these differences, just as any skilled teacher would in dealing with complex curricular material.

The proposed shift in the way we view adult learners means putting ourselves in their shoes. From their point of view, the entering process is not simple and linear but involves juggling questions, obligations, plans, and concrete decisions. Many of these considerations interact; to resolve one requires information about, or resolution of, others. Selecting which courses to take, for example, depends on the program one decides to pursue. In turn, these decisions depend on what future prospects such a program might hold, what prior learning is recognized, how difficult the program is, how long it takes, when classes actually meet, and what kinds of teaching can be anticipated. These issues then relate to the learner's financial resources, full- or part-time work schedules, work demands, family responsibilities, and community activities. Based on their long years of experience at Empire State College, a unit of the State University of New York designed especially to serve adult learners, Steltenpohl and Shipton (1986, p. 638) put it this way:

> College entry signals transition in adult lives. . . .
> Adults must make the transition from citizen-in-

the-world to student when they enter college. At the same time, they may be negotiating transitions related to self, job, or family. These transitions may be conscious or unconscious. All are accompanied by uncertainties and risks as well as opportunities. In addition, new adult students lack confidence in their ability to study and learn. They are uncertain about expectations for college-level work. They do not understand the aims and purposes of liberal education. They lack information about the structure of colleges and universities and the organization of knowledge into disciplines. Their academic skills may be rusty or inadequate. They are strangers in this new world. They do not feel they belong. They feel marginal.

When Walter Adams was director of the Lifelong Learning Program at Appalachian Education Laboratory (AEL), he made detailed studies of adults committed to returning to college. From these studies, he developed a model of the entry process that matches institutional procedures for recruitment and induction with the commitment process for individuals. Figure 1 lays out the model. The top portion gives the recruitment and induction sequence—contacting, informing, evaluating, admitting, registering—which culminates in monitoring student progress. The bottom portion lists the individual actions required for each of the five basic steps: responding to initial information, exploring the personal relevance of program options, deciding to apply for a particular program, finalizing the program selection, and completing registration. Note the frequency of such words as *learning, exploring, clarifying, understanding, planning,* and *seeking.* Such terminology indicates how much learning is required as part of the entry process and how critical that learning is to developing a solid commitment to enroll and stick with it. The range of individual learning and adjustment is startling indeed. Adams (1986, pp. 13-14) sums up his model in this way:

Participation in the admissions process is contingent upon an adult being interested enough to initiate contact with an institution to get information about the programs offered and requirements for admission.

Adults, particularly those who are unsure about themselves or what they want, will delay making contact with the school or making applications until late in the process and then find themselves, usually during registration, in a situation where they need specialized help and counseling at a time when school staff does not have adequate time to work with them.

Adults will have access to and read information about admissions requirements and procedures but will not necessarily understand this information or understand it in the way the institution intended.

The admissions process is conceptualized and operated from primarily an institutional point of view. This involves procedures and services designed to ensure that students meet the information requirements for admissions. There is, however, no systematic conceptualization of the admissions process that takes the prospective student, as a learner, into consideration as well as institutional requirements.

To summarize, the first thing we need to do is to change our basic perceptions of ourselves and of our students—we need to see ourselves as teachers and the students as learners. We are *educators* in the best sense of that word, dealing with some of our students' most significant agendas for learning. How we handle these agendas will make a major difference in the clarity and commitment they bring to their more formal studies. Malcolm Knowles said, "If one thing stands out about adult learning, it is that a self-diagnosed need for learning produces a much greater

Figure 1. AEL Lifelong Learning Program Admissions.

	Admissions Process				Matriculation Process
Step 1	Step 2	Step 3	Step 4	Step 5	
INSTITUTIONAL PROCEDURES					
Recruitment Process →		**Induction Process** →			→
Contacting prospective adult students	Informing prospective adult students	Evaluating prospective adult students	Admitting adult students	Registering adult students	Monitoring student progress
Contacting and attracting adults: (through students, former students, staff, media, etc.)	Providing information	Receiving application information:	Selecting	Starting records	Advising
	Providing application materials	application form, transcripts, medical information, test results, interview data	Assigning adviser	Preparing class rosters	Reporting on exceptions
	Responding to questions	Counseling	Advising	Receiving funds	Counseling
	Interviewing	Receiving requests for financial aid	Orienting	Assigning resources, staff, room	Tutoring
	Administering tests		Placement testing		
			Interpreting academic and placement tests		
INDIVIDUAL PROCEDURES					
Commitment Process →					→
Responding to initial information about learning opportunities	Exploring personal relevance of program options	Deciding to apply for program	Finalizing program selection	Completing registration	Subsequent vocational development tasks (VDT)
Receiving information on school and programs offered	Learning about institution and programs: location of school, programs offered	Understanding program requirements and making tentative program selection	Receiving academic advising	Implementing decision to return	VDT 2 →VDT 3 →VDT 4
			Understanding course requirements and content	Getting schedule approved	
				Completing registration process	

Responding by making written, phone, or personal inquiry	fered, admissions staff, counselors, financial costs, financial aid, transportation options	Setting personal and career goals	Developing a schedule	Paying fees
Assessing relevance of general information	Exploring personal relevance and general implications of information: personal goals, family, work, health, personal crisis, other interests and responsibilities	Providing personal information	Setting learning expectations	Organizing family and work responsibility
General personal factors: self-concept, prior learning experience, interests, and goals		Seeking information	Setting time expectations for courses, major, and graduation	Organizing self to participate in class
Personal and family circumstances		Seeking counseling	Planning transportation	Organizing self to study
Encouragement from other family, friends, students, employer	Clarifying options regarding program graduation requirements	Understanding institutional information	Arranging finances	Implementing transportation plans
Referral by education or community agency	Exploring implications for future: personal growth, employment, career, income, standard of living, social involvement	Planning finances, student loans, financial aid	Understanding results of academic and placement tests	Purchasing learning materials
		Understanding purpose and use of academic tests		

Source: Adams, 1986. Used by permission.

motivation to learn than an externally diagnosed need" (Stelten-pohl and Shipton, 1986, p. 641). When entry education helps our adult learners carry out that diagnosis and successfully achieve the learning required, we contribute significantly to their motivation for learning—and to our institution.

We strongly endorse Adams's (1986, p. 15) orientation toward entry as integrated education:

> The admissions process, when conceived as a learn-ing process, can be a means for adults to transform more general interest in education and career en-hancement into values and goals necessary in devel-oping the commitment to return to school. Such a commitment, when comprehended and grounded in reliable information, can be stated in practical terms, such as an adult applying to a specific school, entering a specific program, and seeking specific outcomes. This involves personal transfor-mation achieved through interactively clarifying knowledge and value to establish goals and develop a plan. A personal plan, as such, integrates knowl-edge about self, and the institution and programs selected, with a concept of a more desirable future to enable the learner to describe how he [or] she will be able to reach his [or] her goal. Learning, when viewed in this manner, illuminates the nature of commitment by structuring and energizing ac-tion in the present with reference to one's concept of the future.
>
> This conclusion reduces to the following in-novation principle: Institutions should cultivate the capacity to help adults engage in self-planned, directed, and initiated learning throughout all as-pects of the admissions process by providing infor-mation and services in a manner that will facilitate their learning and develop a commitment to return to school.

Thus, we need to find ways to help students obtain pertinent information, advice, and counsel across a wide range of topics and according to a schedule and sequence that fit each person's particular background and conditions. Above all, we need to make information and services available in an integrated, coherent fashion.

Seeing ourselves as teachers and our students as adult learners is a shift that must be accompanied by actions that change many practices currently at work. How wide-ranging these changes may be, will, of course, vary from institution to institution.

Entry Education Center

Our most important recommendation is for institutions to establish an entry education center that coordinates the full range of services and programs so that students can build a solid relationship with our institutions.

Maggie, Gwen, Walter, and John remind us that many adult learners return to school with shaky self-confidence, uncertain goals, or minimal experience with bureaucracies. They meet a challenging array of things to be learned, systems to be understood, complex decisions to be made. John's story illustrates the incoherence and indifference students encounter. Small wonder that commitment is so often tenuous, that first semester dropout rates are so high, that program change is the norm, not the exception.

Typically, student services divisions have a set of discrete functions, carried out by separate autonomous units with limited interaction and communication. Recruitment beats the bushes; admissions personnel decide who to let in and by what criteria; orientation, carried out by an entirely different set of staff, occurs after admission and before, during, or after registration. Somehow or other along the way, a central advising staff helps students fill out those five-by-eight cards. Some other offices may be available to help with personal, career, or educational planning questions. However, faculty members and department heads, dispersed throughout the campus, retain detailed knowledge of course and program requirements and final authority concerning what can be credited as part of the "major."

The entry education center would house recruitment, preadmission counseling, admissions, orientation, financial aid and planning, student employment, educational planning, academic advising, developmental assessment, assessment of prior learning, and registration staff. Each student would find the combination of resources needed to address his or her particular institutional, situational, or dispositional barriers. Communication and collaboration would be strengthened among professionals responsible for different aspects of the entry process. Policy changes would be discussed in open meetings with all the appropriate professionals, and implementation by all would follow simultaneously. The major institutional barriers that arise from staff fragmented and dispersed in various locations would be reduced. And the learner would be served in a systematic way according to his or her entry needs, instead of being served by a disjointed contraption organized for bureaucratic or administrative purposes.

Reading Level Analyses

While the complex politics and administrative organization necessary to establish such an entry education center are underway, fundamental gains can be made by examining the reading levels of recruitment literature, admissions information, catalogs, financial aid instructions, and all other print materials designed to interpret the institution's mission, opportunities, expectations, and requirements. When Adams (1986, p. 5) studied admissions literature for two community colleges, he found:

- The college catalogs for both research sites at community colleges averaged at a grade 17 reading level on the five tests.
- The application packet for one site was rated grade 16.5.
- Program information brochures for one site ranged from grades 16 to 17 with a grade 16 average reading level.

- The admissions letters sent to prospective students for both research sites averaged grade 16.
- The student handbooks for both research sites averaged at a grade 17 reading level.

To put these figures in perspective, remember that reading ability for adults in the United States averages at the eighth-grade level. High school textbooks are typically written at the eighth- to twelfth-grade levels. Grade 17 characterizes complex graduate-level reading. With program information and admission materials at such high reading levels, many adult learners have no recourse but to rely on word-of-mouth and face-to-face communication. We tend to say, "Nobody reads. It's right down there in black and white. Why don't they just sit down and read it?"

For a surprising learning experience, take time to read a college or university catalog, including the fine print. Try to understand what a student who wants to get in, get financial aid, and plan a program has to understand from that fine print. Admissions officers, registrars, and financial aid officers have spent years creating the rules and learning the ins and outs. They have to. They are legally liable. But an entering student often has neither the background nor the ability to grasp those complex details.

If we treated the entry process from a teaching and learning perspective, we would not tolerate such texts. Nor would we tolerate the limited resources and short shrift given such key areas of concern for students and for the institution. These documents need to be changed to plain English by someone with skills in straightforward, written communication. Or one might use freshman English classes to test the documents for writing clarity, for organization and expression, and to find the ambiguities or difficult passages and revise them.

Admissions information that is attractive to adults—pictures that show diverse ages and life-styles with easily readable and thoughtful, mature copy—creates a welcoming institutional image. All students moving toward higher education need information about the institution they plan to attend and the best ways to use its learning system for their purposes. These needs are especially strong among adults from working-class homes or educationally disadvantaged backgrounds where few parents, siblings, or friends have attended college. Many admissions procedures, applications, and financial aid forms challenge even experienced college-educated persons. Transitions and crises are often the triggers that propel many adults toward college. What they need upon initial contact is not more crises and anxiety, but easy access and welcoming support.

Recruitment

Reading-level analyses and appropriate revisions can make printed materials more understandable as well as more appealing to and appropriate for adult learners. Oral communication is also important because many students will need personal responses to some of their questions. One solution would be to establish an information booth and a toll-free telephone number staffed by adult learners who are trained to understand and communicate the most basic information and who know the proper sources of information for complex questions.

Programs in the community where adults are already engaged—workshops in their work settings, churches, libraries, or public schools, as well as information booths in shopping centers and invitations through the media—can provide information and encourage prospective adult students to take the first step toward starting or resuming their higher education. Recruitment teams of young staff members and traditional-age students remind adults of the age discrepancy and suggest the unlikelihood of their fitting in. Ideal are small teams of senior faculty, student development specialists, and successful older adult learners who can empathize more readily with adult uncertainties and anxieties.

Seminars that introduce eminent faculty to the community provide an occasion at which interested adults can inquire about entry or reentry. Recruitment staff should accompany such programs when possible. Institutions can also offer "free tickets" that let potential enrollees visit selected classes pertinent to their interests to get a firsthand experience of what being in that environment is like.

In 1984 the Commission on Higher Education and the Adult Learner produced an excellent resource for examining the quality and appropriateness of college and university programs for adult learners: *Postsecondary Education Institutions and the Adult Learner: A Self-Study Assessment and Planning Guide.* The commission was a joint effort of the American Council on Education (ACE), the Council for the Advancement of Experiential Learning (CAEL), the National University Continuing Education Association, and the University of Maryland University College. The *ACE Adult Learner Assessment and Planning Guide*—as we call it throughout this book—was published by ACE and CAEL (copies are available from ACE). It can be used by institutions as a whole or by smaller units within an institution. It provides detailed specifications for educational services that characterize high-quality programs for adult learners. It also provides frameworks for institutional self-ratings and addresses a wide range of program areas (including recruitment) with (1) a list of questions to be answered concerning a general area of policy or practice; (2) an opportunity to describe the current status for the particular area or unit and to record more detailed notes; and (3) a performance assessment section that suggests possible positive and negative factors and provides for an overall rating.

Here are the questions the *ACE Adult Learner Assessment and Planning Guide* asks about recruitment:

1. Are recruitment efforts aimed at special groups of potential adult learners (such as reentry women, professional groups, labor union members, college dropouts) undertaken on a regular basis?
2. Have some populations of potential adult learners been identified after an assessment of community and business educational and training needs?
3. Is a process for evaluating adult learner re-

cruitment efforts in place that enables the program to be continuously improved?

4. Is an advisory committee (which may be multipurpose) available to aid in planning and evaluating recruitment programs and services?

5. Has a marketing consultant been used to help develop or improve the adult learner recruitment program?

6. Have the catalog and program brochures been edited to correct text or photos implying that all students are under twenty-five and to address older students helpfully?

7. Are adults encouraged and enabled to audit or visit classes as part of a program to help them decide whether or not to enroll in a course or program?

8. Are information meetings planned for special groups of adults (for example, women, professional persons, union members)?

9. Are at least some meetings for potential adult learners held at community or employer sites off campus?

10. Are presently enrolled adult learners asked to share their experience with persons attending information meetings?

11. Are participants in meetings asked to complete information forms recording their interests and needs (such as financial aid and child care)?

12. Do promotional brochures and messages include information about proficiency exams, transfer credits, financial aid, career and life planning services?

13. Are persons attending information meetings helped to consider their readiness for entering or returning to college-level study?

Any institution that can answer these questions affirmatively has made significant strides in recruiting adult learners.

Admissions

A system that keeps track of which student is where in the recruitment, admissions, orientation, and program planning process is also important. An example is the Admissions Management Information Tracking System (ADMITS) created by the Appalachian Educational Laboratory Lifelong Learning Program (Adams, 1986). This microcomputer system tracks prospective students through the admissions process and makes it possible to provide assistance for those having difficulty. Has an inquiry from a particular student been dealt with? Did he or she respond with an application? If not, is a follow-up necessary? Is the application complete? Was a request for further information necessary? Did the student reply? Did he or she participate in orientation? Has advising and program planning been completed, resulting in apparently satisfactory enrollment? These are the kinds of questions the system answers.

Admissions decisions should rest primarily on judgments concerning the capacity of the institution to respond to the applicant's educational needs and purposes and on the applicant's current knowledge, competence, and motivation. Admissions forms typically request high school transcripts, test scores, and information concerning participation in high school activities— all of which are difficult for adult learners to obtain and are often useless or misleading. Questions are seldom asked about work experiences or volunteer activities that might provide much more reliable clues to current knowledge and competence. Admissions judgments based on twenty-year-old grade point averages or rank in class and on outdated test scores may bear little relationship to the adult learner's current ability to succeed in college. Once-sharp skills may have become rusty and dull, or significant deficiencies in ability or motivation may have been remedied. When adult learners are asked to take current admissions examinations, their scores may be unduly depressed by anxiety and unfamiliarity with tests. The tests themselves, standardized on traditional-age populations and relying heavily on book learning, may not accurately assess the adult's ability to learn. Admission processes often require commitment four or more months in advance of the enrollment date, but the family and work obligations of many adults often make it difficult for them to be confident about their situation that far ahead. In many cases, part-time adult learners who want to pursue a particular course or two are required to complete lengthy matriculation procedures before registering for the courses that interest them.

Such institutional barriers are especially frustrating for women, some of whom are married to men with professions or vocations that require them to change locations frequently, and some of whom are single parents who move for jobs. Many women find it difficult to put together a college education in the face of continual disruption. Their first responsibilities call for handling a move—getting the children settled in new schools, identifying doctors, dentists, and other support services for the family, learning where to find all the things required for daily life. Then, if there is time and energy left, they can search for a college or university that will accept past credits and offer courses or programs consistent with the educational purposes or degrees they have been pursuing. It is not unusual for such women to bring credits from six, eight, or ten different colleges. Some have been unable to complete even a two-year degree in five or ten years.

Application questions can serve useful educational purposes. Such questions for adult learners might include the following:

- What kind of life do you want to be leading five or ten years from now?
- What are your long-range vocational and professional plans?
- What are your current responsibilities and obligations? Which of these will be continuing?
- What resources for learning do you think would be helpful to you?
- Are there persons, places, instructional materials, or other resources you wish to use in addition to those available here?
- What sequence of learning activities might you undertake to pursue your goals?

- How will you schedule your time?
- What current interests or commitments will you give up?

These questions ask adult learners to consider carefully the significant time, money, and effort they are about to invest. The questions may present problems for potential enrollees who are embarrassed by limited verbal skills or who have never thought seriously about themselves, their future, or their education. Such students may need help thinking through these issues before they are admitted. But if that help and encouragement is not available and if that thinking does not occur, many will not find their way to the educational experiences they need (Chickering, 1973) or will find themselves overwhelmed by challenges they cannot handle. Unfortunately, most of our institutions offer such help only after students are enrolled. That is why preenrollment advice needs to be part of an entry education center.

Following are self-assessment questions posed by the *ACE Adult Learner Assessment and Planning Guide* concerning admission. The critical point is that criteria for admitting adult learners "reflect current conditions affecting learning-readiness rather than the conditions that may have applied when the person was very young."

1. Are adult learners evaluated using the same standards as for traditional-age students in the following criterion areas:
   a. High school grade point average?
   b. Recommendations given by high school principals and teachers?
   c. Scholastic Aptitude Test (SAT) scores?
   d. American College Testing (ACT) scores?
   e. Local tests or standardized tests not mentioned above?
2. Is the quality of recent performance on the job a criterion for the evaluating of applications for admission by adult learners?
3. Is the nature and quality of participation in civic

and community affairs given positive consideration in considering the applications of adults?
4. Is an assessment of the degree of motivation
    possessed by adult learners undertaken as part
    of the admissions process?
5. Are the basic academic skills possessed by
    adult learners appropriately measured and con-
    sidered, regardless of the methods by which
    such skills may have been attained?
6. Are there different admissions requirements
    for different categories of learners (such as full-
    time/part-time, degree goal/no-degree goal)?

Positive and negative factors to be used in evaluating institutional responses to these questions are as follows:

Positive Factors

- Quality of recent performance on a job is an important criterion for evaluating applications for
  admission from adult learners.
- Participation in civic and community affairs is
  an important criterion for evaluating applications for admission from adult learners.
- Admissions procedures include an assessment of
  the degree of motivation toward learning exhibited by entering adult learners.
- Basic skills possessed by adult learners are appropriately measured and considered, regardless of
  the methods by which such skills were attained.
- There are different admission requirements for
  different categories of adult learners.

Negative Factors

- High school grade point average is given significant weight as a criterion in evaluating the applications of adult learners who have long been
  out of high school.

- Recommendations given by high school principals and teachers are given significant weight in evaluating the applications of adult learners who have long been out of high school.
- Scores achieved by adult learner applicants on the SAT many years ago are given significant weight as a criterion in evaluating the applications of adult learners.
- Scores achieved by adult learner applicants on local or standardized tests other than those mentioned above are given significant weight as a criterion in evaluating the applications of adult learners.
- The institution recognizes no differences between adult learners and traditional-age students in evaluating applications for enrollment.
- Admission requirements are the same for all categories of adult learners.

Financial Aid and Planning

For many adults, like Gwen, financial aid and financial planning often mean the difference between attending college and not attending. But a wide range of educational and related financial needs are not being accommodated because the forms and systems, designed for traditional-age students coming straight from high school, do not serve adult learners well. Two major obstacles for adult learners, particularly those who must study part time because of work or family responsibilities, are the attitudes of financial aid professionals and our general institutional priorities. Adult and part-time learners are nontraditional, and they are often seen as nuisances. Going through the whole financial aid process for two or three part-time adult learners instead of one full-time traditional-age student requires more work. Besides, financial aid is finite. Using it to respond to the needs of part-time students can reduce the number of full-time equivalent (FTE) students—the coin of the realm for public institutions.

Just obtaining the necessary information and filling out the forms is often the first obstacle to financial aid for many adult learners. The systems for letting people know about what kind of assistance is available are designed to reach high school seniors or students already enrolled. Little is done to inform prospective adult learners. High school and traditional-age students can get help from counselors and financial aid officers to cope with the numerous forms required by most federal and state programs. Nothing is done to help adult learners cope; those who go to class outside the nine-to-five workday find it particularly difficult.

Success in acquiring necessary information and filling out required forms is a struggle, but adult learners may face a more fundamental obstacle: The formulas used to determine eligibility for financial aid are designed basically for traditional-age dependent students. And those formulas that do recognize independent students seem to assume young adults with a high percentage of effective income available for educational purposes. Prospective adult learners with middle incomes and dependents may find this obstacle insurmountable.

Additional obstacles lie in wait. Financial aid program guidelines often announce that they are designed to offer four years of assistance to recent high school graduates. Such guidelines are not encouraging to adult learners, although there are no legal prohibitions. Work-study programs, an important source of financial assistance, are also designed for traditional-age students. Adults employed full or part time, or who have substantial family obligations, find it next to impossible to participate. Most financial aid programs require information on the income and resources of parents, and some require that parents sign a petition for the applicant. For people aged thirty to fifty who may have their own children, who have not been dependent on their parents for years, and who may be contributing to their own parents' support, these requirements are incongruous. Most aid programs also require that an applicant be pursuing a first degree. But some prospective adult learners already have a college degree, and instead of another degree, they need help in changing careers or updating their skills.

Some adult married women face even more complicated obstacles. Only a married woman whose family income falls below the subsistence level can receive financial aid from a variety of federal, state, or private resources without her husband's signature (Durcholz and O'Connor, 1975). A married woman going to school usually needs to obtain her husband's financial support. Unless she has a supportive employer or an independent income that is not crucial to her family's support, the husband must share his income or be willing to sign for a loan. He must participate in the complex procedures of applying for financial aid—procedures that he might see as revealing his inadequacy as a provider.

What can we do to make financial aid more accessible to adult learners? We can change institutional policies that discriminate against the distribution of financial aid to adult and part-time learners. We can help through monthly tuition payment arrangements and emergency loan funds to help adult learners cope with cash flow problems. We can also look beyond grants, scholarships, loans, and work-study positions and develop links with employers in our communities. Many adult learners are already full-time employees and can enrich their companies by becoming better educated. We can encourage companies that offer tuition reimbursement plans to promote these benefits more openly. We can encourage prospective adult learners to present educational plans and proposals for financial assistance to their employers, and we can encourage businesses and civic organizations to provide scholarships and grants.

For many adult learners, financial planning may be as important as financial aid. Gwen is one example. Another is the adult learner who obtains a government loan and needs to weigh the significant indebtedness he or she will face upon graduation against the potential benefits of working while attending college. We can help adult learners with financial planning through workshops, such as those offered on a regular basis at George Mason University in which the Office of Financial Resources and Planning helps adult learners think in long-range terms about alternative sources of income and the range of expenses they are likely to incur. Workshop topics can include general budgeting, ways of maximizing resources, cost appraisals for education, alternative sources of revenue (tuition reimbursement, second mortgages), tax consequences, ways of managing a negative cash flow, and principles of resource management.

The *ACE Adult Learner Assessment and Planning Guide* lists the following as positive and negative factors to consider as we examine the financial aid and planning programs for adult learners at our institutions:

Positive Factors

- Fee and tuition payment options are sufficient to meet the needs of adult learners.
- Adult learners receiving financial aid are generally able to meet the expenses actually incurred as they pursue their academic programs.
- Family responsibilities and other circumstances typically in the life situations of adult learners are taken into account in criteria applying to the student financial aid program.
- More than one option is available in arranging payment for fees or tuition in programs in which adult learners enroll.
- At least some institution-controlled programs of student financial aid are specifically earmarked for assistance to adult learners.

Negative Factors

- A number of adult learners receiving student financial aid have dropped out or stopped out because of financial difficulties.
- Adult learners have only one option in arranging for payment of fees or tuition.
- An applicant's personal or parental income is the only criterion applying when determining an applicant's eligibility to receive student financial aid.
- No program of student financial aid is specifi-

cally earmarked for awards to adult learners who may qualify and apply.

- Adult applicants for student financial aid must answer a number of questions about the income or status of their parents.

Entry/Orientation Course

For adult learners, orientation workshops should be offered at diverse times and locations, to accommodate their schedules. The workshops need to help adult learners examine their needs, educational interests, and transition issues. A particularly important part of any orientation is contact with faculty and staff: more than anything else, it helps adult learners get started, identify with the institution, or solve problems.

One effective form of orientation for adult learners is an overnight stay. The many benefits of starting their higher education with an intensive residential experience include learning about the institution, the faculty, the staff, and resources for learning, and forming beginning support groups with like-minded individuals. When overnight stays are not possible, day-long workshops, with meals included, can start interactions between adult learners and faculty and staff, and among the adult learners themselves. Opportunities like these help adult learners identify strengths, overcome anxieties, clarify needed resources, and increase their sense of belonging. The educational value of these workshop experiences justifies their being provided on a fee-for-service basis.

But what happens after these favorable beginnings? Because transitions are a process over time, orientation for adult learners needs to continue beyond matriculation. An excellent strategy is to create an entry/orientation course, a life, career, and educational planning course, that helps adult learners address future plans and aspirations, occupational and intellectual interests, and other key concerns. In the early 1980s, Rockland Community College created such a course—a seminar that incorporated adult development theory, learning-style assessment, decision-making strategies, career exploration, educational planning, and life skills development (Viniar, 1984). The for-credit entry course, taught by trained facilitators and offered in a variety of formats, time frames, and locations, is now a well-institutionalized part of Rockland's orientation and educational planning process (Cullinane and Williams, 1983). Several thousand adult learners have used it to develop life portraits, assess their learning and decision-making styles, develop career profiles, and design individualized learning plans. Some departments have created adaptations appropriate for their particular majors. Increasing numbers of such entry courses are being created across the country and provided on both a credit and noncredit basis. These courses introduce adult learners to the institution's programs and services in a holistic fashion and provide a strong base for support groups and developmental mentoring.

Steltenpohl and Shipton (1986) have created a similar entry course for Empire State College adult learners. They describe their basic approach this way:

> In designing our course, we have integrated diagnosis and skill building with rigorous content related to the person (self), adult learning, and the world of higher education. We feature self-assessment, not external diagnosis, and skill building through practical use of skills, not isolated exercises or repetitious drill. We also use an experiential approach to move students from concrete modes of learning toward more abstract ways of knowing. Our major goal is to empower uncertain and anxious adults who feel like strangers in the academic world so that they can become successful participants in a college environment.
>
> The course is designed to capitalize on the interplay between content and process. Learning takes place in a group setting with twelve to fifteen participants. Faculty assume the role of facilitator rather than that of traditional instructor. Students begin with the familiar and personal and move toward the more general and abstract. The study of

adult development immediately engages the student in a process of assessment of and reflection on the self and possible reasons for the decision to return to the classroom. A consideration of oneself as an adult learner and an assessment of one's potential in that role follows logically. At this point the student is prepared to inquire into the purposes of higher education, including the meaning of liberal education. . . .

Our experience also suggested that our students were largely concrete learners. Indeed, based on the Kolb Learning Style Inventory, 71 percent favored concrete over abstract conceptual modes of learning. Kolb's inventory, based on experiential learning theory, measures the relative emphasis an individual places on four learning modes: concrete experience, reflective observation, abstract conceptualization, and active experimentation. Learning style is established by combination scores of abstract conceptualization and concrete experience indicating the degree of emphasis on abstractedness over concreteness, and active experimentation and reflective observation indicating the degree of emphasis on action over reflection. On the whole, our students emphasize concreteness and reflection. Assignments and activities for the group are devised to draw on the students' strengths as concrete learners. Activities include holding interviews and listening to the experiences of former students as well as readings and written exercises. Our goal is to make the group a laboratory for learning how to learn. The outcomes of the activities are shared in a nonthreatening atmosphere. Sometimes this takes place in small leaderless groups, sometimes in the larger group.

This approach has benefits for new, uncertain, and uneasy adult students. It enables students to compare their efforts with the reality of their peers' efforts instead of measuring themselves against some imaginary criteria for college work. The student learns his or her efforts are better than, the same as, or worse than those of others, what the differences are, and, last but not least, the expectations of the college for acceptable work. This learning process builds confidence [pp. 639–641].

The *ACE Adult Learner Assessment and Planning Guide* asks these questions about orientation (Give your institution an A+ if the answer is yes to all of them):

1. Do orientation activities for adult learners include the following:
    a. Attention to ways participants can achieve self-understanding regarding typical adult learning styles?
    b. Content matter relating to pertinence of knowledge and competence from prior experiences?
    c. Attention to professional, vocational, and life-cycle plans and aspirations?
    d. Information about institutional resources available through student services?
    e. Attention to academic program alternatives and requirements of particular concern to adult learners?
    f. Description of "academic culture"?
2. Are orientation sessions for the families of adult learners held?

Developmental Assessment

An important way to encourage personal and professional growth in adult learners is through developmental assessment; an effective tool for developmental assessment is the developmental transcript. Such a transcript, which supplements academic transcripts, is described by Brown and DeCoster (1982). In their Developmental Mentoring/Transcript Project at the University of Nebraska, Lincoln, students assess themselves in the areas of personal identity and life-style, multicultural awareness, interpersonal skills and relationships, academic skills and intellectual competencies, esthetic awareness, and health, physical fitness, and recreation. A goal-planning worksheet helps the students set goals and brainstorm ways to reach their goals. A log of mentor-student sessions details the sessions and summarizes the discussions.

As adult learners prepare developmental transcripts, they assess where they are in the life span and their developmental stage and tasks, learning style, avocational interests, interpersonal skills, leadership abilities, and personal values (moral, ethical, spiritual).

Other tools that might be used for developmental assessment include interviews or essays based on Perry's (1981) scheme and scored by Knefelkamp and Moore's (1982) Measurement of Intellectual Development method; Loevinger's (1976) sentence completion tests of ego development; Rest's (1979) Defining Issues Test based on Kohlberg's (1973) stages of moral and ethical development; the Myers-Briggs Type Indicator (Myers and McCaulley, 1985); Super and others' (1981) Career Development Inventory; Kolb's (1981) Learning Style Inventory; Hettler's (1986) Life-style Questionnaire; Hammer and Marting's (1988) Coping Resources Inventory; and the American College Testing Program's (1983) Adult Learner Needs Assessment Survey.

Based on their assessment, adult learners can set goals for life, career, and educational planning. This kind of goal setting, particularly at the beginning of an academic career, challenges adult learners to look for experiences outside the classroom that they can build on, that can further expand opportunities for growth. To illustrate: As an adult learner assesses prior college-level learning, some life experiences may contribute to the academic transcript and some to the developmental transcript. On her academic transcript, one adult learner documented ten years of experience in organizing and training volunteers for the local art museum and received academic credit for small-group management, art history, and adult education. On her developmental transcript, she documented her skills in interpersonal relations, her organizational ability, and her esthetic awareness.

Throughout the college and university experience, adult learners will add to their developmental transcripts a record of cocurricular and community activities and associated competencies that they see contributing to their long-range objectives and development. Such information documenting these competencies gained through cocurricular programs complements adult learners' academic transcripts and becomes an important prelude to developing a résumé, important to finding suitable jobs upon graduation. To their developmental transcripts, adult learners can also add journal writings that record behavior and serve to encourage personal growth through value formation.

As an adult learner undertakes candid developmental self-assessment, faculty members, student development professionals, and alumni can serve as mentors, that is, as sponsors to help adult learners achieve their dreams and accomplish their developmental tasks. These "developmental" mentors can also help adult learners recognize that each person matters as an individual and that their commitment to education can be larger than their immediate, short-run goals. More is written about developmental mentors in Chapter Six.

An important question that institutions might ask themselves in the area of developmental assessment is: Does the institution offer the opportunity for adults to assess their development beyond the classroom?

Assessment of Prior Learning

For many persons, assessment of prior experiential learning is the key to whether the institution respects and responds to them as adults. This assessment is what Walter wants so he will not have to "start at the beginning." Acknowledging college-level learning derived from work and life experiences recognizes the importance of this background and each person's special strengths. Whether that learning has been derived through business responsibilities, the military, volunteer work, or intensive home study, the adult who can document the learning feels his or her accomplishments are validated. When the institution takes this process seriously and provides easily understood procedures, adult learner motivation increases. Most adults are unaware of the wide range of knowledge and competence they have acquired. Starting college by identifying those areas and having them affirmed by the institution lets the adult learner begin from a position of strength. Unfortunately, the typical practices in most institutions focus on adult learners' weaknesses and areas of ignorance, a focus that exaggerates feelings of inadequacy. Sound and rigorous assessment of prior learning has just the opposite effect. Most adult learners react by saying, "Wow, I didn't realize I knew so much!" When Empire State College graduates were asked about their most significant educational experience during their college career, the assessment of experiential learning substantially outranked all other experiences.

The *ACE Adult Learner Assessment and Planning Guide,* concerning the assessment of prior learning, cites these positive factors

- CAEL and other appropriate guidelines are used for assessing prior college-level, nonsponsored learning and awarding credit for it toward degree requirements.
- A workshop or other experience is offered to assist adult learners in developing portfolios that document prior college-level learning.
- Incoming students may earn credit applying toward a degree through the equivalency procedures and credit recommendation of the *ACE National Guide to the Evaluation of Educational Experiences in the Armed Forces.*
- Incoming students may earn credit applying toward a degree through the equivalency procedures and credit recommendations of the

ACE National Guide to Educational Credit for Training Programs.

- Incoming students may earn credit applying toward a degree through the equivalency procedures and credit recommendations of the *New York Regents' Guide to Educational Programs in Noncollegiate Organizations.*
- Students may gain credit via the American College Testing/Proficiency Program (ACT/PEP).
- Students may gain credit via College-Level Examination Program (CLEP).
- Students may gain credit via College Entrance Examination Board/Advanced Placement (CEEB/AP).
- Students may gain credit via standardized proficiency tests listed in the *ACE Guide to Credit by Examination.*
- Students may gain credit via departmental challenge examinations.
- Degree-relevant prior learning credit awarded by other accredited institutions is accepted for transfer.

In Conclusion

This chapter lays out our recommendations for helping adult learners move in. Our fundamental point is that we need to think of the entry process as an educational experience for most returning adults. We need to approach each of our entering services from an educational point of view and see ourselves as teachers. We need to organize the various group meetings, workshops, and programs as though they were educational activities with clearly identified outcomes for increased understandings and new behaviors. Establishing an entry education center can be the cornerstone of our efforts, ensuring that various services and programs are carried forward in a well-coordinated, integrated fashion. Reading-level analyses and judicious revisions of key documents can assure that they are comprehensible and appropriate for adult learners. Recruitment activities, information sessions, and admissions processes can be carried out in ways that help adult learners address basic questions concerning their orientation toward their education, their aspirations, and their assumptions and expectations concerning the institution. Financial aid materials can be designed that help adult learners work through the complexities of obtaining assistance and help with financial planning and money management. Efficient registration convenient for adults needs to be available, such as computerized registration, registration by mail, or registration that uses credit cards, installment payments, and emergency loans. Orientation workshops can significantly extend and deepen the perspectives brought to life, career, and educational planning that have been triggered by recruitment activities and admission processes. The assessment of prior learning builds a clear sense of current strengths as well as areas in need of further learning. Developmental transcripts can provide a framework for carrying forward systematic thought and reflections concerning desired areas for change.

For most of us in most institutions, the suggestions in this chapter represent substantial challenges. But all do not have to be undertaken at once. Ideally, of course, the whole complex would be addressed in coordinated fashion, while plans are under way to bring the disparate programs and services together under an entry education center. In reality, most adaptations will have to be made piecemeal by units where the motivation, competence, and resources are sufficiently high. Sooner or later the changes in those units will impinge on the policies and practices of others. But in a three- to five-year period an institution can have created additional alternatives for the Maggies, Gwens, Walters, and Johns, alternatives that will make their entry a powerful educational experience and that will improve the match between their purposes and talents and the resources for learning we have to offer.

FIVE

Moving Through: Learners' Concerns in Managing Personal and Academic Lives

The issues, concerns, and challenges for adult learners moving through the educational system change from those they had when moving in. Once in, adult learners must balance the academic with other parts of their lives and find ways to feel supported and challenged during their learning journey. The concern of student development specialists also changes, to a focus on how to develop programs that will help adult learners "hang in there," balance competing demands, tolerate the stresses of an academic environment, maintain a positive perspective, master skills, and gain a new sense of self.

Chapters Three and Four looked at the issues of moving into a system and the issues of orienting adult learners in a system. This chapter looks at the issues of maintaining oneself in a system—of moving through from the adult learner's perspective—and issues of supporting adult learners through the system. As in the previous chapter, we apply the transition model, in this case to adult learners moving through.

In a meeting with a group of returning undergraduate men and women, we asked them to help us understand what they were going through. What was making it possible to continue and achieve? What was holding them back from involvement and participation? Their responses repeated the same messages:

- "Why can't the advisers realize we're different from eighteen-year-olds? We need help and we've got maturity. Yet we're treated like numbers or children. Our needs are not respected."
- "We need a place to meet, to have coffee, to study, to network. Except for one course for returning students during the first semester, we are lost in the crowds."
- "I feel foolish at my age going to the career counseling center. Everyone is so young—even the counselors. They all think I should know where I'm going."

Underlying these concerns is the need to matter, to feel special, to feel respected, to feel noticed. Adult learners come to learning with commitment and eagerness, but for many reasons—no child care, an inflexible curriculum, inadequate counseling, lack of a meeting place for adult learners, no financial aid—they may drop out along the way.

If our institutional policies and practices made adult learners feel that they matter, the adult learners would get involved. They all come with a dream. We can be part of making that dream come true or part of shattering that dream.

The stories of four adult learners follow. They describe how people in their personal, work, and learning environments supported—or sabotaged—their journeys through school. The underlying issues for each learner and implications for that learner are discussed as well.

Valerie: "Look at Me as a Person, Not as a Middle-Aged Woman"

Valerie, a student at University College, has maintained a 4.0 average. She feels she has turned her life around, that she can manage a home, a job, and school. She plans to major in professional studies.

Her husband supported her return to school by fitting his life around hers. He did the laundry, the vacuuming—most of the household chores. However, "At holiday time or in times of crisis he expected me to be available even if I had a test." When discussing supports at school, Valerie mentioned that some of her teachers were insensitive toward her, making negative comments or jokes about her age. One referred to her disrespectfully as a "middle-aged woman returning to school."

On the other hand, Valerie felt the advice she received was excellent. Her adviser always gave her information and the support she needed to stay motivated. The advising process, however, was difficult. For example, students could not easily get through on the phone to their adviser for just one question, and meetings had to be scheduled because advisers were on duty only at certain times.

Valerie appreciated the number of off-campus courses, making attendance easy. However, she wished that books could be placed at the extension sites. Coming to the main campus was difficult for her because the bookstore was not open at times that fit in with her complex work, family, and study schedule.

Underlying Issue: The Chilly Climate—Gender and Age Biases. Bernice Sandler, director of the Project on the Status of Women at the American Association of Colleges, studied the subtle ways in which classroom climates are different, and "chilly," for women (Sandler and Hall, 1982). A chilly climate leads women to conclude that they are not first-class citizens, that their opinions are not central, that their presence is not significant. This climate starts in elementary school. Teachers respond differently to boys than to girls, faculty members respond differently to men than to women students, and the entire community responds differently to male than to female administrators. We live in a His World and a Her World. These biases affect both men and women but seem to have special impact on women.

We need to examine gender issues at home as well as in school, especially the differing experiences of married adult women and men. Some women type and cook when their husbands study; when wives study, some husbands help, but not to the same degree. One major indicator of differences in "his marriage and her marriage" is what some have labeled "the politics of housework." According to Pleck (1981), housework is the issue "liberated" men avoid facing most. Pleck reviewed the conflicting studies that assess the absolute and relative number of hours worked by men and women. In one study, it appeared that when women work outside the home, men's contribution to household chores increases. Confused by the findings, Pleck discovered that the apparent increase in proportion was not because men do more but because employed women do less. The data demonstrate that women experience work overload, no matter how the hours of work are computed. The Institute for Social Research, University of Michigan, surveyed a national sample of 1,575 persons employed twenty or more hours per week. Data, collected by means of a seventy-minute personal interview, showed that (1) employed husbands spent fourteen and one-half hours per week in housework; when they had children under eighteen they spent twenty hours per week in child care, and (2) employed wives spent thirty-one hours in housework and thirty-three hours in child care (Pleck, 1981). Only after the birth of the fourth child do husbands increase their contributions to work around the house (Troll, 1982). Pleck concludes that, although women continue to be primarily responsible for family work, men are taking increasing responsibility and slowly changing behavior.

We have had a gender gap in "care work," with most of it being done by women. We also have had a gender gap in "work work," which is mostly dominated by men. These gaps are closing slowly—maybe imperceptibly at times—but men are increasing their care work and women their work work. In Sweden, both men and women are decreasing work work and investing more hours in play and love (Gunhild Hagestad, conversation with authors, May 1984).

A particular man or woman might behave in any way. But when we look at the obligations, the roles, and the responsibilities—the norms in society that impinge on men and women rather than specific differences among individuals—we see significant gender differences. We need to look at the structure of the society, how the rules and norms are changing, before we can consider how individual women and men respond. Bernard (1981) suggests this approach because the *intra*group differences and variability among men and women are often as great as *inter*group differences. That is, individual men mend and iron; individual women weld and manage. But the general society still pushes in the other directions.

An equally important issue is *ageism* (or age bias), which refers to the stereotyping of old people in our society as generally inferior and useless human beings. But the term can be applied with equal force to the stereotyping of any age group. Ageism is any assumption made about people purely on the basis of their age.

Ageism is made up of a whole network of myths—unsubstantiated beliefs that may be a combination of fact and falsehood and that influence our interaction with others. The premise is that because we know a person's age we can with fair accuracy predict his or her abilities, values, interests, and behavior. Age bias can take three forms (Troll and Nowak, 1976, p. 41):

1. *Restrictiveness*—The belief that certain behaviors are appropriate at certain ages and inappropriate at others. For example, twenty-five-year-olds should be embarked on their careers, and sixty-year-olds should not become doctoral candidates. Evidence indicates that attitudes toward younger adults tend to be more restrictive than attitudes toward older adults.

2. *Distortion*—Lack of congruence between the characteristics that "outsiders" ascribe to an age group and the characteristics that the age group ascribes to itself. For example, it is widely assumed that middle-aged women are bereft when the last child leaves home (the empty-nest syndrome). Recent research shows, however, that most of these women experience a tremendous sense of relief and well-being at this time. Age distortion results from

holding certain stereotyped attitudes toward age groups; in this case, the attitudes happen to be wrong.

3. *Negative attitudes*—Unfavorable or hostile attitudes toward any age group, for example, seeing all teenagers as rude and loud, seeing all older people as dependent or as bad-tempered.

The most insidious aspect of age stereotypes is that they are not imposed from above or from outside but, like all social stereotypes, are part of the belief system of the individual. People who find that they simply do not conform to the stereotype are inclined to feel not that the stereotype is wrong but that they themselves are somehow to blame. Fighting the stereotypes requires inner strength and, frequently, such outside help as counseling.

Because educators share the socialization of other Americans, they inevitably make assumptions about age-appropriate behavior, too. This fact—though difficult to face—is important; the decisions confronting educators are often directly related to what is expected of them, by themselves and by others, because of their age (and their sex as well). Should educators and learners make do with an unsatisfactory way of life because at their age they can expect nothing better? Or should they make a fresh start—go back to school, take up a new career, terminate an unhappy marriage—despite the fear that they will make fools of themselves?

As we pointed out earlier, experts on adult development believe that changes in adults are controlled more by social clocks than by biological clocks (Neugarten, 1968, 1982). Even the severe upheavals of adolescence may be triggered not so much by the biological phenomenon known as puberty as by a shift in the expectations of others: Adolescents can no longer act like children; suddenly they must grow up. The implications of the social-clock metaphor are central to the functioning of counselors. Presumably, social conditions can be altered more easily than biological conditions. What was appropriate at an earlier historical period, when medical, social, and economic conditions were different, may not be appropriate today. As educators, we must take a fresh look at the adult years. When we move away from the assumption that certain events are inevitable and right at certain ages, we can move toward helping students, and ourselves, explore new options at every age.

Implications for the Learner. Valerie's transition is facilitated by her strengths and her good coping strategies. Her 4.0 grade point average gives her a great sense of accomplishment. However, the classroom climate has indeed been chilly for her. Instead of feeling angry when the teacher referred to her disrespectfully as a "middle-aged woman returning to school," she felt demeaned. (She might benefit from some assertiveness training.) Such biases in the classroom against women, especially older women, need to be confronted. The consciousness of faculty and staff needs to be raised about sexism, ageism, and aging. As someone has wisely pointed out, bias against age is counterproductive, because those who hold this bias will, in fact, inevitably become part of the stereotypical group. Policies on sexual harassment also need to be widely publicized.

Valerie is fortunate that her husband is supportive of her return to college. He shows it by fitting his life around hers and by doing household chores, not just "helping her" do them. Many female adult learners must add the role of student to their other responsibilities. Our societal consciousness also needs to be raised concerning the politics of housework for employed women, women attending college, and men or women who work or study at home.

Mary: "Hang in There!"

Mary, originally terrified about her capacity to learn and cope, has become so hooked on the learning process that in a few more years she will become a certified public accountant. What factors hooked her?

Her family was proud of her and participated fully in running the house, without making her feel guilty. They just cooperated and assumed that she was entitled to study and get ahead. In addition, they realized that her studying would eventually help the entire family financially. However, many times she chose to participate in family activities rather than study. As she put it, "When you are married and have children, you want to be part of holidays, birthdays, and there when you are needed." The pressures were internal.

She found her advisers accessible and always supportive. In addition, she came to enjoy the content of most of her courses. Her initial comments were all positive. After probing, she admitted that several times she almost quit. The reason: Her accounting courses required driving to a campus sixty miles from home. Her other courses were offered near home. This 120-mile round trip exhausted her. She had so many competing demands—her family, her job, her studies—that this additional demand seemed like the last straw.

Underlying Issue: Options. Sussman's (1972) *options-maintenance model* underscores the relationship of options to well-being. When individuals see no options, they feel trapped and caught. Pearlin (1982) claims that self-esteem and confidence are eroded when people feel forced to stay in a low-level job or an unsatisfactory marriage because they see no options.

Sussman discusses two levels of options: structural and psychological. *Structural options* are related to the availability of options, such as child and family day care, academic tutoring at flexible times, and financial aid for the adult learner taking one course at a time. Many potential adult learners become actual adult learners when the structure of educational opportunities changes. For example, before the advent of learning and extension programs via long-distance telecommunications, many rural adults were unable to participate in formal learning programs.

Psychological options are related to the individual's skill in perceiving and utilizing alternatives (Sussman, 1972). The comments of two sixty-year-old men, from a discussion in which each was assessing his options for learning, serves as an illustration. One said, "I doubt the local university will take older students. I'll not apply." The other disagreed, saying, "The demographics are for me. I'm in a growing age cohort so I know that the institution will take me." Clearly, assessment of actual options, as well as perceiving and utilizing them, is an individual matter.

Another category of options emerges here: that of *created*

options. The history of oppressed groups in this country—women, older people, black people, and other ethnic minorities—reflects a shift from a time when they accepted that they had no options to a time when they fought to change the opportunity structure. Similarly, through efforts of such organizations as the Council for the Advancement of Experiential Learning and the American Council on Education's Commission on Higher Education and the Adult Learner, learning options have been created for older learners.

Consider the story of a thirty-six-year-old construction worker who became paraplegic as the result of an automobile accident. After the initial physical battle to survive, he became preoccupied with how to live. Not surprisingly, he saw no options at first. His initial attempt to build a new life was aborted when his application to law school was rejected. Although discouraged, he wrote his mother, "I want to share with you the perspective I now have on my future. Because of your love and support I am facing the future with courage, hope, and curiosity." His use of the word *curiosity* showed that on a deep level he would make it—he would be in control and create options. And, in fact, he applied to and was accepted at a school of architecture, drawing on his interest in building and his experience in construction.

In a study of how clerical workers cope with transitions, we asked, "Generally, in change situations how many options do you perceive?" Ninety-four percent saw more than one option. Then we asked, "For the transition you are currently undergoing, how many options did you perceive?" Over 34 percent saw only one option. This indicates that individuals usually see several options, but under stress or in the middle of a transition that has significantly altered their lives, many often freeze and can see only one option—which seriously affects their ability to cope (Charner and Schlossberg, 1986).

Thus, options can be objective or structural (at one time there were few opportunities for older learners on college campuses), subjective or psychological (the person assumes that because of age he or she will not apply to undergraduate school, medical school), or created (the person believes he or she can find or assemble a new alternative).

Implications for the Learner. Now in the middle of her transition, Mary has learned to persist. Although she was terrified during her entry period, she found that she could do the work and be successful. Her self-esteem has improved steadily. She has an excellent support system from family and advisers, the kind of support one would wish for all adult learners. From time to time, Mary found the competing demands on her almost too much to bear; she felt trapped and could not see her options. But whenever she thought of quitting school, someone— usually a counselor—showed her there were options and helped her perceive and utilize her psychological options more effectively. She could seek more help at home or negotiate with her instructors so that missing an occasional class would not diminish her opportunities to learn. She learned to create new options for herself.

Educational support services can be designed to help learners mobilize their energies and persist in their efforts. More structural options can be offered to adult learners through a reevaluation of the scheduling of classes, for example, which would have helped Mary greatly. Student development specialists have a unique opportunity to engage in two kinds of activities; creating supportive options for their adult learners and teaching adult learners how to perceive and create their own supports both inside and outside the college community.

Art: "Mastering New Skills"

After Art's mandatory retirement from the army, he wanted to develop new competencies and make a life plan for himself. Returning to school for further training seemed the logical way to cope with his retirement and plan for the future. "I resolved not to be a hang-around, not to keep going back to the old outfits. I felt that going to school would be a more positive way to move into a new life. At first, I just took courses— sort of exploring. After a year, I saw what I wanted and focused on getting my degree in political science. Just when I thought I had direction and felt comfortable in school, the —— hit the fan at home."

The biggest support was his adviser, who was a "sympathetic voice in court." His peers were another important support: He reached out to other adult learners and started a Thursday night dinner group.

Art was doing well at the university. He was intent on becoming prepared for the rest of his life, his grades were A's and B's, and he made "some of the closest friends I have ever had." But he became very depressed and almost threw everything over because of the tension his return to school was causing at home.

His wife, who expected him to get another job, was highly agitated when he returned to school. After two years of living on his cut income, she told Art that she did not intend to live at this reduced level any longer. She saw that Art would be at least two more years in school and she could not take it. She asked for a divorce. This of course was not the main reason for the divorce. It merely brought older, unresolved problems to the surface. Art's return to school was the trigger, not the cause.

Art felt pushed in two directions: by the pressure from his wife to leave school and get a paying job, and by his internal pressure to get prepared so that in the long run he would have fulfilling work at a higher level. Art visited the career counseling center and found there was a day-long workshop on life planning for adults. (He felt fortunate that there was such a service for adults; however, he found it only by chance.) With the support of his peer group and his adviser, through career counseling and an opportunity to work in an internship situation that really excited him, he decided to opt for education and end the marriage.

Underlying Issue: The Drive for Competency. The theme of competence is identified by White (1976a), who believes that most theories of human motivation overlook the constant striving of individuals to become more fit, more competent. White sees this tendency not as a negative drive, whose sole purpose is to relieve tension, but as a positive force, akin to a child's compulsion to explore and manipulate the environment. It is the expression of a universal need to expand boundaries, investigate the world, and achieve mastery over it. White distinguishes between *competence* (in the objective sense of fitness or ability) and *sense of competence* (a subjective state), the more crucial construct in explaining human behavior. We all know people who are competent in a particular area (such as academic study) and yet feel themselves to be incompetent in general; it is often vitally important to their well-being that they become aware of their strengths and abilities.

The validity of White's view was dramatized at a presentation by Roger Gould, where he asked the members of his audience to identify the personal issue that currently concerned them most. By means of a lecture and a demonstration counseling session with a volunteer from the audience, Gould showed that such personal issues related to an aspect of their lives with which they were tinkering. This tinkering was an attempt to overcome childhood prohibitions and to "change one's boundaries of self-definition." Pointing out that people in the process of change are often preoccupied with feelings of their own inadequacy and incompetency, Gould emphasized that these feelings should be welcomed as an opportunity to confront deficiencies. Such a confrontation can serve as a stimulus for growth, of "enfranchising oneself as a competent person" free from parental strictures (Gould, 1978). Thus, White's concept of an inherent human drive for greater competence and Gould's idea that recognition of incompetence is the first step in actualizing this goal are complementary.

The move from incompetency to competency is usually made in two primary ways: by changing oneself and by pursuing and learning new activities. The process can be difficult. Gould (1981), noting that people are extremely vulnerable at times of transition and change, found that they often protect themselves from changing by "catastrophizing." For example, a fifty-five-year-old woman was afraid that if she took up writing as a serious career, it would provoke her husband. Frequently, when people tinker with incompetency and try to forge new patterns, they are afraid that if they think and behave differently, the sky will fall in. According to Gould, "The catastrophe prediction phenomenon guarantees a slow rate of change and a dialectic stability when it operates as a healthy dynamic. When it operates in an exaggerated fashion as an unhealthy phenomenon, it causes people to be 'stuck,' paralyzed, and unable to grow by integrating their new experiences in life" (p. 45).

A broad perspective on learning motives is offered by

Kuhlen (1963), who suggests that adult behavior in general is impelled by two *metamotives:* (1) a positive drive for expansion and growth, and (2) a self-protective drive based on anxiety and insecurity, to compensate for perceived inadequacies. Obviously, both motives may be present in the pursuit of education; that is, adults may seek to improve their social skills and interpersonal relations or simply to expand their knowledge of the world, or they may be pushed by the fear that without further education they will lose their jobs, their friends, or their cognitive powers. In Cross's (1981) model explaining participation in lifelong learning, she incorporates the individual's drive for competency with the opportunities or barriers the individual faces when attempting to express this need for competency, thus suggesting that the psychological need for competency must be seen in a larger context.

But the drive for competence is lifelong. White (1976b) contends that people continually need to expand, explore, and achieve mastery over the world and over themselves. As they grow older, they continually try out new coping mechanisms that can potentially increase their feelings of competence.

Implications for the Learner. After retirement from the army, Art explored and found a goal that would give his life meaning. His motivation was strong and his search for mastery of new skills was important to him. His sense of competence was high, bolstered by the evidence of competency in his courses.

Although Art did not find support at home, he actively developed peer support. And he viewed his adviser as his biggest supporter. Art's family situation caused him a great deal of pain and anxiety. The tension he felt at home almost made him give up. Under stress, he could have been motivated by a self-protective drive to compensate for his perceived inadequacies. But he expanded the boundaries of his self-definition, stopped catastrophizing, and found his strengths. Finally, through sorting out his options, he chose school over the marriage.

Janice: "A Need for Involvement"

After two years in school, Janice, a widow with two children, decided to put school on a back burner. Her need for a sense of community and productivity was not being met by the university. She felt isolated at school, where she had no opportunity to socialize; she felt isolated at home, where her activities were limited to child care and studying. Her grades went down. She dropped out of the university and became a real estate agent, investing in property that she refurbished at a profit.

At the beginning, Janice got support in two ways. The counselors told her "You can do it," and even more important, they told her how. She did well in her classes—and yet she withdrew.

With all this support, what went wrong? First, she kept commenting on the fact that it was "by chance" that she found out about the returning student program. In addition, after this course, returning students had no systematic way to keep in touch. School became just a place to leave quickly after class. Without a social life, sense of community, or place to go for chatting and studying, Janice found the school experience isolating. She wanted to meet other adults and to feel productive, both at school and at home. In addition, Janice had trouble writing term papers and her grades suffered as a result. She needed help organizing her time and figuring out how to get the library books she needed when they were either missing or on reserve. She knew that an office dealt specifically with study skills, but she felt too pressed for time to search it out, to risk wasting as much as a day she did not have. It was easier to drop out. School was becoming a drag.

Janice's children are supportive. However, the demands and mechanics of being a single parent are complex. She would spend the early part of the evening helping her children with their schoolwork, then start on her own projects. She had many all-nighters. Despite the initial support of friends in her community, as time went on most were no longer available for emergency help. To pay for outside help, she needed to work for money.

When we discussed her personal strengths and liabilities, Janice commented that she had coped with multiple losses—a baby who died, a husband who died suddenly, and a relationship turned sour—through her religious faith, friends, and therapy.

Underlying Issues: Lack of Community and Role Over-load. At the same time that adults have the need to feel individual and special, they also have a need to be connected to a community, to belong. Myerhoff (1978) underscores the essential paradox of the human condition—that people simultaneously need separateness and community connectedness. These twin needs explain the limitations of experimental learning arrangements like long-distance learning and external degree programs. These innovations address only the need for individualization and may neglect the issue of community in learning.

Baruch, Biener, and Barnett (1987) contend that the dual need for competency and intimacy can best be met through investment in work and family roles. In their examination of "role overload (typically defined as having too much to do) and role conflict (typically defined as feeling pulled apart by conflicting demands)" (p. 131), they find that a person's investment in two spheres of life is not the cause of overload or conflict; rather, the cause is the imbalance of psychological demands and control in each sphere. Role overload for parents of young children can be debilitating, an overload especially heavy for the single parent.

When individuals can feel in control in another area, their feeling of being out of control overall—often associated with the parent role—is diminished. Baruch, Biener, and Barnett suggest that work for women may serve as a buffer against stress from other areas. We suggest that learning can also serve as a buffer, when organized so that learners can experience a balance between the needs for "autonomous achievement . . . and connectedness and attachment" (Baruch, Biener, and Barnett, p. 134). This research presents a new way of thinking about the topic of role overload or competing demands. Investing in multiple roles can be beneficial to mental health when the quality of the role involvement allows control or mastery and pleasure or attachment. The learning role can be one that provides opportunities for quality role involvement.

Implications for the Learner. Having coped with many losses in her life, Janice turned to college to meet her needs for achievement and involvement. During her first semester in the returning students program, she was able to have a sense of community through friendships she developed in her classes. When the semester was over, however, she had no systematic way for her to meet her friends. Had there been even a lounge, a place to meet others, an ongoing support group, or easily available academic advising, she said she would have undoubtedly remained at the university.

Janice had few supports at home and experienced mostly the demands and role overload of being a single parent—performing parenting tasks alone and making all the decisions alone. Her neighbors and friends were less and less able to give her help and support. She felt more isolated and overloaded than ever.

Janice's learning environment was not stimulating enough to fulfill her desire for a sense of community. By dropping out of school and starting to work as a real estate agent, she felt more in charge of her life. She developed relationships at work that were satisfying. The work and her new relationships, unlike the college experience, served as a buffer against the stresses of single parenthood.

The Conceptual Framework for Moving Through

Our conceptual framework suggests directions professionals might take in designing interventions for adult learners moving through. Each learner—like Valerie, Mary, Art, and Janice—has different needs, yet all need help in sustaining their involvement in higher education and in continuing to feel they matter to the institution. The transition model helps us understand each adult learner's needs through its structured approach to predicting, measuring, and modifying reactions to change. The model builds upon the work of Lowenthal, Thurnher, and Chiriboga (1975) and their study of four groups in transition. These researchers found that people bring potential strengths and weaknesses to each transition. In Chapter Two we described these potential resources or deficits as the four S's: situation, self, supports, and strategies. Here we can apply the four S's to adult learners in the midst of learning.

Take the situation. As each adult learner progresses, his or her situation changes. Art found himself in divorce proceedings, needing money and support; Valerie needed help sorting out sexism and ageism; Mary would have benefited from easier access to courses; Janice had competing demands and not enough support from the school. We can assess each person's situation by looking at it in context with other demands in life, to see how the learner evaluates the total situation. By knowing an adult learner's particular situation, we can design interventions tailored to that individual.

The self element refers to the adult learner's strengths for coping. Is the adult learner basically optimistic about the outcome of the process? Can the adult learner deal with the ambiguity inherent in any planned transition? Does he or she have a repertoire of positive experiences? Some individuals are better able to deal with the middle transition period than others.

Supports are particularly critical for adult learners. An inventory of external supports and options suggests ways the institution can help the adult learner in this essential area. Art's lack of support at home, for example, was compensated for by his strong relationship with his adviser and fellow adult learners. Another adult learner, who lived with a chronically ill mother, received words of encouragement from her mother when she entered school. But as she became more involved with school, her mother began to make last-minute demands for food and medicine, usually as the student was leaving for her long drive to class. The lack of support from her mother tipped the balance, and she dropped out. She might have persisted with her plans if she could have brought her mother to a family care center at the school.

Many people write and talk about support as if it were an absolute entity that one either has or does not have. Support actually exists in degrees; there are some areas in which advisers and significant others are very supportive but others in which they are not. The amount or kind of support needed varies from one person to the next, but a certain amount is essential and can make the difference in how people cope with transitions.

Support for adult learners comes from many sources, including families, friends, and institutions.

When we looked beyond the most frequent description of the family as being "very supportive" in a study of adult learners, we found apparent differences in the types of support— both desired and received (Schlossberg and Warren, 1985). These differences appeared to be related to gender roles. What was left unsaid, but implied by the male adult learners, was that they did not think of spouse support in terms of relieving them of household duties, because their wives were already doing that. Rather, they viewed a supportive wife as one who understood the importance of the student role they had undertaken and was willing to make few demands on their time or attention, leaving them free to fulfill the role of adult learner.

What about support from children? Adult learners referred to the excitement and pride their children felt about their achievements. A seventy-year-old lived alone, but his children and grandchildren gave him a big party when he finished his A.A. degree, complete with college banners and special touches. However, it would be misleading to believe that it is all thrill and pride on the part of adult learners' children, especially when the learner is female. Children still identify mothers as caretakers; they may feel the loss of their mother's everyday attention and make demands that sabotage her learning.

We were curious about the role of friends in helping adult learners sustain their learning efforts. Friends were rarely spontaneously mentioned. When asked whether their friends were supportive, male adult learners responded that friends did not enter into the picture, one way or the other. The female adult learners generally said their friends were supportive, but few of the learners considered their friends to have been significant enough to mention them without being asked about them. The adult learners who did speak of friends as playing a prominent role for them were women. This probably reflects the greater importance that women in our society place on interpersonal relationships. Gilligan (1982) found that men value personal achievement over personal relationships, and that women tend to reverse those two values. Other studies support Gilligan's contention. When confronted with a situation demanding a choice between personal achievement and helping a friend, males tend to opt for personal achievement, while females choose helping the friend.

One adult learner reported more support from friends who had college and university degrees. Another learner said there were a few friends who just could not understand why she never had time to go to lunch and "play." In a few cases, the returning women adult learners reported a friend who either returned with them or whom they influenced to return later. One could assume support from these friends. In one noteworthy case, a friend played a critical support role. The adult learner gave up her home and literally moved in with her friend for the duration of her student status in order to cut down on living expenses. Many adult learners make friends when they return to school—friends who share their interests and the learning journey.

Our most pressing concern in this book is the role that institutions of higher learning play in supporting their adult learners, and in the next chapter we will examine the variety of ways student development professionals can offer support. But first, we need to emphasize that just laying out the welcome mat to older adults is a form of support. In talking about the institutions, one adult learner said she chose a particular school because she believed it to be "such a caring place that I thought it was important to go there."

The word *caring* captures the essence of the kind of support the adult learners talked about most. Caring meant the learners were made to feel that their special needs for information, guidance, and encouragement were perceived and that the institution, through its individual representatives, cared about those needs and was doing its "darndest" to meet them. Most of all, caring was the sense on the part of each individual adult learner that he or she mattered. As one learner put it, "They treated you like you were the only person there, calling you by your first name and all." Having individual advisers and faculty who were knowledgeable, accessible, and advocates for them was important—it was having someone on the staff in your corner, so to speak. For some, a caring adviser provided special support; for others a teacher, and for still others, a special program, such as the returning student program or the adult student information center.

Many adult learners spoke in one way or another of the difficulty in getting information about services and programs available to adults. They had numerous suggestions for more and better advertising of programs by institutions. Adult learners wanted access not only to courses but to the guidance of the college or university staff. Further, being in a time of transition in their lives, they were looking for emotional support and encouragement. It meant everything to believe that there was at least someone—an adviser or professor—who understood their needs and cared enough to help.

What strategies best enable adult learners to cope? We speculate that if adult learners had more coping strategies, they would be better able to stay in school and deal with the competing demands, change of goals, lack of financial and day-care assistance, and many other issues and problems. Pearlin and Schooler (1978) point out that there is no single, magic coping strategy; rather, the creative coper can employ a number of coping strategies in relation to the situation, self, or supports. They categorize these strategies as those that (1) change the situation, self, or external supports; (2) change the meaning of the situation, self, or supports; and (3) enable one to relax in the face of stress. The individual faced with a divorce ultimatum, for example, can try to change the situation by negotiating for time or seeking marriage counseling. Or the person, like Art, can decide that marriage is a restrictive state and that divorce would offer new opportunities for growth, thereby changing the meaning of the situation. Or, the individual could employ relaxation techniques by jogging, swimming, meditating, or even laughing. Consider the physical therapist who suggested that the tightness in a patient's shoulders could be the result of tension and asked, "Can you lessen the stress in your life?" The patient responded, "Sure, if I can give my children and their problems to you."

Lazarus and Folkman (1984) indicate that time often is a healer and problem solver all by itself. Another effective coping strategy is knowing when to do nothing. Student development professionals can help learners expand their coping repertoire to deal with the long learning journey.

The transition model, then, can help us help adult learners assess their situation, self, supports, and strategies. The model suggests what activities each individual might (or might not) undertake so that he or she can cope more creatively with the learning process and its issues. It also describes how individual reactions change. For example, what adult learners need when moving in—learning the ropes, gaining confidence—is not the same as what adult learners need when moving through. What they need most when moving through is support, and support is what institutions need to structure and provide. Some adult learners, like Art and Mary, need support as they continue their search for competence. Some, like Gwen, need support through such structural help as day care and financial aid and planning. Some, like Maggie, need support through counseling or therapy, or through tutoring when academic problems arise. Some, like Janice, need support through being connected with the community and with others in their same situation.

Janice found the campus very frightening at first. She wondered, "Do I have all my marbles? Will I ever find a niche? Will being older make me feel too different and out of place? Why can't I read the class listings?" Fortunately, she found out about the returning student program, which she claims saved her life. The counselors in the program pushed her to take the entry/ orientation course for returning students. At first she arrogantly refused, thinking she didn't need this "Mickey Mouse stuff." She found out how wrong she was. The course was the best experience she had. She met others in the same situation and had a chance to air her feelings about being in her new role.

But Janice left after two years. Her concerns and issues during the middle period were clearly different from her earlier concerns. She no longer needed to learn the ropes; she needed to feel productive and connected. She needed to feel that she mattered, that she was part of a community, and that her need for involvement was recognized and addressed.

More and complementary directions we might take in

designing support for adult learners are suggested by the underlying issues most adults confront as they move through. Chickering's (1969) vectors of human development can provide a compass for thinking through the needs of these adult learners. Some, like Mary, are uncertain about their competency to deal with academic content; others, like Valerie, are concerned about their competency to deal with competing demands. Some, like Art, are concerned about who they are and where they are going. They may have entered or reentered with one learning agenda, like Janice, but later questioned whether that is really what they want.

Chickering's issues of developing competence, managing emotions, developing autonomy (interdependence), establishing identity, freeing interpersonal relationships, developing purpose, and developing integrity certainly were concerns of Valerie, Mary, Art, and Janice. They were also the concerns of the adult learners in the group meeting described at the beginning of this chapter. Specifically, all these adult learners were involved in gender issues, apparent lack of options, the need for developing mastery and competence, and becoming involved despite the inevitable competing demands.

In fact, no matter what the interviewed adult learners expressed as their major concerns, they all referred to competing demands. Just as many high school seniors must deal with competing demands of academic requirements, extracurricular activities, college applications, home responsibilities, and often part-time work, so too, must returning single parents deal with making money, studying, and child care. And other adult learners are caught among the competing needs of children, parents, school, and work.

In Conclusion

Once adult learners are well entrenched in the institution and know the rules and norms, their concerns and issues change. The underlying issues—or agendas—identified in this chapter for adult learners moving through include: the need to be seen as an individual and not be stereotyped as middle aged or older; the need to cope with competing demands for time and energy in family and work; the desire to master new skills—personal, professional, and academic; and a sense of belonging, a need to matter to the institution.

Among institutional responses for meeting the multiple issues of their heterogeneous adult learner populations are these:

- Vigilance around gender and age issues both in the institution and at home
- Identifying and creating options that will enable learners to remain in the learning situation
- Encouraging personal, professional, and academic competencies
- Developing a sense of community for all learners, whether part time or full time

But whatever their issues, vectors, agendas, or roles, all adult learners moving through express a need for support, both personal and institutional. Support of all kinds is central to the success of returning students, and the next chapter examines the various ways higher education professionals can offer this essential support.

SIX

Creating Programs to Foster Educational Progress

As Valerie, Mary, Art, and Janice tell us, their need for achievement and success continues as they move through the institution. The first few weeks of the first term are usually the most crucial in determining which students will continue, but the saga of role responsibilities and transitions continues throughout subsequent terms and years. The adult learner faces the realities of hard work once the initial excitement fades and the anxiety of starting school at a nontraditional age recedes. It takes effort to plan time to study, pass tests, prepare papers, and balance school with the many other obligations of family, career, and community. One striking difference between adult learners and most other students is that, for adult learners, school is not the primary focus; it is just one of many demands competing for their time and energy.

Institutions that pull new students into the pipeline and treat them all the same, preferring administrative convenience to attention to students' needs, are grave travesties of higher education. Adults accustomed to being treated as competent individuals in their home, work, and community activities are shocked when they are suddenly part of a herd—without status or recognition of their individual talents—in classes, assemblies, and cafeterias. Having their names replaced by Social Security numbers on most forms symbolizes for many a loss of identity.

Revamping Student Educational Services

The "bag lady" of Chapter One could not find a place to sit or receive messages. Janice, in the preceding chapter, felt so isolated that she withdrew. The frustrations of John's odyssey in Chapter Three are all too common. We need to move from institutional convenience to learner convenience. We need to change from a treatment orientation to a prevention orientation—to see ourselves as educators and collaborators with learners. We need a comprehensive and coherent system of supporting educational services and programs that puts learner needs first.

General systems theory views each person as a complex individual operating within a system in which concepts such as sick or well are irrelevant. When people in the system develop symptoms, the system must be modified because it has become dysfunctional—the fault lies with the system, not the people. Our colleges and universities have dysfunctional characteristics for many learners, especially adult learners. Nevitt Sanford (1966, p. 49) said, "If an institution is a system of subsystems, and if a change in any one of them can change the whole, then it should be possible to make certain modifications in a college program which would reduce overall rates of mental illness among students or increase the overall level of their development." So that we can build truly responsive learning systems, we need to strengthen our understanding of adult learners and their interactions with all supporting services and programs.

Adult learner transitions and developmental tasks, which rarely lead to severe emotional disturbance, are best addressed through education and changes in the environment, that is, through prevention. Prevention activities can promote conditions that reinforce positive mental health and lower the incidence of emotional disturbance. As the adage says, "An ounce of prevention is worth a pound of cure." Albee (1980) proposed a formula regarding the incidence of emotional disturbances:

$$\text{Incidence of mental disorders} = \frac{\text{Organic factors} + \text{Stress}}{\text{Competence} + \text{Coping skills} + \text{Self-esteem} + \text{Support}}$$

This formula means that when we increase an adult learner's competence, coping skills, self-esteem, and support and reduce his or her stress, we promote positive mental health and reduce the incidence of emotional disturbance. By shifting to a prevention orientation, our colleges and universities become caring institutions that promote adult learners' strengths.

A prevention orientation means that administrators, faculty, and student development professionals need to become increasingly proactive—to use their skills and experience to identify and design intervention strategies for such potentially vulnerable target subpopulations as single parents, displaced homemakers, and unemployed workers. Such strategies can include programs to strengthen self-esteem, build confidence, and improve competence and coping skills through education, social engineering, and modeling. Support groups can be developed that help adult learners develop a sense of competence, identity, and integrity. Stressful environmental circumstances can be eliminated or lessened. And training for self-empowerment—a way to give adults strategies for taking more control of their lives—can be provided for all members of the learning community.

Student educational services have traditionally been organized along functional lines of orientation, academic advising, counseling, housing, and student activities. Often little communication and minimal integration exists among these various services. Students bring complex problems but experience fragmented and compartmentalized responses. In recent years, services for such special subpopulations as minority, handicapped, and international students, who may be particularly at risk for not completing their education, have been integrated across functions, with program coordinators acting as advocates for their group. Students in these groups feel supported; they have a sense of belonging to their institution.

We are not proposing a whole new set of parallel services for adult learners. We are proposing a structure that clusters educational services and support programs, that has a prevention and education orientation, and that emphasizes developmental issues using a transition framework. Different groups of students can use the services in different ways. Major criteria for measuring effectiveness in such a system of services and programs are flexibility and responsiveness to the needs of all learners.

How can the problems facing adult learners in the moving-through stage, like those faced by Valerie, Mary, Art, and Janice, be confronted? What can we do to make the agendas of adult learners our agenda? How can we promote learning throughout their higher education careers? When we view ourselves as educators and the students as learners, we set different priorities. We view admissions as a learning process. We view the entire college environment, as well as the home, the workplace, and the community, as the learning context for the adult learner. We recognize that adult learners are in transition and that the college or university experience is one of their transitions.

We know from Astin's (1986) research that students who feel they are involved in their institutions are most likely to stay until they graduate but that students who are not involved, do not feel that they matter, are more likely to drop out. The 1984 National Institute of Education report *Involvement in Learning* used the concept of involvement to recommend important changes needed for the survival of higher education. Those recommendations are perhaps more important for adult learners than for traditional-age students, because adult learners often feel isolated and different.

Involvement directly strengthens self-esteem and support, two key elements in Albee's prevention formula. The more the adult learner is involved, the greater the feelings of self-esteem and support. This concept also works in reverse order: To get involved, the adult learner must have some self-esteem and feel some support. We propose three main areas of change in the support dimension.

The first area of change is recognizing the difference between adult learners and traditional-age students and acknowledging adult learners as a vital force in the institution. Such recognition means allocating space, personnel, and budget and demonstrating that adult learners are valued throughout the institution. Such acknowledgment means taking a new look at educational services for adult learners, developing an awareness of the overload of commitments many of them already handle, and revamping our student educational services. As students said in the last chapter, "Why can't advisers realize we are different than eighteen-year-olds? We need help and we've got maturity. Yet we're treated like numbers or children. Our needs are not respected." We suggest starting with an adult learner support center than can involve and service adult learners in ways that make them feel they matter.

The second area of change is connecting each adult learner, possibly through the adult learner support center, to a recognized member of the institutional community—a faculty member, administrator, student development professional, or staff person—who can serve as a developmental mentor. A developmental mentor is one who cares and sponsors (as will be explained later in this chapter). We see a mentor and an academic adviser working together to refer an adult learner as needed to academic support services: career and personal counseling, financial planning, residence life (for the small number of adult learners who live on campus), family and health care, and other services such as parking, transportation, food services, or the bookstore. The support services, such as career counseling, may make referrals back to the mentor and academic adviser. In other words, through a connection to a member of the college or university community, each adult learner will have access to and be part of a network of services and programs that make up a system for serving adult learners effectively.

The third area of change is in the structure of institutional services and programs. This change responds to: "I feel foolish at my age going to the career counseling center. Everyone is so young—even the counselors. They all think I should know where I'm going." Staff persons in the counseling center should be mature and interested in meeting the needs of adult learners, and at least one staff person in each of the other service areas needs to be specifically responsible for adult learners. Professional development for all staff members, including clerical staff, on adult issues will help ensure effective service for adult learners, as does the reminder that we are all adult learners. And institutions can encourage their faculty and staff to continue with their own education—to practice what is being preached. This area also includes recognizing that adult learners have an overload of commitments already, that adult learners have multiple responsibilities, demands, and needs. It involves adjusting class schedules, locations, and program offerings, as well as faculty and bursar office hours, to accommodate adult learner schedules and needs. It means changing to a prevention and educational orientation for career and personal counseling, learning resource centers, and health services for adult learners. Such services as residential life, child care, and transportation are also adjusted to meet the special needs of the mostly commuting adult learners. In other words, adult learners need services that are provided at times and places convenient for them, through programs that serve their specific needs, and by staff who understand adult issues and can help students like Mary "hang in there."

A comprehensive reassessment of current services and restructuring to accommodate adult learners may be required, but helping adult learners get involved and building support for them are essential for the successful future of our institutions and represent important challenges to higher education.

Adult Learner Support Center

A place to matter is important to adult learners. Janice actually dropped out because she felt so isolated. These concerns were expressed in Chapter Five: "We need a place to meet, to have coffee, to study, and to network. Except for one course for returning students during the first semester, we are lost in the crowds." Adults interviewed in Chapter Five echoed the "bag lady" in Chapter One, saying that having a place to meet, a quiet place to study, and a place to receive messages and make phone calls would make all the difference in their feeling that the institution cared.

Memphis State University is an institution that demonstrates its support by allocating space for adult learners to meet. The large Adult Information Center, located in the Student Center, makes adult learners feel recognized and supported. It contains sofas, chairs, desks, tables, file cabinets, bulletin boards, a telephone, a coffee pot, tea bags, a dictionary. Adult learners from throughout the institution use this room to study, wait between classes, eat, drink coffee, meet their friends, plan programs, or discuss meaningful issues. Such groups as the Adult Student Association, Warmline, Women's Studies Group, Graduate Student Support Group, Parenting Group, and Career and Midlife Change Group meet there weekly or monthly. In addition, the Counseling and Personnel Services Department sets aside room primarily for student use to encourage a sense of connectedness, a feeling of community.

Staffing any adult learner support center should be a student development professional who is familiar with adult development issues, empathizes with adult learners, and, of course, wants the assignment. This professional can provide coordination and continuity, serve as adviser and liaison to the adult learner association, facilitate group meetings, act as a referral source for adult learners, develop and disseminate an adult learner survival manual, and coordinate a babysitting referral system or co-op. A message machine would allow adults to call the center at their convenience evenings or weekends to ask for information. Work-study adult learners can assist and help with mailings. Institutions that set up and staff such centers give adult learners a strong signal of support and mattering.

Another signal can be organizing an adult learner association, like Art's Thursday night dinner group, to support social, recreational, and educational programs and events. Such an association could be an important advocate for adult learner concerns, even though many adult learners may not have time to participate actively or often.

The Adult Student Association at Memphis State University has a booth at registration to give new adult learners information on services such as orientation, career, personal and peer counseling, and a babysitting referral system. The association publishes a newsletter and sponsors family outings and parties. It also serves as an advocate for adult learners, for example, by successfully working to change academic policy so that part-time students are now eligible for the dean's list and academic awards. The association also presents its own "We Believe in You" award to the adult learner who has overcome the most obstacles to return to education. A recent recipient was a single parent of three who worked as a waitress by night so she could pursue business studies by day.

Florida Atlantic University (FAU)'s Lifelong Learning Society, with over 3,000 members, assists nontraditional, older students with orientation, registration, and general adjustment to the university. The society brings an opportunity for lifelong learning to thousands of retired and semiretired area citizens by providing a program that allows Florida residents aged sixty or older to audit courses for free, as well as by sponsoring enrichment courses and a fitness/wellness program. The university received special commendation for the Society for Innovation and Change in Higher Education by the American Association of State Colleges and Universities "for extremely well focused programs meeting pressing national needs in unique ways" (Ostar, 1988, p. 2). The society works closely with the FAU Foundation to promote academic, research, and public service programs and has an executive director employed by the university.

Adult learners today are aware that they have a real stake in student activity-fee funds, even though they often leave student government to traditional-age students. A further signal that adult learners matter is the use of student government funds to finance the adult learner association and other adult learner activities.

Questions adapted or taken from the *ACE Adult Learner Assessment and Planning Guide* to help institutions assess their commitment to adult learners include:

1. Has the institution allocated space for adult learners to study informally and to meet other students?
2. Is the space provided with a message board and a telephone for use by adults?
3. Are staff assigned who are sensitive to adult learners and who can facilitate programming relevant to adults?
4. Has an adult learner organization been established to serve as an advocate for adults and to plan programs to meet their needs?

5.   Is there a newsletter or other publication that provides information and news about adult learners?
5.   Are student government structures and functions so designed as to encourage participation by adult learners?
   •   Have the structure and functions of student government been reviewed to ascertain whether they accommodate the interests and needs of adult learners?
   •   Do any adult learners now hold elective or appointive offices in the student government structure?
   •   May voting in student government elections be done by mail or at times and places convenient for adult learners?

Developmental Mentoring

Mentoring is mentioned in various publications of the last decade. Levinson and others (1978) recognize in their research the importance of the mentor—a nonparental sponsor—in the achievement of career dreams. Thomas, Murrell, and Chickering (1982) propose ways that developmental theory can be used by mentors to help students of any age, race, or sex accomplish their developmental tasks.

Daloz (1986) shows that mentors are often the most effective teachers for adult learners. He tells of rural Vermont adult learners in the external degree programs at Johnson College and Norwich University. Daloz, who compares the college or university career to a journey, describes the work of dedicated mentors as they hold a hand here, pat a shoulder there, and say words of comfort or praise, guiding their adult learners through the maze of learning obstacles. Daloz's mentors are required to be in the classroom as well as on the external degree circuit, in student educational services, or connected to an adult learner support center.

We take these ideas one step further. We suggest the use of developmental mentors—faculty, staff, or student development professionals trained in human development and committed to working with learners over the entire learning journey. We see developmental mentoring programs, designed to respond to the development tasks facing adult learners, as a key to their involvement in our institutions. We also see developmental mentoring as interacting with academic advising and with academic support services, career development, personal counseling, and cocurricular activities. The process is illustrated in Figure 2.

Figure 2. Developmental Mentoring Process.

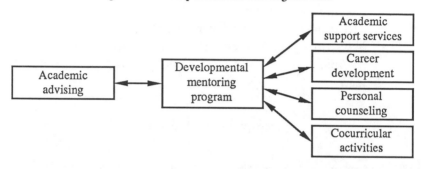

Students usually have assigned academic advisers—a faculty member if they have declared a major, a student development professional if they have not. Developmental mentoring goes a step beyond academic advising and can be the bridge for adult learners who want to explore their own development or plan interdisciplinary and cocurricular activities that augment their academic program—although Winston, Miller, Enders, Grites, and Associates (1984) point out that academic advising also needs to be developmental and to address these issues. We suggest that student development professionals, for whom studying adult development theory is a professional responsibility and for whom listening is an occupational skill, can serve as effective developmental mentors to adult learners.

What will an effective developmental mentor do? The developmental mentor can be the sustaining influence in the life of the adult learner throughout his or her college or university experience. The mentor can provide challenge, support, and vision as the learner moves through the developmental tasks and stages (Thomas, Murrell, and Chickering, 1982). A mentor provides encouragement and helps adult learners increase their psychological options through perceiving and using various alternatives (Sussman, 1972). Developmental mentors help adult learners plan coherent use of all parts of the learning system.

As the adult learner moves into the institution (and prepares the developmental transcript as described in Chapter Four), the developmental mentor can help the learner set goals and plan a sequence of learning experiences and activities, including nonformal activities, that will contribute to achieving those goals. For example, the developmental mentor would encourage an adult learner whose goal is to become a professional writer to contact a community newspaper or local trade magazine to begin building links to professional publications and gain important and useful competencies to add to his or her developmental transcript.

Developmental mentors who have clear understandings of developmental theory can assist adult learners through the assessment process (to be incorporated into the developmental transcript). For example, using Perry's (1968) scheme, the developmental mentor can help the adult learner at a dualistic stage (that is, who thinks in *either/or* terms) understand the choice between two different stances regarding family and school. An adult learner at the multiplistic stage (that is, who is capable of understanding several points of view) can be helped to see the variety of options opened by pursuing alternative activities in the institution and in the community. An adult learner at the relativistic stage recognizes that there is no single truth and that all knowledge is relative. This learner can be helped to clarify values regarding the impact of different ideological stances leading to making commitments. The final stage of commitment occurs when a person accepts a plurality of views but commits to a course of action or a set of values. In helping a person move from one of these stages to the next, both challenge and support are needed (Sanford, 1966).

Developmental mentors who are knowledgeable about psychological type and the Myers-Briggs Type Indicator (Myers, 1980) can help adult learners assess their personality type—according to the Indicator—and show them how their assessed type affects their choices (Lynch, 1987). For example, adult learners who are extroverted may choose activities that involve working with groups, whereas those who are introverted may choose activities that allow them to work alone. A preference for sensing or intuition may influence the choice of majors and careers. A preference for thinking or feeling often influences decision making. A preference for judgment or perception may influence the spontaneity of life-styles. (For specific applications of the Myers-Briggs Type Indicator in higher education, see Provost and Anchors, 1987.)

Developmental mentors can oversee adult learners as they move in, move through, and move on. Adult learners who feel out of sync can be helped to see that learning is actually a lifelong process, that attending college at any age is beneficial. Using Chickering's (1969) vectors, developmental mentors can help adult learners identify those areas that are fairly well settled and those they are renegotiating. Adult learners who feel overloaded can be helped to realize that investing in multiple roles is favorable when the quality of the role involvement allows control or mastery, pleasure or attachment. Developmental mentors can help adult learners apply the transition model and analyze their four S's—situation, self, supports, and strategies.

Developmental mentors can also help adult learners negotiate and use the system—by providing general information about academic requirements and making any needed referrals to the learning resource center; by suggesting such career development activities as assessing career interests and strengths, exploring careers through computer or library searches, interviewing professionals, volunteering, and designing a relevant practicum; and by pointing the way to residential life experiences, individual counseling, self-help support groups, and such educational programs as assertiveness training and couples' enrichment.

We also suggest that student development professionals, with their knowledge of adult development theory and experience in working with adults, can serve equally effectively as organizers, coordinators, trainers, and facilitators of developmental mentoring programs that involve other caring faculty, administrators, staff, and alumni. Such involvement creates a bridge between professionals and adult learners. Faculty and staff, as adults themselves, may find that adult learners mirror how they feel or trigger their anxieties, creating opportunities for heightened awareness and mutual learning. (Such mirroring of their own concerns may be why some faculty feel threatened by adult learners in their classes.) Just as adult learners willing to share life and work experiences in the classroom can add a richness and reality generally missing from textbook-based discussions, so faculty who share their experiences and insights in the classroom and in advising can form significant connections with their students and model the best of developmental mentorship.

An important role for the director of any developmental mentoring program is that of advocate for adult learners. Information on adult-learner needs must be gathered and fed back to departments, faculty, and advisers for action. Schedule changes may be needed, for example, when only beginning classes are offered in the evenings and adult learners report they are finding it difficult if not impossible to take the advanced courses they need to complete their degrees. Or changes in registration may be needed if adult learners report they are finding classes filled with traditional-age students who have early or special registration privileges.

To find out whether the institution provides developmental mentoring relationships for adult learners, one might ask these questions:

1. Are developmental mentors available to all adult learners who request the relationship?
2. Are mentors available in the evening? On weekends? At different locations?
3. Are mentors educated in adult development theory? Are professional developmental opportunities provided to increase their knowledge?
4. Are mentors made aware of the array of experiences in the institution and in the community that will facilitate the development of the adult learner?
5. Are mentors assigned in a systematic manner?
6. Is the developmental transcript available for adult learners who request it?
7. Are the mentors professionals who really care about adult learners?

Academic Advising

For adult learners, academic advising is particularly crucial. When they move into the institution, they already feel behind. Academic advisers for adult learners need to understand the assessment of the prior learning process to help adult learners gain recognition for their college-level learning in work, service, or volunteer experiences. Many adult learners pursue further learning solely for pragmatic reasons and want to make sure that every course they take fits their educational goals. Advisers need to make sure adult students are aware of degree requirements and of any prerequisites for the courses they want to take—and advisers also need to have a theory base for defending curricula requirements.

But educational plans and goals can change as adult learners move through and acquire more knowledge and experience. Adult learners need academic advisers to help them review their educational plans periodically so that educational programs can be modified and adjusted as necessary. Advisers need to be knowledgeable about institutional policies on dropping and adding courses, and about the financial implications of interrupting course work for family or career reasons.

In general, adult learners need academic advice throughout the term, rather than at registration only. The advising process was difficult for Valerie, even though her adviser was excellent. She could not easily contact her adviser on the phone for just one question. When advisers are available only at certain times, often those times do not match the available times of adult learners. Some advisers need to be available for calls and appointments early in the day; others in the evenings, on weekends, or at different locations. Helping adult learners negotiate the system and select appropriate classes and instructors who encourage (especially the first few terms an adult learner is back in school) are among the most important contributions academic advisers can make.

Academic advisers for adult learners may be faculty in academic departments with a special interest in this group, or student development professionals in a central advising center.

Academic advisers may use cognitive developmental models, such as Perry's (1968) scheme, to help adult learner advisees make choices about education programs connected to their professional goals, particularly when the adult learner has not requested a relationship with a developmental mentor. Academic advisers with specialized training may also serve as developmental mentors.

Like developmental mentors, academic advisers—particularly faculty—need professional training in adult development theory and issues and in listening skills. Knowing about the institution's policies, educational programs, and requirements is essential. Advisers should also know about the staff and programs of the academic support services, including career and personal counseling, and have the skills to make referrals to those services on campus and in the community.

Through extensive interviews, DeCoster and Mable (1981) found that students complained most about academic advising of all services. The following questions from the *ACE Adult Learner Assessment and Planning Guide* can help determine whether an institution gives adult learners access to the services of academic advisers who are competent to assess their academic needs and help them plan academic programs attuned to those needs:

1. Is the academic advisement program:
    *   Designed to meet the unique needs of adult learners?
    *   Carried out by advisers trained to advise adults, assess academic needs, and plan programs in light of adult life experience and situations and adult development theory?
    *   Available in evenings? On weekends?
    *   Available at off-campus locations?
    *   Coordinated, or integrated, with related programs of personal and career counseling?
2. Do adult learners enrolled part time have to

pay a fee in order to receive academic advisement?
3. Is computer-assisted academic advising tailored to the needs of adult learners available?

Academic Support Services

Many adults fear that they will not be able to perform academic work. Some of these fears are based on previous failures, some on the length of time their education has been interrupted, and some on myths about "rusty brains" or "old dogs." Some adults actually do lack writing, reading, and computing skills. Other adults, like Maggie and Janice, need help with study skills and time management. All students need library and learning resources available to them at convenient times and locations. Services related to developmental mentoring and academic advising should be accessible to mentors, advisers, faculty, and students.

Academic support programs or learning centers can offer resources that diagnose strengths and deficiencies and help build the necessary skills to begin college-level work. With encouragement and hard work, practically all adults can overcome learning handicaps. Having professional staff in the academic support programs or learning centers will provide the essential continuity and consistency, and having adult learners serve as helpers and tutors in the centers will provide important role models. These peer counselors and tutors can be employed and trained by the institution. This kind of support could be crucial to helping an adult learner break through skill or anxiety barriers.

For adults pressed by many competing demands, time management is essential. Adults removed from the academic scene may have an unrealistic view of the time it takes to study. Many have a compulsion to be thorough and exacting in taking notes, reading, and preparing for tests. Some have forgotten how to use their time efficiently for a system that measures progress by in-class exams, and they may have difficulty studying for multiple-choice questions or organizing their thoughts for essay exams. Guidance from a support program might help them better manage their study time.

The learning preferences of adult students are also important to their efforts to achieve. For example, adults who prefer extraversion and sensing may want classes that are practical and oriented toward group activities, those who prefer introversion and intuition may want class activities that allow them to work alone creatively and contemplatively. The Myers-Briggs Type Indicator (Myers and McCaulley, 1985) shows adult learners that their learning preference as well as their reading, writing, and listening skills are influenced by psychological type as reflected in their individual preference scores. When adult learners find themselves in classroom situations that differ from their learning preferences, learning specialists can introduce compensatory strategies.

Programs that teach adult learners about Kolb's (1984) learning cycle show students the importance of concrete experiences, reflective observation, abstract conceptualization, and active experimentation. Many adult learners seem at first to prefer a curriculum based on concrete experience, but the more they learn in an atmosphere that introduces theory in a nonthreatening, collaborative manner, the better they are at adjusting to abstract conceptualizations. Learners can integrate all four learning styles, as described by Kolb, by being exposed to different curriculum formats and the modes of thinking of a variety of disciplines. As adults gain knowledge about their learning style, they assume more power in their own learning process and become increasingly active in determining their learning outcomes.

An example of effective academic support services is the Educational Support Program (ESP) described by Manske (1987). ESP's emphasis is on "Everyone can learn how to learn." Staff involvement includes recruiting and orientation, providing ACT/SAT preparation workshops in public libraries, and offering continuing education and intensive English for internationals. Adults intimidated by entrance exams may go to their local library to learn more about the tests, or they may come to continuing education programs. No grades are issued. Once they find that they can be successful in the classroom setting, they are more likely to enroll in the university. ESP staff also help adults who do not pass entrance tests and who, in Tennessee, must take state-mandated courses to remedy learning deficiencies and participate in required learning labs where they receive intensive tutoring. In these courses, supplemented by computerized instruction, enthusiastic teachers help adults overcome deficits in math, reading, writing, and foreign language.

The ESP's main mission at Memphis State is retention. Special learning centers are open long hours and are free to all students. For adult learners, the Math Learning Center is often the most important—mathematics is frequently the barrier that keeps adults from pursuing desired careers. With encouragement, complemented by computer software packages to teach basic mathematics skills, adult learners can overcome these deficiencies. The Math Learning Lab helps them as they complete remedial courses to progress to college algebra and calculus, for example. The lab also helps students who must take algebra for a nursing degree or provides statistical help or computer classes as students undertake required research. Many adult learners also use the Math Learning Center as a study hall, a tactic they believe helps them conquer their anxiety about math.

The English Learning Center helps adult and other learners in writing essay exams and term papers. International students or others with language problems are assigned tutors trained in teaching English as a second language. This increases the effective use of their intellectual capabilities in the college environment. The Foreign Language Learning Center provides help to adult and other learners beginning a language or to those who have delayed taking a language because they are anxious about completing the requirement to graduate. As in the Math Learning Center, computers help, but instructors are the key. In all centers, learning specialists trained in adult developmental theories use a variety of methods to teach students how to learn and how to move toward becoming independent critical thinkers and model builders.

At all higher education institutions, the library is one of the most important resources for students. Usually the library is in the province of academic affairs. In some institutions, the library is not open late at night or on weekends, making it difficult for adult learners with limited discretionary time. For classes held at satellite locations, library resources may be limited or nonexistent. Phone service, which would help an adult learner with references or save a trip to the library, also may be restricted.

The *ACE Adult Learner Assessment and Planning Guide* asks the following questions to find out whether adults enrolled in academic programs have available to them the academic support services they need:

1. May adults enroll in remedial courses or developmental programs that will enable them to improve basic knowledge or skills (reading, writing, mathematics, study skills, etc.)?

2. Are remedial courses or programs for adults available in the evening? On weekends? At remote locations or in correspondence and/or mediated format?

3. Is the progress of adult learner enrollees monitored to identify quickly those having academic difficulties?

4. Are records kept to show rates of retention for adult learners? Reasons for adult learner dropouts or stopouts?

5. Have at least some academic departments undergone self-study to identify academic support services needed by adult learners?

6. Does the institution have a peer assistants' program for adult students who are experiencing academic difficulties? Are those assistants adult learners themselves?

7. Are accelerated, advanced placement, or honors courses or advanced learning experiences available for exceptionally well-qualified adult learners?

Questions to ask to find out whether an institution's learning resource center provides programs and services identified as especially useful to adult learners are as follows:

1. Are learning resource centers open evenings? Weekends?
2. Are decentralized learning resource centers available to adult learners (either branch campus facilities or cooperative arrangements with other facilities)? Open evenings? Weekends?
3. Can adult learners receive information from the learning resource centers by phone?
4. Can persons enrolled in off-campus courses or programs secure needed materials from learning resource centers without undue difficulty or delay?
5. Does the learning resource center have instructional materials and telecommunications equipment for use by persons who cannot come to all classes in which they are enrolled?
6. Are computers and software available to assist adults in their learning?

To find out whether the library provides programs and services identified as especially useful to adult learners, ask these questions:

1. Are the campus libraries open evenings? Weekends?
2. Are decentralized library services available to adult learners (either branch campus facilities or cooperative arrangements with other facilities)? Open evenings? Weekends?
3. Can adult learners receive information from the library by phone?
4. Can persons enrolled in off-campus courses or programs secure needed books and related materials without undue difficulty or delay?
5. Does the library have instructional materials and/or telecommunications equipment for use by persons who cannot come to all classes in which they are enrolled?

Career Development

Career development is a particular concern for adult learners moving in and moving through. In fact, information collected from adults at fourteen colleges in the Higher Education for Adult Mental Health Project, using the American College Testing Company's Adult Learner Needs Assessment Survey, indicated that the highest need felt by adults is for career information (Lynch, Doyle, and Chickering, 1984; Kelly, 1985). Adults especially want to know about the prospects of jobs in their locality, given their educational plans.

Yet many adults returning to education with specific occupational goals do not know much about the qualifications needed, the characteristics of the work setting, or the life-style generated by an occupation. And the vocational decision-making skills of other adults who return to education "to better their situation" may be as unsophisticated as that of many younger students. Still other adult learners, satisfied with their work situation, plan to use their added credentials only to advance within their occupation or company.

One effective way to help these adult learners with career development is through courses integrating adult development theory, learning styles, and career information with a planning process, such as the life, career, and educational planning seminars given as a part of entry education at Rockland Community College and at Empire State College as described in Chapter Four. Life planning workshops, like the one Art found especially helpful (Chapter Four), can be part of career counseling centers.

Another way is through the Career Development Inventory (CDI) (Super and others, 1981). This is a tool for assessing career knowledge on scales of career planning, career exploration, decision making, world of work information, and knowledge of preferred occupational groups. The CDI evaluates a person's progress toward planning a career and making the commitment to seek a job in that field. It makes clear that there is an orderly process in making career decisions and helps adult learners at the beginning of their higher education careers plan the steps needed to progress in an orderly way toward their goals.

As adult learners moving through explore career interests, career counselors can help them see the components of their careers over a life span, as described by Super's (1980) life career rainbow. Super's comprehensive approach to life's many roles is a way of acknowledging—and reminding adult learners of the value of—their careers as students, spouses, parents, workers, professionals, leisurites, citizens, and community contributors.

Career counselors can help adult learners sharpen their focus on the future by asking such questions as:

- How much career planning have you done?
- How much training is needed for the type of career you are planning?
- What information do you have about the work setting?
- What requirements do you have about locations, travel, salary, and work climate?
- How does the career you have chosen fit with your personality preferences and learning style preferences?
- How close to completion is your résumé?
- What have you done about preparing for an interview?

If the adult learner is approaching an entirely new field, the career development professional needs to provide different information than for an adult learner staying in the same career field. And if the adult learner has never before been in the workplace, the career counselor must be particularly supportive and encouraging.

Computer-assisted career development programs are excellent supplements to career counseling that can help adult learners explore new fields (as well as familiar fields). One such program is DISCOVER, which was developed by Joann Bowlsbey (1987) for the American College Testing Company to help career counselors work with adult learners. Others, such as SIGI PLUS, have been described by Johnson (1986).

DISCOVER is a career and guidance system that allows users to investigate their interests, abilities, values, and experiences and receive results instantly for use in exploring educational and occupational options. The DISCOVER system's extensive files put vast quantities of essential information about occupations, colleges, specialized training programs, and financial aid literally at an adult learner's fingertips.

The first of six modules explains the career planning and

decision-making process and offers an assessment device that prescribes appropriate DISCOVER modules for the user. The second module introduces the frame of reference of the world of work and includes the ability to search for occupations and educational programs by cluster, region, and job families. The third module consists of self-assessment exercises regarding the individual's interests, abilities, life and work experiences, and values, and the fourth module identifies occupations that may be appealing to the user based on the formulation in module three. Learning about occupations, the fifth module, provides in-depth information about these alternatives and helps identify tentative choices from the list. Descriptions of such areas as work tasks, work settings, training needed, employment outlook, and income can be searched and printed.

The relationship between occupations and educational training is introduced in the sixth module, which includes possible paths of training based on tentative choices of ten or fewer occupations and on the ability to select majors or programs of study related to those occupations. Education data files consist of information about two- and four-year colleges and graduate schools as well as national trade and technical schools and military training programs. (A new capability calculates expected family contribution for college expenses and information about national financial aid programs.) The occupations and related education programs can be localized at the user's site and automatically printed out. Special features of the DISCOVER program particularly useful for adult learners are its ability to "turn on" additional modules and its functions dealing with careers and life transitions and with external degree program search and the documentation of prior learning options.

Other useful programs for adult learners moving through are career encounter programs, such as those described by Heitzmann, Schmidt, and Hurley (1986). At one university adults visit work sites and talk with professionals in their prospective fields before the pressure of getting a job descends on them. One twenty-seven-year-old man had completed his B.A. in education but did not want to teach and thought he wanted to write a novel. Through career counseling he went on a career encounter to the local television station. He later took courses in television camera work, volunteered at the television station, practiced at the local cable company, and now has a career as a camera operator in New York. He did not write his novel, but he found he could be creative in other areas.

Are career counseling and career development services that are oriented to the needs of adult learners available at an institution? The *ACE Adult Learner Assessment and Planning Guide* offers the following questions to find out:

1. Are career counseling/career development services:
   - Designed to meet the needs of adult learners (for example, counseling regarding career change, job needs versus family needs)?
   - Staffed by persons trained in counseling adult learners?
   - Available evenings? Weekends?
   - Offered off campus?
   - Offered to student spouses?
   - Offered prior to enrollment as well as after enrollment?
   - Facilitated by interactive computer-assisted services such as DISCOVER, SIGI PLUS?
2. Do adult learners enrolled part time have to pay a fee in order to receive career counseling/career development services?

Personal Counseling and Mental Health Services

Many adult learners need personal counseling programs as they move through the institution. A challenge for counselors helping adult learners is remembering that movement is developmental and that crises are opportunities for change. By helping adult learners identify and build on their strengths and see themselves as part of a support group or system—family, community, professional, or recreational—counseling shifts from a treatment to a prevention orientation. This is a systems approach in which counselors can seek ways to change the structure of the educational system, improve interactions within the system, and reduce stress in the environment.

Counselors and psychologists with a prevention orientation can develop support groups with such themes as "Building Self-Esteem," "Coping with Transitions," and "Developing Capacities for Intimacy and Autonomy." Focusing on prevention in couple and family counseling, they emphasize the structure of the relationships, communication behaviors, and problem solving rather than diagnosing, taking histories, finding causes, or attaching blame (Schlossberg, Troll, and Leibowitz, 1978).

Counselors of adult learners help establish support groups for specific target populations at risk—single parents, reentry women, veterans, or retirees, for example. Support groups that focus on gender and behavior help to empower adult learners so that they can cope with the chilly classroom and campus climate, for example (Sandler and Hall, 1982), or address "His World/Her World" issues. Counselors can also help organize self-help programs for recovering alcoholics, recurring dieters, abuse victims, or the math-test anxious, for example, and encourage wellness programs and the flow between the physical and mental health subsystems.

Particularly helpful for adult learners are programs like one university's Warmline, in which adult peer counselors provide information and support to older-than-average returning or first-time adult learners. Jo Chickering and Jane Clement (1987) list Warmline's major objectives: (1) to reach out to returning students and to welcome them to campus; (2) to provide encouragement and information about resources on and off campus in order to ease the problems of returning to college; and (3) to help groups discuss problems involved in returning to campus. Warmline is staffed with volunteers who are graduate students in counseling, adult learners themselves, and committed to Warmline for at least one semester. Their weekly training—and continuing support—emphasizes how to make effective referrals, transitions in adult life, communication and counseling skills, and program development. Volunteers provide adult learners with information on how to obtain such services as child care, personal and career counseling, and career and financial planning workshops. They also provide supportive peer counseling to adult learners returning to school after career changes or such life changes as divorce or widowhood.

One forty-year-old woman who was a first-time adult learner said that Warmline peer counseling connected her to career counseling, a connection that helped her stay in school and find her way to a career in audiology after fifteen years of being a word processor. One man who had entered and dropped out of college several times and who was a recovering alcoholic asked Warmline for an AA group. Since there was none on campus, the Warmline coordinator started an Alcohol Information and Support Group and the man served as co-facilitator. Warmline tells adult learners that the institution cares, that they matter. Had Art talked with a Warmline peer counselor when he first started having marital problems, perhaps he and his wife would have been referred to a marital therapist and the marriage might have been saved. If Janice had met a Warmline counselor who could tell her about the adult learner association and the adult learner support center, perhaps she would have felt more of a sense of support and community and stayed in school.

Counselors can help students change their boundaries of self-definition and develop both competence and a sense of competence as White (1976b) suggests. By using Gould's (1978) hypothesis and helping an adult learner recognize his or her incompetence and confront deficiencies, a counselor can help that adult learner take the first step toward becoming a competent person. Counselors can also help adult learners see their personal and career transitions as opportunities to learn and develop rather than as catastrophes.

Perhaps the most important thing a counselor offers is a view of the learner's options. Mary was able to "hang in there" when a counselor showed her that there were other ways she could seek help at home and that she could negotiate with her professor about making up work when she had to miss a class. When adult learners see only one option, they limit their capacity to cope. Counselors, mentors, and advisers who help adult learners by presenting other alternatives in nonthreatening, nonjudgmental ways help learners move toward their goals and fulfill their potential.

Here are the questions to ask to find out whether an institution has personal counseling or mental health services designed to meet the special needs of adult learners:

1. Are personal counseling/mental health services:
    *   Designed to meet the unique mental health needs of adult learners (such as transitions or midlife crisis assistance, marital, family, and divorce counseling, support groups)?
    *   Staffed by persons trained in counseling adult learners (knowledgeable about adult development theory, etc.)?
    *   Available to adults evenings? Weekends?
    *   Available off campus?
    *   Available to students' spouses and children?
2. Do adult learners enrolled part time have to pay a fee to receive personal counseling/mental health services?
3. Do counselors of adults show that they care about adults and that they matter?

Cocurricular Activities

Recreational and athletic activities can help adult learners rediscover competencies or acquire new ones that contribute to good health, longevity, and lifelong recreational skills. Theatrical, musical, artistic, and lecture programs can significantly enrich a liberal education, but adult learners often hesitate to attend such programs because of babysitting problems or fatigue. The more that faculty and staff help encourage attendance and participation, the more likely adult learners will recognize the importance of such activities to their total education. A ticket office can also help improve access to such activities and events both on and off campus and in the community. Adult learners may have more interest than traditional-age students in visiting museums with their children or attending the local symphony or community theater.

Adult learners often question the use of their portion of activity fees for such activities as intramural athletics. Adult learners could benefit more from individualized sports and from fitness and wellness centers that promote healthful physical habits. Such centers can administer wellness life-style questionnaires, such as the one developed by Hettler (1986), to predict life expectancy based on current behavior and to suggest changes for greater longevity. The centers can sponsor programs that contribute to wellness—such as those involving walking or nutrition improvement—and can provide treadmill, flexibility, and blood pressure tests, for example, so that exercise and recreation programs can be developed to reduce the chance of a heart attack or stroke. Experiments with cafeteria-style benefit packages, now being explored in business and industry, suggest a possible approach to activity programs. All students could choose from a menu of activities those directly relevant for them at this period of their lives.

Questions to ask to determine whether cocurricular activities (recreation, athletics, clubs) at an institution include activities appropriate for, and accessible to, adult learners are as follows:

1. Do cocurricular programs include events responsive to the interests of adult learners?
2. Are recreational and athletic facilities open evenings and weekends and are they available at satellite sites?
3. Are adult learners involved in planning cocurricular activities or are their interests surveyed about off-campus activities?
4. Are cocurricular programs open to students' spouses and children?
5. Must adult learners through required fees pay for a number of student activities they do not often use?
6. Is there a listing of community facilities with fees that might be of interest and be more convenient for adults and their families?

Residential Life Services

We often view residential, on-campus life as appropriate only for full-time traditional-age students. We also often view the typical adult learner as a commuter who comes to campus only to attend classes and use the library. But adult learners also live in our residence halls. When they do, they generally prefer the privacy of suites or special quiet sections, although multigenerational living arrangements can simulate an extended family and stimulate much learning and sharing.

Riker (1981) describes alternative housing programs that particularly appeal to adults. These include short-term residential programs, such as weekend colleges, that offer intensive learning programs for interested adults; elder hostel programs that provide academic and recreational programs with residential facilities; and special programs for residents of nearby retirement communities or for alumni, who may be encouraged to return for graduate studies.

Research by Chickering (1974) shows that traditional-age students in informal residential settings change more and learn more from each other than they do when they continue to live at home or in off-campus apartments. Sharing opinions and learning to accept differences—and gaining a sense of a scholarly community—contribute significantly to the educational experience. In fact, residence halls represent one of the best laboratories for learning tolerance for differences and the meaning of a pluralistic society (Barger and Lynch, 1973).

So that adult learners can participate in these benefits, residential-life staff can cooperate with faculty in setting up the short-term, intensive residential experiences that appeal to adult learners and that can provide an opportunity for them to put aside family and work responsibilities and concentrate fully on being a student, on learning through sharing ideas with classmates and faculty. These short-term residential experiences can be planned in conjunction with specific courses (such as the entry education courses) or at periodic intervals throughout the career of the adult learner moving through. Developmental mentors can also help adult learners plan with faculty for these experiences.

Married and single-parent adult learners are often housed in villages, or residential communities, separate from campus. The villages generally provide the privacy adult learners prefer, and institutions should make sure that self-governance organizations and educational programming are available to meet the special needs of the adult-learner residents. Sponsoring a newsletter covering family housing and activities will help develop a sense of community and contribute to retention, involvement, and the sense of mattering.

Residential life services can also assist adult learners who are new to the community by providing packets of welcoming information as well as by making information available about apartments or convenient low-cost housing. Information about local schools may also be helpful.

Questions from the *ACE Adult Learner Assessment and Planning Guide* to ask concerning whether residential life at an institution provides services responsive to the needs of adult learners include:

1. Are residential life services:
    -   Designed to take into account the unique housing needs of adult learners (such as singles or quiet sections, family housing, off-campus housing)?
    -   Staffed by persons trained to serve the needs of adult learners?
    -   Open evenings? Weekends?
    -   Provided by mail? By phone?
2. Do adult learners enrolled part time have to pay a fee in order to receive services from the housing office?
3. Is institution-controlled housing used for residential-type seminars or workshops appealing primarily to adult learners (such as credit or noncredit courses, short-term intensive learning experiences)?

Family Care

Some women can return to college only if they can find good, inexpensive, and convenient child-care services. Returning to school is much easier when child-care programs that are educational for the children and convenient for the parents are available. Most institutions recognize the need for child care and are beginning to provide facilities for young children of students and staff. The University of Florida, for example, has several Baby Gator nurseries for children of students, which are subsidized through student government funds. The University of Washington, another example, has a successful child-care voucher program that provides portable vouchers to student parents for the purchase of child-care services at any cooperating child-care facility. According to Morris (1984), this program's objectives are (1) to assign first priority for child-care assistance to those student parents who demonstrate the greatest financial need, (2) to assure equity in distributing child-care assistance by using an application process open to all student parents, and (3) to enable student parents to select personally acceptable child care from the community.

What many adult-learner parents want is not all-day child care but care for the time they are attending classes or working in the library. Some adult-learner parents, especially single parents, also need such care in the evenings and on weekends. Drop-in child care for children of students and staff is provided in an innovative program at State Technical Institute at Memphis. Parent effectiveness training is provided and parents are also taught how to read to their children. Colleges of education could use this kind of care for their laboratories and at the same time train their students in early-childhood education and enhance a sense of community and mattering.

When the institution cannot provide child-care facilities, it should ensure that referral sources are available to adult-learner families who are new to the community. Cooperative babysitting can be sponsored by the local campus ministerial group or the adult-learner support center or association. Residential life staff can facilitate cooperative babysitting in campus family housing. Student development staff can initiate, or serve as an advocate for, such needed services.

A growing number of adults today care for elderly parents or handicapped family members. They, too, need relief from their caretaking responsibilities to attend college. A comprehensive family care center offering services for elderly and handicapped family members (as well as young children) could help many more adults take advantage of the opportunity to return to school. A comprehensive center could also help alleviate the stress of the "sandwich generation" adult learner who must make several stops and separate arrangements for day care for his or her young children, elderly parents, or handicapped family member. The dream for such a center would be meeting all such needs for adult learners.

The major question we need to ask in assessing family care at an institution is this: Are family care facilities provided to facilitate the education of adult learners?

Health Services

Comprehensive health services resemble a health maintenance organization and serve students of all ages and their families, as well as faculty and staff and their families. They also reduce absenteeism for all students, faculty, and staff. The institution has a responsibility to provide such health services for its members—or to act as a referral source to service providers in the community. Particularly helpful for adult-learner parents may be a well-baby clinic in family housing or some central location, which can serve a preventive function and keep emergency trips to the pediatrician at a minimum.

Institutions connected to medical schools and teaching hospitals can use the comprehensive approach to provide exemplary health services on a health maintenance basis rather than on the traditional medical model. For institutions without this capability to act as a referral source for the local medical community, feedback from students of all ages about such referrals is important. Is the physician or health professional aware of the student's needs? Does the professional respond in an appropriate and timely manner? Would the student recommend the professional to other students? Accountability among health care providers can be life-enhancing; accountability among student development professionals as referral sources can be the link to that enhancement.

Questions to ask in assessing treatment of adults in the health care area are: Does the institution provide health services that are responsive to adult learner needs and to the student's family? Does the institution make provisions for referring students to competent health care providers in the community?

Other Services

What other services do institutions need to provide for adult learners? The student educational services division can conduct assessments of adult-learner needs on a regular basis. Institutions can develop their own surveys or use surveys developed elsewhere, such as the one designed by Florida International University's Adult Student Office, which ascertains the types of programs most needed, or the Adult Learner Needs Assessment Survey developed by the American College Testing Program, which provides individual and group data on perceived needs for educational planning, academic skills, career and job information, and interpersonal relations.

Services that may need improvement to help adult learners feel they matter include food and employment services, bookstores, and financial aid and planning. Food services are generally available, yet often adult learners feel the need for a special place for them to meet and eat with other adult learners and faculty. The bookstore may not be open at times convenient for adult learners, such as after evening classes and on weekends. Employment services need to help adult learners as well as traditional-age students get part-time jobs. Financial aid and planning can be crucial, as noted in Chapter Three, for both full-time and part-time adult learners.

Transportation and parking are major sources of concern to many commuter students, the majority of whom are adult learners. Frequent comings and goings mean that fair and equitable parking arrangements are essential for adult learners who drive. For other students, share-a-ride programs can provide connections throughout the community. Student development staff can serve as advocates for adult learners who depend on public transportation.

Many adult learners are concerned about safety, especially when attending night classes. Adequate lighting and security are vital. Another approach to safety is the Indiana University–Purdue University (Indianapolis) Learn and Shop College Credit Program (Gruebel, 1983), in which adult learners, primarily women, can enroll in courses given in the relative safety of public shopping malls, where parking is free and convenient.

Questions from the *ACE Adult Learner Assessment and Planning Guide* that help assess other services for adults at an institution include:

1. Does the institution have a mechanism for gathering information from adult learners to identify needed campus services?
2. Are food service facilities designed, located, and operated in a manner that meets the needs of adult learners?
3. Does the institution have an adequate program to promote personal safety, especially for learners attending night classes?
4. Can adult learners qualify for student employment opportunities?
5. Is public transportation easily available for adult learners?
6. Are parking arrangements distributed in such a manner that adult learners are treated equitably?

In Conclusion

Supporting services are essential for helping adult learners remain in our colleges and universities. Without recognition and a sense that they occupy a viable place in the institution, a sense that they matter to the institution, adult learners will not feel that they belong. Administrators, faculty, and student development professionals need to make every effort to provide the support that makes a difference. Students like Valerie, Mary, Art, and Janice need the advocacy of an adult-learner association and a place to meet, such as an adult support center. They also need someone with whom they can connect—as developmental mentor, academic adviser, counselor, faculty member—to make them feel involved.

A new perspective on support services, a new prevention orientation, means a restructuring and a rededication to serve adult learners more effectively. It also means extensive advertising of the services and resources available for adult learners. And because adults are so diverse and busy, that advertising must take various forms, such as orientation programs for adult learners and their families, adult learner newsletters, and ads in campus and local newspapers and on radio. A peer counseling program like Warmline can reach adult learners who need specific information about services. More than anything, this new prevention perspective makes a statement that adult learners matter, telling adult learners that the institution recognizes them as people with legitimate claims.

Moving On: Challenges Adults Face in Developing New Life and Work Roles

How can we conceptualize adult learners moving on? Adult learners are still students, but more than students; they are still in the system but outside it, too. They are ending one series of transitions and looking ahead to what is next. Higher-education professionals work hard to involve adult learners at the beginning, to create a climate that makes adult learners feel they are welcome and matter, and to support them as they progress through the system. But as adult learners prepare to leave, the support programs and professional attention often diminish. Yet there is an important task at hand: to help adult learners look back at why they came, what they got, and where they are going. Adult learners need to know how to use the institution for help with their futures, so that they can successfully invest, attach, and care about new beginnings, new institutions, new activities.

To gain clues about endings, beginnings, and "what's next," we interviewed four adult learners who had the end in sight. The vignettes describing these learners suggest underlying issues: change during the adult years, age discrimination in the workplace, beginnings and endings, and a reappraisal of possibilities. They also suggest ways to use the transition model to understand and help these adult learners as they move on to new beginnings. (Chapter Eight will describe culminating services that institutions can offer to provide support.)

Carlo: "I Am Changing, and My Needs Are Changing"

Carlo is single and twenty-seven years old. He lives at home with his Italian family so he can afford college expenses. In high school, Carlo was a good student and worked in a number of jobs. He started as a stockperson in the supermarket and became assistant manager soon after he graduated. He took courses at a community college, dropped out, and later went to the university at night to study engineering. He soon found out engineering was not for him, so he dropped out again and worked successfully in pharmaceutical sales. When his company was sued, he became interested in law.

Through some experiences that his best friend had, Carlo became aware of the oppression of minority groups and felt challenged to work to relieve that oppression. He knew that he needed to finish undergraduate school to be admitted to law school. Once admitted, he knew he would have to go full time, because there was no night law school in Memphis. So he quit his job and moved back with his family and pursued his studies in liberal arts as a first step. When we interviewed him, he said, "For a long time I floundered around trying to decide what I wanted to do. Finally, I realized that law was what I wanted. I recognized that there was more to the world than just making money. I wanted my life to count for something." Carlo will graduate in another year, and he needs help with the steps to come. He asked, "What do I need to do to get admitted to law school? I know I have been changing and my needs are changing."

Carlo's situation is one in which many young adults find themselves today. They have returned home for financial reasons or for support in completing the process of separation from the family. Carlo is clear about his goal now, and this clarity of purpose helps in the development of his identity. His sense of self has greatly improved from his "floundering around" days. He has a positive emotional support system in his large extended Italian family, although his father's health is failing and he cannot ask his family for financial help with his college expenses. His strategies for coping include his ability to concentrate, his determination to reach his goal, and his drive to be involved in issues and policies that "help people," so that his life can "count for something."

Although the university helped Carlo when he first reentered by assigning him an adviser who was encouraging, his needs have changed. He needs a different kind of help now that he is about to graduate and apply to law school.

Underlying Issue: Change in the Adult Years. We had not realized until our interviews how many adult learners had been dropouts, seemed to have developed on a different timetable, and seemed to be marching to a different drummer. Perry (1981) describes three deflections from growth as students move from one stage to another of intellectual and ethical development. In *temporizing,* the first deflection, students simply wait, reconsigning the agency or motivation for a decision to some event that might turn up. Students who report temporizing often express a sense of guilt or shame—an uneasiness over a failure of responsibility with which they feel helpless to cope.

The second deflection Perry describes is *retreating.* Students who retreat take a dualistic position often accompanied by childlike complaints and demands. *Escaping,* the third deflection from growth, involves the more complex reactions of alienation. For some students, escaping becomes a settled condition, but for many it is a time of transition after which comes a resurgence of vitality and involvement. During the transition "the self is lost through the very effort to hold on to it in the face of inexorable change in the world's appearance. It is the space of meaninglessness between received belief and creative faith. In their rebirth *they experience in themselves the origin of meanings, which they had previously expected to come to them from outside"* (p. 92).

Evidence supporting the possibility of change all through life comes from the Harvard Grant Study, which covered thirty-five years of the lives of more than 200 men (most of them with significant ability and from high socioeconomic backgrounds), beginning when they were college sophomores. According to Vaillant (1977), "When the Grant Study was started, the hope was that it would allow prediction, that once all data were in, college counselors could interview sophomores and tell them what they should do with their lives. This was not to be. . . . life . . . is more than an invariant sequence of stages with single predictable outcomes. The men's lives are full of surprises" (p. 373).

If we placed the sophomores in the study into two groups, depending on how well adapted they were, and then looked to see what had happened to them by the time they were thirty, forty, and fifty, we would find many surprises. For example, some of the worst adapted had changed, had developed, and were much better adapted. Our interviews with adult learners also demonstrate that such change is possible, given the proper conditions. Vaillant writes, "Adults change over time. If we view lives prospectively, they look different from our retrospective view of them. . . . if we follow adults for years, we can uncover startling . . . evolutions . . . developmental discontinuities . . . that are . . . great" (p. 372).

Male adult learners like Carlo are struggling with the issues of career commitment, identity, and purpose. The issue of "Who am I?" often becomes intertwined with what Vaillant labels career consolidation. Vaillant points out that the Grant Study confirms the adult life patterns outlined by Erikson (1959) but that between the decade of the twenties, the stage of intimacy, and the forties, the stage of generativity, Erikson left an uncharted developmental period. Vaillant calls this an intermediate stage of career consolidation, a period during which men translate their hobbies and ambitions into occupational terms. Men need to have this period of career consolidation, which then frees them to deal again with the issue of intimacy and to move on to generativity. Successful resolution of this period results in commitment, contentment, and valuing of the individual's work.

These issues of commitment, contentment, and valuing of work crop up periodically over the life span. People are constantly starting over, constantly realizing that as their identity shifts so does their career commitment. Thus, issues of career commitment come and go, ebb and flow, related to that part of an individual's identity that is generally best expressed through work.

Recurring education provides chances for people all through life. Presumably, people develop and are ready for new learning at different times—there is no one timetable for everyone.

Implications for the Learner. For Carlo, the issue of change throughout the adult years is one that he has recognized. After floundering for a few years, he identified the career he wanted. Once his goal was set, he knew what he needed to do. Now that he is looking toward law school, he again recognizes the changes he is encountering. He had a supportive adviser when he entered the university, but now he requires information about applying to law school. The institution needs to have such information readily available for students.

As Carlo looks to his future as a lawyer, he will be focusing on a time of career consolidation. Compared with traditional-age students, he will be a little older than others graduating from law school. However, for Carlo, the time he spent floundering was a time that helped him discover his life goal. Using Perry's (1981) scheme for deflections from growth, that time could be called either temporizing, retreating, or escaping. Because his recovery was so marked and his dedication to growth so determined, we see his in-between period as escape. His need to make his life count for something can be viewed as a move to a higher level of commitment.

Virginia: "I'm Too Old to Get the Job I Want"

Virginia is fifty-six years old and is about to finish her degree in advertising. She returned to the university three years ago, after her husband of thirty years divorced her and married a much younger woman. Virginia had been a homemaker. She raised four children who have finished college and are now in different stages of engagement, marriage, and divorce. She also has two grandchildren who live close to her. Virginia could have been satisfied to stay home and be the babysitter for her grand-children. Although she had never worked outside the home, she was involved in many volunteer activities, including coordinating the docents of the art museum. The divorce ended in bitterness. She was forced to find a way to support herself. She received the house, half of their few joint assets, and rehabilitative alimony until she could finish her degree.

When interviewed, Virginia said, "I am afraid that I am too old to get the job I want. I have heard that the big advertising agencies only hire young people so they can mold them according to their practices." Virginia was almost terrified of graduating because she would no longer have any financial support from her ex-husband and she did not want to sell her house.

Underlying Issue: Fear of Age Discrimination in the Workplace. There is no doubt that age discrimination does exist in the workplace. In a work setting, age distortions may manifest themselves in personnel practices that work to the detriment of the individual employee and, ultimately, to the organization itself. In a survey undertaken to determine the extent to which age bias and age stereotypes are reflected in administrative decisions, Rosen and Jerdee (1977) found that because older workers are viewed as "relatively inflexible and resistant to change, deficient in creativity and mental alertness, and lacking the capacity to deal with crisis situations," managers often fail to give them feedback that might improve their work performance, to support their career development and retraining, or to offer them opportunities for promotion.

Sex differences are also visible in recent research on how men and women are viewed in the workplace. Management students were asked to rate both the attractiveness and unattractiveness of men and women in relation to applications for managerial jobs. Whatever the job level, attractiveness was an asset for men. For women, however, it was not. In fact, unattractive women got the highest ratings for managerial jobs. The reason seems to be that attractive men are seen to be more masculine, whereas attractive women are seen as more feminine and thus indecisive, passive, and emotional—traits that do not go with being a successful manager (Heilman, 1980).

A related finding is that while men tend to turn inward

as they grow older (becoming more concerned with interpersonal relations and with expressive rather than instrumental goals, becoming more "feminine"), women tend to turn outward, becoming more involved in the external world, moving from a passive to an active stance (Gutman, 1977). The implication seems to be that some older women are at least as well suited as older men to positions that demand executive ability.

For the divorce transition, 1974 was the first year that more marriages were terminated through divorce than through the death of a spouse (Troll and Hagestad, 1985). The increase in divorce also affects women and men differently. More women suffer financially; more women than men will not spend their older years married. In an article in *The Washington Post,* one of the 140,000 women over forty-five divorced in 1981—nearly 30 percent more than a decade earlier—was quoted as saying, "I am a dumpee. . . . You feel so dumped. The rejection is unbearable after so many years of love and devotion. To think he could pick up with somebody else so quick" (Morse, 1984, p. B5). Divorce is difficult for everyone, but women suffer loss of income, often loss of pension payments and health insurance, and loss of remarriage possibilities.

Implications for the Learner. Virginia's situation is one that is scary for many older women who are forced into the work world for the first time. However, Virginia has many strengths. She knew that her life was not "over," even though the man to whom she had devoted her life did not want to spend the rest of his with her. She has her children and grandchildren for support, and she has an aging mother who depends on her, too. As a member of the "sandwich generation," Virginia has many competing demands. These family supports are reinforced by her old friends and neighbors. In the past Virginia relied on her husband to provide the strategies for problem solving; now she has learned that she has the capability to develop her own strategies. Her interest in advertising is exciting to her. She has looked forward to the day when she can work in this field and support herself.

What Virginia heard about advertising not being open to older people may be true of some firms. However, Virginia does not want to leave Memphis and her mother and her grand-children. She is willing to work hard, she will be dependable, and she has many creative ideas that will help her progress in her chosen field. Many employers are reassessing their needs and realizing that older workers are reliable, creative, and dedicated employees. What Virginia needs now from the institution is support in dealing with her fears and advocacy in approaching the job market.

Bruce: "I Wonder If I Made a Big Mistake"

Bruce is an art major about to graduate. He realizes that he will have a difficult time supporting himself. He is thirty-five and single. He lives with a long-time partner who is a legal secretary and who has helped Bruce travel to New York for several important photography exhibits. After working for many years in a photography studio, Bruce went back to college because he wanted to improve his technique so he could go into art photography. Now he wonders whether he should have taken education courses so that he could teach art, have a steady income, and do art photography on the side. He wonders whether he should continue on to graduate school and whether he will ever have the opportunity to prove he can capture all the images he holds in his mind.

Bruce knows that when he leaves the university, he will be giving up the support system he values—his friends, his adviser, and the faculty members he has come to know and who have inspired him. Lately he has been depressed and has not felt like completing his projects. When interviewed, he said, "I know I can go back to my old job at the photo studio, but I have put a lot into getting this degree. Now I wonder if I made a big mistake. No one told me that I should consider other possibilities—like art education."

Underlying Issues: Beginnings and Endings. We energetically study the entering student. After the first year, our interest and understanding seems to taper off. This trend—focusing much attention and energy on the entering process and paying little attention to the leaving process—is not unique to higher education. In an informal discussion with Peace Corps Special Services staff, we were told of the contrast between the ways Peace Corps volunteers were actively oriented to their Peace Corps roles but were casually left to figure out what came next once they were separated from the Corps. For those who left early—because of family or health problems from inability to cope with all the stresses—there was no formal program. Those serving their entire time were sent a packet of materials and invited to attend a one-time conference. Although more attention is now being paid to the leaving process, leaving the Peace Corps is still difficult for many volunteers. They are leaving a situation where they mattered very much to others, where they felt important, significant, and useful. They are returning to their home country and moving back into the everyday life of being a graduate student or looking for a "mundane" job. Volunteers often report that they are not emotionally prepared for this part of the transition. Whether the volunteers stay their full term or leave early, they are in great need of help with exiting and reintegrating back home.

Adult learners and higher-education professionals are also uncomfortable with the ambivalence in the moving on stage. A model of grieving helps explain the difficulties for adult learners and the inadequacies of the helping program. Marris (1974) suggests that the "concept of grieving could be applied to many situations of change which we would not ordinarily think of as bereavement" (p. 1). He suggests that most people have a conservative impulse. Change of any kind can create anxieties, forcing a person to establish new roles and to "recover a meaningful pattern of relationships. Loss disrupts the ability to find meaning; grief represents the struggle to retrieve meaning."

For some adult learners, graduation forces a reformulation of goals. As one set of goals is reached—finishing a degree—there is an inevitable letdown; for as Marris suggests, once again a sense of purpose must be reconstructed. The adult learners moving on are giving up classes, advisers, and the goal of becoming, but have not yet moved to a new set of activities and self-definition. Change involves loss as well as new possibilities, in what Marris calls "the articulation of ambivalence" (p. 98). Marris points out that grief works itself out not by substitution but by reformulation. The "process of externalizing ambivalence is, I think, a crucial aspect of the management of change" (p. 99). Marris argues that grief is the inevitable response to loss, even when the loss is one that is desired—like finishing a degree. There are contradictory impulses—a yearning for the past and the push to formulate new agendas. "Although the circumstances are not tragic . . . since in this case the gains usually outweigh the losses, the threat of disintegration is similar" (p. 89). Over time, learners reconstruct a sense of self and their environment, developing a sense of purpose.

Bridges (1980, p. 90), writing about transitions, says: "Considering that we have to deal with endings all our lives, most of us handle them very badly. This is in part because we misunderstand them and take them either too seriously or not seriously enough. We take them too seriously by confusing them with finality—that's it, all over, never more, finished! . . . At the same time we fail to take them seriously enough." It seems as if no one takes seriously an adult learner's completion of a degree.

Bridges discusses the transition process as having three phases: endings, neutral zones, and beginnings. We can therefore view the task of moving in as an end to something else and the task of leaving as an opportunity for a new beginning.

Sutton and Kahn (1986) hypothesize that prediction, understanding, and control can serve as antidotes to stress and strain. The pain cannot be taken out of change, but if the pain can be understood, and if understanding the transition process can help with other transitions, the individual feels in control. We suggest that rituals might help in prediction, understanding, and control. In referring to the needs of Peace Corps volunteers as they leave, one staff member said, "They need some rituals to help them deal with their forthcoming role change." For many adults a formal graduation ceremony is a temporarily significant ritual, but it does not help them deal with next steps. Student development professionals might acknowledge the paradoxical nature of this phase in the learning process by helping those about to complete their program develop meaningful rituals.

In *Rites of Renewal* (Maryland Public Television, 1985),

the late anthropologist Barbara Myerhoff discusses the role of rituals, ceremonies, or rites of passage that help people deal with marginal states by marking "the transition of an individual from one phase of life . . . to another." Rituals can help people make sense out of the contradictions and paradoxical nature of many transitions, including those of adult learners as they move on.

According to Myerhoff (1984), rituals have three stages. In the first, the individual or group is segregated or made separate, as in ceremonies for graduation, retirement, and marriage. In the second stage, the individual moves into a feeling of being "betwixt and between" the old role and the new role—what Victor Turner (1969) labels "liminality." That person is still a baby and not a baby; still a worker and not a worker; still an adult learner and not an adult learner. As Myerhoff says in the film: "That middle stage, the marginal one, the liminal one, is an especially interesting one because that's where the person is neither one thing or another." Adult learners with questions about their future are neither here nor there.

The final stage of the ritual, Myerhoff says, is "reincorporation . . . back into society . . . with a new identity." The final phase of this transition for adult learners is signified when they articulate an identity that connects them with their futures. "I am going to be working as an engineer, living in a condominium, and not studying anymore." "I am going to take a year off and travel." "Now that I have finished school, I can get the divorce I have planned for." In other words, adult learners are identifying with their new, next roles.

The problem is that for many transitions, the existing rituals are inappropriate. Myerhoff devoted a great deal of energy to teaching people how to develop rituals for themselves that would have personal meaning, help them deal with the ambiguities of their in-between state, and connect them to their pasts and futures.

An example is a divorce ritual, portrayed in the film. The minister calls together the divorcing parents and has them repeat an oath of caring, because of their past as parents and lovers—even though their love for each other has vanished, even though they are disconnecting for their new future lives. The minister then calls up the children and has the parents pledge their care, concern, and love for them. Finally, he includes the grandparents, in-laws, and friends in the ceremony. Many watching this film cry—probably because they have intimate experience with pulling apart, with losing community, self-definition, and supports.

How does all this relate to the learner exiting from school? For some, a brief acknowledgment is all that is needed; others need "a hand reaching out," meaning "We will help you plan for your career now or for as long as you remain an active alumnus of our institution." Still others need to be encouraged to view their lives as a continuous interweaving of learning, work, leisure. But whatever the need, the mission becomes clear: Student development professionals must make the culmination an important part of the transition process, deserving and needing as much attention as entering. This becomes a new challenge with exciting possibilities.

Implications for the Learner. Bruce is experiencing a loss of structure and is not sure what the future holds for him. His depression can be helped through talking with others who are also anticipating the loss of structure of friends, advisers, and faculty and the routine of classes and college work. Bruce would like the security of knowing that he can support himself, and he needs help in trying to find out whether art education is what he really wants to pursue, whether he is willing to take the risk to produce those images that he holds in his mind, and whether he can make a living as an art photographer.

Bruce may also need a way to accept the ending and greet the possibilities of new beginnings. Some form of ritual would help him see that his education has been important in his total development and that he is ready to move on and take the risk of applying his education in the art world.

Amanda: "I Need to Reevaluate My Possibilities"

Amanda, forty-three, is married, and her two children are in junior high school. Her husband has been a successful businessman, but he has recently been diagnosed as having cancer.

She will need to stay in the vicinity when she finds a new job. She has majored in English with a minor in journalism. Although teaching would provide her with more flexible hours to be with her children and her husband, she does not want to teach and therefore did not take education courses leading to state certification in English. Amanda has thus eliminated some careers by her choice of a major and preferences for work environments. Yet there are many other career opportunities for someone with her talents, interests, and experience.

Amanda has been writing articles for the school paper and a community newsletter, and she has helped edit a brochure for a major volunteer agency in town. When she used the DISCOVER computer career program, she found that she liked to help people but that she preferred to work on projects alone. Previously, Amanda had worked as a secretary, and she has held a part-time job in an insurance agency while going to college. Now she is ready for a job that will use the education she has been receiving. When interviewed, she said, "I have always dreamed of being a writer—someone who could influence the values of others through writing."

Amanda has a strong sense of self and knows that she can accomplish her goals. She has learned various strategies for coping but realizes she needs specific help in preparing a résumé, finding job leads, and interviewing for a job. She has a deep spiritual faith that has been shaken somewhat by her husband's illness. She also recognizes that she may become the sole support of her family. She acknowledges her need to balance her family life with her work life and church life. However, she is eager to progress now that she has spent her time and energy in accomplishing her educational goal.

Underlying Issue: Reevaluation of Goals and Possibilities. Commencement is a good time to look again at life-span concepts and possibilities, a time for reevaluation, for planning, for sorting out the meaning of all this learning. This might also be the time to help learners realize that learning is a perpetual experience.

Much of a personal reappraisal revolves around dreams. Our dreams, imagined possibilities of what may be, are a key to

our identity. Do women submerge their dreams for their husbands? Does midlife transition become a crisis if an individual
realizes his or her dream has been submerged? The reevaluation
of the dream occurs at marker times, such as retirement or
death of a loved one. Levinson and others (1978) found that
the men in their study spent a great deal of energy building life
around a dream. This means, of course, that as an individual
pursues one line of work or one life-style, other options—other
jobs, other relationships—are ruled out. As time goes on, there is
a growing sense of lost opportunities, and a process of disillu-
sionment sets in, complete with "what if's" and "if only's":
"What if I had taken that job in Oshkosh?" "If only I had gone
to college . . . " "What if I had followed that advice and done
such-and-such?" For some people, this time of questioning—
of regrets—becomes a time of thinking almost obsessively about
what might have been.

This questioning leads us to consider the role others play
in our lives. Levinson also discusses the role of an individual's
spouse in the realization of his or her dream. Does a person select a spouse who encourages or sabotages his or her dream?
An Australian movie, *My Brilliant Career*, portrays a heroine
who refuses to marry the man she passionately loves for fear of
losing her dream of becoming a great writer. She is afraid he
will unwittingly sabotage her dream. Levinson points out that
when women lose their dreams by supporting those of their
husbands, deep resentment creeps in.

A few more words about women, at least those who are
married: They not only reappraise their own dreams but the
dreams they had for their mates. If their own lives are not
everything they thought they would be, they suffer. But they
also suffer over their husbands' lives. Most women have a dream
for their husbands: he should be the most successful or best
contractor, doctor, lawyer, policeman. In reappraising their own
dreams, they may also reexamine their husbands' dreams and
wonder, Is this what it is all about? Data show that men's
dreams mostly relate to their careers, whereas women's focus on
relationships (Gilligan, 1982).

Carl Jung (1953) focused on a person's sleeping dreams as

a way to tap into the personal and the collective unconscious. For him and his followers, dreams are a window on the soul. Analytical psychology helps individuals examine their dreams as they progress toward individuation. He believed that personality dimensions existed in pairs of opposites and that we are all striving toward balance and wholeness. He emphasized that we could not live the second half, or afternoon, of our lives using the program for the morning. The second half of life is a time for reappraisal and for looking at deeper meanings.

Another aspect of reappraisal is to consider how the different parts of one's life fit together. Is there balance or imbalance? The wellness model developed by Hettler (1986) at the University of Wisconsin, Stevens Point, provides a paradigm for looking at the fundamental aspects that must be balanced for a well-functioning, healthy, happy, and productive life. According to the model, the six dimensions we need to consider (and that we can assess by using Hettler's Life-Style Assessment Questionnaire) are intellectual, social, emotional, physical, vocational, and spiritual:

- *Intellectual:* This dimension entails the practice of creative, stimulating mental activity. The intellectually well person uses all resources available within and outside the classroom to improve skill and expand his or her potential for sharing with others. Intellectual and cultural activities and human and learning resources all are utilized to grow in this dimension.
- *Social:* Development in this area includes contributing to the common welfare of one's human community and physical environment by emphasizing the interdependencies with others and nature. It also includes the pursuit of harmony in one's family.
- *Emotional:* Awareness and acceptance of one's feelings is the premise for this dimension. The emotionally well person maintains satisfying relationships with others while feeling positive and enthusiastic about his or her life. Goals in this dimension are to appropriately control one's feelings and re-

lated behaviors, to realistically assess one's strengths and limitations, to develop autonomy, and to learn to effectively cope with stress.

- *Physical:* Regular physical activity, cardiovascular flexibility, and strength are all signs of the physically well person. Knowledge about food and nutrition and the appropriate uses of the medical system is also encouraged, as is medical self-care when warranted. Finally, the use of tobacco and drugs and excessive alcohol consumption are discouraged.
- *Vocational:* This dimension deals with attitudes toward one's work. One needs to prepare for and seek jobs in which personal satisfaction and enrichment in one's life is the result.
- *Spiritual:* The spiritually well person is involved in seeking the meaning and purpose in human existence and in developing a strong appreciation for the depth and expanse of life and natural forces that exist in the universe.

The Wellness Model is a proactive approach that makes clear that high-level wellness means "giving care to the physical self, using the mind constructively, channeling stress energies positively, expressing emotions effectively, becoming creatively involved with others, and staying in touch with the environment" (Ardell, 1977, p. 13). It means not accepting the medical concept that the absence of illness is the norm for health and instead means regaining a role in one's personal health, one's potential for education, growth, and self-actualization.

Implications for the Learner. Amanda is faced with much reappraisal of her possibilities. Her life as a student is coming to an end, and she needs help in finding a professional position. Her husband's illness has shaken some of her religious beliefs, and she is faced with the prospect of his debilitating illness and early death. Her dream for his continued success in business and their opportunity to grow old together has become sharply limited.

For a while, Amanda, like many other women, had put her own dream on the shelf to marry and raise children. Returning to college has been her way of preparing to fulfill her lifelong dream of becoming a writer who can influence the values of others. Unlike the heroine in *My Brilliant Career*, she did marry her love and had children, but now she has the opportunity to follow through on her dream. She thought she had it all, until she was faced with the reality that her husband may die and that she will be the sole support of her family. How can she hold to her dream and confront the realities of her life?

Amanda can seek help from her minister, a campus chaplain, or a counselor sensitive to spiritual issues as she reevaluates. Her mentor/adviser can use the wellness model to help her examine how she is balancing the different parts of her life. And a placement counselor can help her with next steps in finding an appropriate job.

The Conceptual Framework for Adult Learners Moving On

Our conceptual framework, built on transitions, involvement, vectors, and mattering, helps us understand adult learners and the educational environment. It also helps us develop programs that assist people as they experience learning transitions.

Transitions. Keeping in mind the underlying issues raised by adult learners moving on—change in the adult years, age discrimination in the workplace, beginnings and endings, and reappraisal—we return to the transition model for guidelines. The four S's—situation, self, supports, and strategies—provide a framework for helping adult learners cope with their particular ending-beginning situations, identify their strengths to reinforce a positive sense of self, obtain supports as they move into the next transition, and develop strategies to deal with these endings and beginnings.

The situations of individuals as they face the end of formal schooling vary. Some, like Carlo, need specific help with next-step educational or career plans; others, like Bruce and Virginia, need strategies for implementing career plans; and still others, like Amanda, need job placement and reflective support. Many would benefit from more general life planning for avocation, vocation, family, and citizenship roles. Some are in stressful situations and need to rush into next steps, like Amanda and Virginia or the woman or man needing to earn money because he or she is the sole support of self and small children. Others can move slowly because they are in an intact family and have financial support. The real question is how the situation has changed their roles, relationships, routines, and assumptions, and how completing the formal part of the transition and moving on will again change roles, relationships, routines, and assumptions. For those whose college experience was not very disruptive, the change will not be as great as for those who invested heavily in education by changing and rearranging work and family roles.

The sense of self is being reevaluated by each adult learner moving on. Many, like Bruce, are questioning their choices, and many, like Virginia, have fears about what is next. Some, like Carlo, who knows his direction, are feeling very strong. Others, like Amanda, have resources for coping with their reappraisals and progressing toward their dreams.

Psychologists who study the adult personality ask whether there are orderly, sequential personality changes related to age and if so, whether these personality changes cause changes in behavior. Studies of adults eighteen to eighty confirm the broad hypothesis that human personality changes perceptibly as people grow older. These changes in personality are caused not by the passage of time but by the various biological and social events that occur with the passage of time. Adult development from youth to old age can be seen as a process of adaptation in which personality is the key element. Bruce, Virginia, Carlo, and Amanda surely have the strengths of personality to adapt effectively to the change process.

Supports are needed by most people as they leave school, the Peace Corps, a marriage, or a job: this is clearly an area for creative intervention, for intervention tailored to individual need. For some, support will take the form of helping with anticipation and identification of what comes next; for others, it will take the form of helping with implementing an already articulated goal; for still others, it will consist of helping with balancing work and personal roles. As we saw, Virginia and Amanda need help with résumé writing; Carlo needs support with law school applications; Bruce needs support thinking about next steps; and Amanda needs help in reappraisal and job placement. The mentor, the adviser, and career planning and placement become central supports at this time. In other words, adult learners need culminating education, just as they need entry education, and we see this as an area of future growth for student development specialists.

To determine how each learner could be helped to deal with this phase and to take advantage of available resources, we first need to assess each adult learner's strengths and weaknesses. Possible coping strategies that might be incorporated in any adult learner's repertoire include those identified in the Pearlin and Schooler (1978) study; these coping strategies "constitute but a portion of the full-range of responses people undoubtedly call upon in dealing with life-exigencies" (p. 5) but still provide a systematic method for examining strategies. The following outline is adapted from the study. Questions or descriptors illustrate each strategy or coping response.

1. Responses that modify the situation and are "aimed at altering the source of strain" (p. 20).
    *   *Negotiation:* "How often do you try to find a fair compromise . . . sit down and talk things out?"
    *   *Optimistic action:* "When you have difficulties in your work situation, how often do you take some action to get rid of them, or to find a solution?"
    *   *Self-reliance versus advice seeking:* "In the past year . . . have you asked for the advice of a friend . . . relative . . . doctor . . . other professional?"
    *   *Exercise of potency versus helpless resignation:* "How often do you decide there's really nothing you can do to change things?"
2. Responses that control the meaning of the problem in order to "cognitively neutralize the threat" (p. 6).
    *   *Positive comparisons:* "A device . . . [to enable] a temporal frame of reference . . . captured in such idioms as count your blessings."
    *   *Selective ignoring:* A "positive attribute . . . within a troublesome situation. When you have difficulties in

your work situation, how often do you tell yourself
that they are unimportant, try to pay attention only
to your duties, and overlook them?"

- *Substitution of rewards:* "Hierarchical ordering of
life priorities . . . to keep the most strainful experiences within the least valued areas of life. If I have
troubles at work, I value other areas of life more and
downplay the importance of work."

3. Responses that help the individual manage stress after it has
occurred to help "accommodate to existing stress without
being overwhelmed by it" (p. 7).

- *Emotional discharge:* "Expressive ventilation of feelings: How often do you yell or shout to let off
steam?"
- *Self-assertion:* "When you have differences with your
spouse, how often do you fight it out?"
- *Passive forbearance:* "When you have differences with
your spouse, how often do you keep out of his or her
way?"

Each of our adult learners uses these coping strategies.
Carlo is altering the source of his stress by seeking advice about
next steps in applying to law school. Virginia is controlling the
meaning of her problem by neutralizing the threat through
some selective ignoring, especially in relation to the threat from
her ex-husband. She realizes she cannot change the fact of her
divorce, but she can look for her strengths in approaching the
work world. Bruce can manage his stress by expressing his feelings of ambivalence and loss to his friends, his partner, and his
adviser. Amanda is using substitution of reward to help her control the meaning of her problem. She knows that she has stress
at home with her husband's illness, so she is seeking a rewarding
work experience to help her cope. Each of our adult learners
might also assess his or her coping resources and learn ways to
improve them by using the Coping Resources Inventory developed by Hammer and Marting (1988). This inventory measures
coping resources in five domains: cognitive (positive appraisal of
self and others), social (supportive social networks), emotional

(affective range and expressibility), spiritual/philosophical (value systems), and physical (health promoting behaviors).

Involvement. Astin's (1984) theory of involvement can be looked at as a continuum from high to low involvement. Those adult learners, like Bruce, who are highly involved in the learning process may feel a sense of loss and mourning upon moving on. However, people's degree of involvement shifts over time. Take the case of one man who had just finished a program in business. He had become the financial director at a car dealership during his last year of classes and was so involved in his new worklife that he did not take the time to graduate. He was involved, but with work and not school. His apathy about school did not reflect mourning, loss, or separation. Rather, it reflected the excitement of being a worker in the "real world."

Student development professionals must perform a delicate balancing act: Without intruding, they must work with adult learners who are in all degrees of involvement, reminding them that learning is a process that continues over life and that educational institutions are for "whenever needed" and for evolving purposes.

Vectors. Chickering's vectors can help us identify adult learner agendas and focus on the best ways to help adult learners better achieve competence, manage emotions, become interdependent, establish identity, free interpersonal relationships, clarify purpose, and develop integrity. People all through life are continuously dealing with these issues. The moving-on adult learners we interviewed were in the process of clarifying purpose, achieving competence, and establishing identity. For many, their new identities were connected with activities outside of formal schooling. They were also managing their emotions, handling interpersonal relationships, becoming more interdependent, and developing a new sense of integrity.

Mattering. We need to develop systematic ways of connecting with adult learners both to help them view learning as continuous and to help them recognize that their learning involvement will vary as they balance their many spheres of life. We must focus continually on adult learners' agendas—such as "Who am I?" "Where am I going?"—if we are to make them feel they matter and that their welfare is of concern to us. Only when we design and put in place multiple programs and strategies designed to reach adult learners will we be sure that adult learners know we are here and that we care.

In Conclusion

Adults are dealing simultaneously with endings and beginnings as they leave an institution. There is no formula for understanding this time, since each individual's endings and beginnings are unique; but we can help by (1) labeling this period, so that individuals can better understand their conflicting feelings, and (2) prodding institutions to attend more to those leaving.

EIGHT

Providing
Culminating Programs
for Adults

When we asked adult learners about the educational services their institutions provided for them as they prepared to move on, they all mentioned the many ways in which they had been helped at the beginning—with entry/orientation classes, with readily available advisers. And they all seemed concerned with career plans and said they needed help with, for example, writing résumés and getting information about teaching certificates and law aptitude tests. Yet not one of them felt entitled to get such help from their institution. In fact, they had never even thought about asking for such help. This response surprised us. Entitlement and narcissism are considered to be national diseases, yet here we found a group of adults who did not feel entitled. In addition, many student development professionals report they have not thought about creating explicit and systematic programs to help adult and other learners as they move on, nor have they felt any pressure to put money, energy, and programs into this phase of the learning process.

This chapter emphasizes the importance of providing specific programs for learners moving on, and it explores how institutions can best help adults in the final phase of learning look to the future. Special culminating services are particularly important for adult learners. For when institutions do connect with their adult learners enough to recognize their needs for culminating education, it often means the adult learners moving on are once again being shortchanged. When they entered, they may have been victims of the attitude, "Since they are older and have more experience, they already know what they need to do to succeed here." Now that they are leaving, they may not get needed help because of reasoning that runs, "Since they are older and more experienced, and since they have been in the institution *all this time,* they know what services are available and how to ask for them and *certainly* they are assertive enough to ask for any services that are not readily available." Such attitudes on the part of faculty and staff often leave adult learners bruised. Perhaps these attitudes form the basis for the lack of entitlement felt by many adult learners.

Barriers to Culminating Education

Just as there are barriers at entry (Cross, 1981), there are barriers at exit. These barriers can also be conceived as situational, institutional, and dispositional. Situational barriers to exit include being place-bound and finding a lack of employment open to older workers. Institutional barriers include advisers who are not available, policies that do not facilitate adult learners' graduation, and lack of communication about placement services. Dispositional barriers include fear of the job market, a belief that one is too old to start a new career, expectations that one should land a job with the first interview, and a lack of confidence. With education and persistence, these barriers can be overcome.

While some adults, like Carlo and Amanda, are looking forward to graduation and their future roles, others, like Virginia, are afraid of what the work world holds. No doubt there are some adults who are bored with college and are eager to get on with their lives. Certainly, a slight depression is obvious among some adults, such as Bruce. Perhaps the depression is due to a loss of structure, including loss of goals, classes, and friends. Underneath the depression may be anger—anger at advisers and the institution, anger at their own passivity or inability to ask for help, and fear of the unknown future. Under the anger is hurt and disappointment with the institution as well as with themselves.

How can we help relieve such students' boredom with the institutional environment and their anxiety as they face the final stages of formal higher education and the uncertainties of life and work? How can we help them gain a perspective that will provide a bridge from our institutions to whatever future they choose? Their major and academic courses represent just one aspect of their total development. What they seem to need most is a handle to help them make sense of their learning and understand how it fits with the realities of the work world. Because adult learners are so diverse, no single theory will suffice to help them through this maze. However, teaching them some of the career development theories and letting them understand how they can approach their futures may be a way of giving them that needed handle.

Most institutions do provide career planning and placement services. Perhaps what is most lacking is communication about those services and how they apply to adult learners. What individuals need at this stage—culminating education—is parallel to what they needed at the beginning—entry education. In Chapter Four, we described how an entry education center helped adult learners see the admissions process as a learning experience (Adams, 1986). So, too, a culminating education center can help adult learners view the events and the culminating process leading to graduation as a part of the learning process—the lifelong learning process.

Traditionally, student educational services have given low priority to the culminating process. The services usually offered by career planning and placement offices are (1) placement services geared toward on-site interviews by company representatives seeking bright, young graduates, and (2) training in techniques for résumé writing, job search, and interviewing. In some institutions these services are separated administratively and may even compete for student participants. In other institutions, placement is seen as the province of the various colleges or departments, and job bulletin boards may be most visible in departmental lounges.

Culminating educational services help adults reflect on their learning and focus on their future. Three additional major components of culminating educational services, which can be integrated into the culminating course or stand as separate elements, are reviews with developmental mentors and academic advisers, referrals for career planning and placement services, and referrals to transition groups.

Culminating education should be considered an important part of the learning process, an essential winding up of the work toward a degree and of the development of the learner as a self-educating person. This time can be spent in integrating learning from academic and cocurricular sources and in making the transition to a new world of work and a life enriched by higher education.

Culminating Course

A culminating course similar to the entry/orientation course can help adults integrate their learning and take important steps toward the future. The objectives of such a course are to integrate significant learning from courses, programs, and life experiences through interviews and discussions; make plans for the future—immediate, short term, and long range; and facilitate the transition from the institution.

Some of the theories about learning and development presented in earlier chapters of this book can enrich the theoretical base for the course. Concepts about integration of information can help learners recognize their part in the self-educating process.

To integrate means to form or blend into a whole, to unite or incorporate into a larger unit. When we ask students to integrate the learning they have acquired over a period of years, we are asking them to find the meaning of that learning for themselves. Some models of maturity and development may help in understanding this goal.

Heath (1968) describes *maturity* as "growing coherence" and classifies becoming progressively integrated as the third stage in the development of the mature personality: "Increasing differentiation and synthesis and greater complexity mark the mature person" (p. 13). Essentially, maturing involves the development of a more unified personality. Heath suggests that becoming more integrated can be demonstrated through increased skills in analytic, relational, and synthetic thinking and in systematic problem solving; development of a value system or world view; increasing congruence between one's self-image and one's behavior; and increasing ability to be more intimate and open in relationships.

In presenting her six stages of ego development, Loevinger (1976) sees the integrated stage as the last stage, which few people ever reach. She sees most Americans as being in the self-aware stage, which is a transition from stage two, the conformist stage, to the conscientious stage. In the conformist stage, the individual is concerned with appearances and social acceptability, tends to think in stereotypes and clichés (especially moralistic ones), and is concerned about conforming to external rules. An individual in the self-aware stage is increasing in self-awareness and the ability to think in terms of alternatives, exceptions, and multiple possibilities. In the conscientious stage, the individual's interpersonal style can be described as intensive, responsible, mutual, and concerned about communication. Loevinger adds "respect for autonomy and interdependence" for those in the autonomous stage (stage five) and "cherishing of individuality" for those in the integrated stage.

In whatever ways we help adult learners move toward an integrated stage or level, we know that they must become more complex in their thinking and in their interpersonal relations. Their entire education at our institutions should support the development of this complexity. However, the current system of majors and courses usually does not provide an integrative experience in which students can reflect on their learning and conceptualize its meaning for themselves. Thus, it becomes important for the faculty of the culminating course, the developmental mentor, and the academic adviser to serve as focal points for helping the learner integrate learning and plan for the future.

Reviews with Developmental Mentors
and Academic Advisers

At the beginning of the adult learner's last year at the institution, interviews should be scheduled with the mentor and/or adviser. Perhaps if Bruce's teachers or his adviser had reached out to him and discussed his possible future, he would have been less depressed by his losses. Just as the portfolio assessment of prior learning can constitute academic credit for many adult learners, a review of learning and the significance of that learning in accomplishing life goals will help adult learners gain a closure perspective as well as a sense of accomplishment. This process can be profitably carried out in the culminating course or on an individual or a small-group basis, in which adult learners share their perspectives on their learning and their futures with the mentor as facilitator.

Although some institutions are in the process of outcomes assessment, few ask for evaluations of their total program or of their responsiveness to their learners. Reviews and individual or small-group sessions will provide far more effective feedback on outcomes both to students and institutions than will senior theses and standardized tests of minimal academic competency. In preparation for the oral reviews, adult learners can be asked to prepare an evaluation form on the program and on their experiences at the institution. Questions that can help adult learners integrate their knowledge include:

- For what reasons did you choose this major?
- Has it met your expectations?
- How have your goals changed over your time here?
- What has been your most meaningful learning experience here?
- What has been your least meaningful learning experience?
- What has helped you learn the most effectively?
- What could be done to improve the program?
- What cocurricular activities (campus, professional, and community) have added to your learning?

- What meaning have you found in your education to help you live your life?

Focusing on the future helps adult learners plan ahead and see lifelong learning as an ongoing process. Questions to be posed include:

- What goals do you have immediately after graduation?
- What goals do you have for the next five to ten years? The next ten to twenty years?
- How do you envision your life changing in work, home, and leisure?
- How do you plan to cope with these changes?
- What role will learning (formal and informal) have in your further development?
- If you conceptualize yourself as a lifelong learner, what can help you continue the process?

In reviewing the adult learner's academic transcript and evaluation of program and experiences form, the academic adviser may offer the adult learner the opportunity to voice praise and complaints about the academic program. There may still be time to alter the selection of some courses to make them more appropriate to the adult learner's goals. If not, then the chance to have a say about the program and its effects on the adult learner will help ameliorate any uncomfortable feelings toward the department and the institution. This opportunity to summarize and synthesize in a review can be a powerful learning experience for the adult learner, and the information obtained from the review—treated anonymously and confidentially—can be important to both the academic unit and the institution.

As the developmental mentor reviews the adult learner's transcripts and evaluation, the mentor can help the learner find meaning in his or her experiences in moving through the institution and help the adult learner integrate the thoughts and feelings precipitated by completing an evaluation form. In addition, if goals were written when the adult learner entered the institution, they can be reviewed to see what the learner has accomplished.

Early research on reasons for returning to college showed that it was often for practical purposes—to increase job opportunities, to improve income, to be able to advance one's career. More recent research indicates that for many adults the goals include becoming better educated and informed, achieving personal satisfaction, and helping to solve personal and community problems. The reasons given by today's adult learners usually reflect these changing goals as well as a deeper understanding of the benefits of education and an awareness of learning as a lifelong process. In fact, for some adults, learning seems to be addictive, as exemplified by those who start college at thirty-five and go from a bachelor's to a master's and even a doctoral degree without stopping.

Developmental mentors may have interviewed their mentees early in college using Perry's (1981) framework for the measurement of intellectual and ethical development. As an alternative, the adult learners may have written essays based on Perry's scheme, and the mentors may have had the essays assessed using Knefelkamp and Moore's (1982) Measurement of Intellectual Development scoring process. Comparing the earlier assessment of developmental level with findings from a similar interview or written essay during a culminating course or interview, mentors can help mentees evaluate their intellectual and ethical development as they moved through the institution. Similarly, Rest's (1979) Defining Issues Test provides mentors or faculty with assessments of moral and ethical development that can help adult learners determine their development in these areas. Reflection on cognitive growth and moral/ethical development may help adult learners realize they have gained more from college-level learning than simply the content of courses. This examination may include a reflection on spiritual growth and the role of religion and values in the person's life.

Mentor interviews can also clarify needs for other culminating educational services. The academic adviser or the developmental mentor may find that the adult learner requires additional career planning and placement services. Certainly, the adviser or mentor can make strong suggestions that the soon-to-be-graduate adult learner complete placement forms. The adult learner also needs to decide which faculty or staff would be appropriate to ask for letters of reference. The adviser or mentor might suggest ways to approach these faculty with a résumé before the end-of-semester rush. The placement office usually maintains a data file on students that includes letters of recommendation. The usefulness of this service to the learner should be stressed.

Just as the academic transcript will continue to be important to the adult learner, the developmental transcript can provide valuable information for writing a résumé. The mentor can help the adult learner identify skills and abilities derived from cocurricular activities and determine how to best state them on a résumé. If the adult learner has participated in a cooperative learning experience, a practicum, or an internship, the adviser or mentor can help the learner conceptualize how these experiences will add to the résumé. Such a discussion best precedes work with the placement staff on developing a résumé and an interviewing style.

The mentor or adviser can also assess the adult learner's requirements for other services to help in the moving on process. If the adult learner is passive and somewhat depressed, like Bruce, perhaps a referral for counseling or assertiveness skills training would help. Or students with family problems triggered by imminent graduation, like Virginia or Amanda, could use the empathetic ear of a psychologist or personal counselor. Workshops on the transition into the world of work can also help adult learners move on. The culminating course together with the series of interviews and group sessions serves as both a summary of what the adult learner has gained and an assessment of what the adult learner needs for successful moving on.

Advisers can also provide important assistance for those adult learners who choose to go on to graduate school. Carlo, for example, needs information about law schools and how to take the LSAT. Advisers can also help adult learners think about how further education might or might not contribute to their career goals. Bruce needs assistance in deciding whether to risk trying to be an art photographer or to go to graduate school, get a master's degree in art education, and become a teacher.

Advisers in major areas can help adult learners considering graduate school by asking them such important questions as:

- What graduate programs offer the kind of education that will facilitate accomplishing your goals?
- What professional schools will give you the opportunity to fulfill your expectations?
- What is needed for you to apply for these opportunities?
- Where do you take the Graduate Record Examination?
- How can you prepare for the LSAT? MCAT? Business Exam?

The learning resources center can help with the last three.

Many adult learners considering further education are place-bound, and it may not be possible for them to go to other institutions. Arranging for them to talk to adults currently enrolled in graduate or professional schools at their home institution can provide a helpful and realistic picture of requirements and expectations.

Referrals for Career Planning and Placement Services

The needs of the adult learner about to move on are different from those of the adult moving in and unsure about a career. The services of the career planning center may be known to adult learners in the exploration stage but may never occur to them as a help for moving on. Bruce, for example, could have been helped by the career planning center to clarify his other options with a B.A. in art. Adult learners are at all different stages in their development and have a variety of needs. A few come to the institution with a goal in mind and pursue their education without deviation until that goal is reached. Many others are unsure of themselves and their goals and explore (Carlo calls it "floundering") until they discover what seems right or better to them. Still others are unsure even after they have declared a major and have taken most of the courses to graduates. Many may also flounder *after* they graduate.

Placement services are not career planning services. They have a different purpose: Whereas career planning is usually educational, placement is generally instrumental. Some adult learners need to recycle through the career planning process to explore alternatives and focus on career possibilities before targeting a specific job area. Placement serves a more limited function of matching applicants with employers. When a moving on adult learner seeks a job placement, the necessary exploration of and focusing on career goals have usually taken place. Yet some adult learners close to graduation and needing jobs may not be ready, and a career planning or placement counselor will need to assess their career maturity and decide which service will be most helpful.

Because Virginia had gone through the preliminary planning steps and clarified what she wanted to do with her advertising major, the placement center could provide a great deal of assistance in helping her find an appropriate job. What a placement center offers adult learners like Virginia are orientation sessions for registrants; an employer information library; current job listings locally and nationally; workshops on job search, résumé writing, and interviewing; on-campus interviews with employer representatives; a data file for each registrant; mailing of placement files to specified employers; and individual employment counseling.

Alumni can continue to use these placement services for five years or longer after graduation in most institutions. The University of Maryland, for example, offers a Career Check-Up Program for alumni, faculty, staff, and graduate students in a series of four weekend sessions. It is an intensive, experiential, "fun-filled" program that focuses on the participants' strengths. Tools are provided for clarifying values, identifying and prioritizing skills, enhancing personal power to choose a more rewarding life-style, believing more fully in oneself, setting personal life and career goals, making more effective decisions, considering career and life-style change, assuming more responsibility for one's life, and expanding one's vision of what is possible (Ritter, 1987). Participants take the Myers-Briggs Type Indicator and do extensive (ungraded) homework assignments before the workshop and between the sessions. They report that the program has been very helpful to them.

Many placement centers provide special sessions and

other services for adult learners to help them recognize their strengths and prepare for employer contingencies. For example, despite federal antidiscrimination legislation regarding hiring practices, many employers use subtle ways to weed out older, often more qualified applicants. Placement center staff who are advocates for adult learners provide encouragement and teach adult learners more effective approaches to handling innuendos about age and experience and such questions as "How long do you expect to work?"

Placement publications also contribute to preparing adult learners for employment. For example, the following suggestions are contained in a brochure that was published for graduate students:

> You will be glad to know that career opportunities abound! Your fine educational credentials are impressive; however, the degree alone will not guarantee success. If you were an established professional, what qualities would you look for in your future associates? You will probably mention the same factors that most employers are seeking now:
>
> 1. They are looking for someone whose college record indicates an ability to handle the technical phases of the work and who will continue to enhance skills and capacities.
> 2. They are looking for someone whose background indicates that breadth of interests which promises a well-rounded person and citizen.
> 3. They are looking for someone who exhibits initiative and enthusiasm for hard work.
> 4. They are looking for someone who displays an ability to communicate clearly—a characteristic which is often underestimated in its value to success.
> 5. They are looking for someone who possesses that priceless ingredient—integrity.

6. Lastly, they are looking for a select someone
   with whom they will be proud to practice
   their profession in the years ahead [Warren
   and Madden, 1986, p. 2].

Amanda's journey through placement services will serve
to illustrate the important kinds of help she and other adult
learners can receive. After Amanda's mentor helped her integrate her learning and experience using a developmental transcript, the mentor referred Amanda to the placement center.
There Amanda was told about an orientation program for new
adult registrants. At the orientation program, she heard about
the services available to adult and other learners. She learned
what she could expect from the staff and what her responsibilities would be in order to make the best use of the services. She
was surprised to find that the placement counselor was close to
her age and had gone back to school when her youngest child
entered kindergarten. Amanda began to understand the importance of placement services for establishing her own file, including her academic transcript and letters of recommendation
from faculty and others. She learned that listings of local and
national jobs were already available and that she would be able
to make appointments with representatives from large corpora-
tions in the near future.

Amanda took the application materials and completed
her college interview form. She knew that exams were coming,
and she wanted to have her file completed so that she could apply for interviews with the company representatives scheduled
for the next semester. Although she had applied for secretarial
jobs before, Amanda had little knowledge of how to do a job
search, complete a résumé, or interview for a professional position. She therefore scheduled an appointment with the placement counselor.

When Amanda talked with the counselor, she found that
the freshman entry/orientation course she had taken had helped
in developing her career goals. Her academic adviser had helped
in planning her program. The talks with her developmental mentor had helped her clarify who she was and what she wanted

from life. The placement counselor helped her to review her goals and to get more specific about her immediate career aspirations. She learned that seeking a job would become a full-time job in itself and that she had to commit herself to the time, energy, and money to get positive results. The counselor assigned her the task of writing long-term goals and gave her this model from the University of Southern Mississippi to help her conceptualize the process:

> Goals should be stated as clearly and concisely as possible. The more specific you are, the easier it will be to carry out your plans. Try to think of goals as cities plotted on a map. Your long-term goal represents where you want to end up on your journey. This long-term goal should be defined clearly and concisely in writing. Reaching this desired destination may become impossible without a series of smaller plans called short-range goals. These are immediate goals and should link together in achieving a long-range goal. In the example of a map, plotting a course of action as cities to travel through facilitates movement toward your destination while giving you a sense of accomplishment. Clarifying your goals and setting a course of action for achieving those goals will help you get out of life what you really want [Anderson, 1983, pp. 2–3].

Amanda wrote her long-range and short-term goals. Eventually, she hoped to become feature editor for a major religious magazine. In the meantime she wanted a job that would allow her to write articles, edit copy, and work in a creative environment. She knew that she might have to support her family if her husband's illness worsened. When she submitted her goals to the placement counselor, they talked about the realities of the local job market. The counselor suggested that Amanda spend some time looking at current job listings and using the employer information library in the placement center.

The counselor reminded Amanda to use all her contacts

to help find the desired job. Amanda talked with her senior writing professors and asked for letters of recommendation as well any job leads they might hear about. She contacted the head of the volunteer agency for whom she edited the brochure, asked for a letter of reference, and described the kind of job she was seeking. Of course, she talked to her family and friends about her career aspirations.

The counselor also suggested that Amanda attend workshops on job search, résumé writing, and interviewing. In the job search workshop, Amanda learned that she had begun the search process none too soon—often a year is needed to adequately research the job market. In many cases, 50 to 100 contacts result in only one or two offers. Timing is another important factor. Amanda was reminded that the world was not waiting for her: She was encouraged to keep good records, including copies of all letters sent and all replies received. She learned to keep an appointment calendar, with reminders of when and where to go for interviews, and when to conduct follow-ups on interviews. Often persistence and a show of interest are as important as experience in the field. Amanda was shown how to prepare a research data sheet on a prospective company, including names of company executives, types of products or services, new projects, the financial situation of the company, and types of positions available. The final part of record keeping was to take notes immediately following an interview to assist in the follow-up letter and the possible subsequent interview.

The job search workshop exposed Amanda and the other participants to numerous sources of job information, including placement center files; personal contacts; direct mail; advertisements in newspapers, professional journals, and newsletters; the state employment service; and the U.S. Civil Service Commission. She learned that some executive recruiting firms and some employment agencies may have useful listings but that caution should be maintained before signing any contracts. She learned, too, that interviewing persons for information about one's field of interest may produce leads as well as give valuable information.

The résumé writing workshop was also helpful. She learned

the difference between chronological, functional, and analytical résumés. She was reminded of the importance of using action verbs in describing her skills and learned how to state a career objective that would capture the eye of the potential employer and yet not limit her opportunities. She learned what to include and, more important, what not to include in a résumé. (Since her age was of some concern to Amanda, she was told not to include it, for example.) She learned how to write effective cover letters to accompany her résumé and got tips about completing employment applications.

Amanda found the interviewing workshop quite challenging. She had never thought about the importance of dressing properly for an interview or about what neatness conveys to the employer. Nonverbal communication, including eye contact, body posture, composure, and loudness of voice, was stressed. She learned that looking the interviewer in the eye without staring conveys a message of composure and self-confidence and that avoiding eye contact projects low self-esteem. The participants role-played interviewing and were encouraged to continue practicing after they left the workshop. Some of the tips Amanda found helpful were:

- Arrive on time.
- Greet the interviewer by name.
- Bring a résumé and be able to talk about your goals.
- Listen carefully.
- Be as relaxed as possible yet project an image of being enthusiastic, confident, sincere, and dedicated to achievement.
- Indicate a willingness to assume responsibility.
- Stress your qualifications without exaggeration.
- Find out to whom your position reports.
- Thank the interviewer.

She was given a list of questions that employers often ask in interviews and was encouraged to prepare her own answers. She was also told to develop some questions that she might ask potential employers.

After Amanda completed her résumé, she took it to the

placement counselor, who made a few suggestions for changes. Then she had it printed. She made an appointment for an on-campus interview with a company representative who was looking for an English major to assist in writing the company newsletter. However, Amanda found that the job would require her to relocate. The interview experience was a good one, and she learned to be more relaxed and to ask questions. She also answered a local newspaper ad for a copy writer. She asked the placement service to forward her file to the employer, but apparently the firm wanted someone with sports writing experience. The next interview with an on-campus representative was a disaster: he made her feel that she was too old, that a person with her background could never fit with his company. Somewhat shaken, Amanda talked with the placement counselor again. She needed to have her confidence rebuilt. The counselor suggested a transition group to help Amanda with her self-esteem. (More about Amanda later.)

Referrals to Transition Groups

Transition groups are another service helping adult learners bridge the gap between the institution and the outside world. Bruce's depression and Virginia's anxiety might have been addressed by an individual counselor or alleviated by a group experience. The counseling service can offer transition groups for adults in their last year or semester, or the culminating course might include group alternatives.

Transition groups are named for their different themes, such as "Making the Plunge into the Professional World," "So You're Considering Graduate School," or "Coping with Graduation and After." Although a counselor is the initial leader, much of the responsibility for the content and process rests with group members themselves. More often, it is peer support that is needed at this stage. Moving from a leader-structured group to a peer-support group requires planning and flexibility by the leader.

In transition groups, the counselor helps the group members learn about transition theory. Specifically, they examine the four S's—situation, self, supports, and strategies. This process helps them face the endings and the new beginnings. The members of the group recognize the three stages through which they are moving:

1. They are breaking away from an old situation (being in school).
2. They have a period of liminality (betwixt and between).
3. They become part of a new group or situation.

Members of the "Making the Plunge into the Professional World" group first examine their *situations*. A few adult learners in this group have never worked outside the home. Most others have held only clerical, manual, or fast-food jobs. But now they have prepared to fulfill roles in management or as beginning professionals. Group members also recognize that because they are older, more will be expected of them, even though they do not have the work experience of others their age. To attend to the *self* aspect of the transition, each member makes a list of personal and professional strengths. In examining their *supports*, group members acknowledge the contributions of family, friends, professors, and each other. The counselor helps them recognize that having this peer support means they are not alone in going through this process, and that knowledge helps. Finally, members list *strategies* for coping with this transition, taking advantage of placement services or contacts in finding a job.

A variation on this group is the Job Search Support Group for Adult Students at Iowa State University, reported by Arp, Holmberg, and Littrell (1986). After an initial interview, the program focused on exposing the hidden job market; developing cohesive relationships to maintain momentum during the job search; retaining individual responsibility for the search; and enhancing the self-image of job seekers. In six sessions, adult learners and recent adult learner alumni set weekly goals, became aware of barriers and resources, and shared experiences to give each other support. Each session asked a pertinent question, for example:

- What is holding you back?
- What skills do you possess?

- Where do you fit into the job market?
- Does a résumé make a difference?
- What can you expect in an interview?

By the time of the follow-up session, four out of ten participants had found jobs. The others said they had a good foundation on which to build further job searches.

The "So You're Considering Graduate School" group starts with assessing why each member is considering graduate or professional school. Situations will vary, but many group members will have decided that they need more education to allow them to work in their career goals or to offer the kind of life-style they are seeking. One important focus of this group is the "professional student syndrome" or "Is going to graduate school a way of avoiding the real world?" Supports may come from faculty more than from family. Because many adult learners have been at their undergraduate education for a long time, they may question their own motivations for graduate school, especially in light of its implications for the family. Is now the best time to be going to school? If I stop now, will I ever return? Perhaps the most important support is an internal determination and an ability to persist, which the group leader can recognize. Strategies certainly include ways to apply to graduate and professional schools. Information about taking the GRE, LSAT, and MCAT is shared. Some members may need a referral to the learning resource center to learn ways to prepare for these exams. Others may need encouragement as they bone up on their own. It is important to recognize that graduate school can be quite different from undergraduate school. To recap, by taking stock of these four S's, members can determine whether this is a "good" time to go to graduate school (*situation*), whether their level of maturity is such that they can deal with being a student again (*self*), and whether they have the supports and strategies to make it.

The group focusing on "Coping with Graduation and After" is composed of adults who are not sure what they want to do when they graduate. They are having difficulty with graduating because it means an end to relationships and an end to a structure that has come to have meaning for them. They may be feeling depressed and may not be aware that they are anxious about the future. With the prospect of graduation, what the adult learner has found most meaningful in life—learning—is coming to a formal end. Graduation may also be accompanied by the breakup of a marriage that was being held together by the routine of school. In the past it was common for marriages to fall apart when the husband graduated from law or medical school; today a growing number of divorces are occurring when the wife graduates with a B.A. in business and begins a new life in the corporate world. The group helps members cope with these personal and family problems that often accompany graduation and new professional opportunities.

As in all transition groups, the members look at their four S's. What is their situation now that they are leaving? Do they see themselves as complex and autonomous? If so, they will be more likely to deal with the ambiguities when they leave a structure. What supports can they expect as alumni? What are their personal and community supports as they forge their new identities? What strategies can they use as they cope with the transition ahead?

Each group member will assess the four S's differently, according to individual strengths. For example, for one the situation may be favorable, while for another a pending divorce may make the situation particularly bleak. The assessment of strengths and weaknesses will enable each person to figure out which S to work on.

Each group can develop its own ritual to help in the transition. The "Making the Plunge into the Professional World" group might develop a ritual in which individuals come to the group dressed professionally, acknowledge the learning that has taken place at this institution, and declare their strengths and abilities to make a contribution in the professional world. In the "So You're Considering Graduate School" group, the role of graduate student may not feel much different from the old undergraduate student role, but a ritual will help to make the break and acknowledge the change in status. The "Coping with Graduation and After" group should take time to acknowledge that learning is a lifelong process. Part of the ritual ceremony might be a sharing of meaningful pieces of writing and ways they might continue to be learners throughout life no matter what their circumstances.

Let's return to Amanda. She chose to attend the "Making the Plunge into the Professional World" group. She talked about her situation and especially about how she had felt when she went for the interview that bombed. She questioned her whole attempt at entering the professional world and wondered whether she wouldn't be better off getting a full-time secretarial job and maybe writing on the side. The group members encouraged her to keep trying and to go for other interviews. At the next session she talked about her husband's illness and what the group's support had meant to her. She described her strengths as persistence and the desire to write. A few weeks before graduation, Amanda was able to find a job writing for the educational department of a large hospital. The group applauded her courage and determination to pursue her dream. During the ritual she again thanked the group members for their support and encouragement and told them to be watching for her article about her experiences in a new religious magazine.

Commencement ceremonies, with families in attendance, can be the icing on the cake. All group members should be encouraged to attend this final ritual. The camera flashes and shouts of "Right on, Mom!" and "We knew you could do it, Dad!" amid strains of "Pomp and Circumstance" make the adult learner know that all the struggles, all the late nights have been worth it.

Institutions serious in their commitment to adult learners can assess their programs in culminating education or placement by applying the following questions, adapted from the *ACE Adult Learner Assessment and Planning Guide:*

1. What courses or programs exist to help adult learners integrate their learning and plan for the future?
2. Have placement services been established to serve adult learners?
3. Are placement services open evenings? Weekends? Available at different sites?

4. Does placement work cooperatively with local, state, and federal employment agencies to help adults find appropriate jobs?
5. Have résumé-writing and interviewing materials and services been adapted to adult learners?
6. Have support groups or other programs been developed to help adults make the transition from the institution?

Culminating Education and After

Helping adult learners feel that they matter to the institution is the role of every administrator, faculty member, and student development professional. If we provide an atmosphere of care as learners exit, they will remember the institution with care.

One way to assure this climate of care for adult learners is to give more recognition to their contributions while they are enrolled. At graduation time, most of the awards go to traditional-age students. Why not have special awards for adult learners who have overcome great obstacles to return to college, who have contributed to community and campus activities? Of course, academic honors should be acknowledged, whether the adult or other learner has been enrolled full or part time.

Assurances that adult learners are welcome to use the library and to continue to use the placement service may help them feel that the institution continues to be a part of their lives even after graduation. This union of graduates with the institution is probably more important to adult learners than to traditional-age students because more of them tend to live and to remain nearby. Allowing or encouraging graduates to take courses even though they are not enrolled for a graduate degree recognizes the link and loyalty between the alumni and the institution. It also acknowledges the importance of lifelong learning.

In Conclusion

More emphasis needs to be placed on culminating education not only for the sake of adult learners but also for the prosperity of the institution. Often the adults who return to a college or university later in life are already successful members of the community. Sometimes they are leaders and have influence with trustees and state legislators. It behooves the institution to acknowledge their contributions and to find ways for them to identify with the institution other than through attendance at football games.

If we provide what Daloz (1986) terms "an education of care," we provide support, listening, challenges, and vision. Support takes the form of giving structure, expressing positive expectations, sharing ourselves, and serving as advocates. We offer challenges by setting tasks, engaging in discussion, heating up dichotomies, constructing hypotheses, and setting high standards. Providing vision includes modeling, keeping tradition, offering a map, suggesting new language, and presenting a mirror. Whether through a special culminating course, work with a mentor or adviser, career planning and placement services, or transition workshops, culminating education can be education of care.

NINE

Payoffs to Learners from Improved Educational Support

Now that we have proposed model services for adult learners in higher education, we need to ask: What are the potential payoffs for these learners in terms of enhanced mental health and self-esteem, improved clarity of purpose, and increased skill in learning how to learn? What could the adult learners in our vignettes hope to gain if institutions were to change their policies, procedures, and practices as we have suggested? What could adult learners expect for themselves at each stage of the transition—moving in, moving through, and moving on? What would it mean to adult learners to feel that they matter?

In this chapter, we first examine how the implementation of our suggested changes would influence the adult learners we have encountered as they move in, move through, and move on. Next we consider the importance and results of mattering to adult learners. Then we look at the mental health payoffs to the adult learners and some of the current notions about what makes for mentally healthy and well-developed individuals. Finally, we review some ideas about the value of learning how to learn and summarize the payoffs for the adult learner.

Moving In

We recognize that we do not know those adults who did not enroll because of barriers that were too many, too high. If situational barriers such as needs for dependent care and for transportation were removed through changes in policies and practices and through better advertisement of the services available, many adult learners would have less difficulty in moving in. The same is true for institutional barriers: Changes in the reading level of the recruiting brochures and advertisements as suggested by Adams (1986), for example, would reduce or remove barriers to basic information and would help attract more adults who would benefit from further education. Similarly, information about the learning process and positive feedback would help to dispel such dispositional barriers as feeling too old to learn.

In our new and improved institution, Maggie ("I need to find out who I am") could come to the entry education center, talk with a developmental mentor, and get help in assessing her specific needs. In a system that is open to new recruits and that sees admissions as a learning process, she could explore with her mentor, adviser, or counselor those aspects of her concerns that keep her from setting goals and making commitments. Through interviews with her mentor and use of assessment instruments such as the Myers-Briggs Type Indicator and the Career Development Inventory, Maggie could discover who she is, what she wants, and where she wants to go—to search for her identity. She could join in the entry/orientation course on life, career, and educational planning or be referred to the career planning center for help in exploring possible careers. Warmline peer counselors could provide support throughout her move into the institution. Payoffs for Maggie would be an increased sense of competence and clarification of her purposes.

Gwen ("I want to move forward, to accomplish and achieve") would find the assistance she needs in the entry education center. She would find that she is not "too dumb and stupid to go to college" after all. She would be validated in her progress toward her nursing degree by her adviser or her mentor and by her instructors. Because the new orientation program would include spouses and family members, Gwen's boyfriend and her mother could be enlisted in giving her support. If her boyfriend were less threatened by Gwen's achievements, he could be more supportive and not make her feel so dependent on him. Further, if she could be helped with financial planning, she would feel able to accomplish more of her education on her own, giving her a sense of autonomy and pride. So the payoffs for Gwen under the new program would be greater autonomy, increased self-esteem, a sense of competence in achieving her goals, and a validation of her need to achieve. In addition, she would have an effect on her family system and perhaps inspire her boyfriend to continue his own education.

Walter ("Do I have to start at the beginning?") is a successful businessman. Starting college at fifty is a way for him to gain recognition and to be an example for his children. Early advising and an assessment of his prior college-level learning would help him feel affirmed and assured that he is not starting at ground zero. He would find, for example, that much of the learning he has gained from his business experiences, his self-study of history, and his leadership in politics could be aggregated through assessment of prior learning and portfolio processes to fulfill introductory course requirements in management, history, and political science. By gaining recognition for his prior college-level learning, Walter could be a model for his children and inspire their educational efforts. Payoffs for Walter would be an increased sense of competence, greater self-acceptance, and clarification of purpose.

For John ("Just show me the way!"), any reduction in his admissions red tape odyssey would be a benefit. If the changes proposed by Adams (1986) were made, John would find a receptive admissions office willing to track down the details and unwilling to send him scurrying through the institutional maze. Facilitating transcript evaluation by the registrar's office would eliminate most of John's trips, phone calls, and appointments with faculty, department heads, and registrar personnel. Payoffs for John would include getting on with his education, having a sense of being accepted and respected for the adult learner he is rather than being demeaned by the bureaucracy, and, importantly, having a greater sense of control over his life.

Moving Through

The frustration of an adult learner moving through is exemplified by the powerful image of the bag lady in Chapter One, shuffling from class to class in winter with one bag for her books and another for her boots. She is disenfranchised, with no place to sit, to receive messages, or to make phone calls. Worst of all, she tells us, is that "I have no dignity."

If the bag lady were to attend our new and improved institution with a policy of recognizing adults, much of her frustration would disappear. If her institution had an adult support center, she would have access to a message board, as well as to a telephone for making calls and finding out about her sick child. She would have a place to sit and to study between classes and, who knows, maybe even a locker for storing her books and boots. Payoffs would be a greatly improved sense of self, a stronger feeling of autonomy, and best of all, restoration of her sense of dignity.

For Valerie ("Look at me as a person, not as a middle-aged woman"), raising the consciousness of faculty and staff about ageism and sexism would increase her opportunities. If she did not find the chilly climate for women that Sandler and Hall (1982) found on most campuses, she would feel more like a first-class citizen. She would know that her opinions were respected on a par with those of male students. She would feel that her presence was significant, that she mattered. By having her own perceptions changed about the way she is treated on campus, payoffs for Valerie would include gains in sense of competence and strength of identity. She might even explore with her husband, who is already somewhat supportive, his role in "the politics of housework," thus relieving her for more active involvement in her educational experience. Confronting the basic prejudices against age and gender can bring greater opportunities to be fully functioning for men and women, young and old.

For Mary ("Hang in there!"), the counselors who helped her recognize her options made all the difference. The competing demands of her family, job, and studies almost made Mary quit several times. When she learned to evaluate her options, her self-esteem and confidence increased. Just as the thirty-six-year-old paraplegic rejected from law school could find the courage and curiosity to create his own options, so, too, Mary could cope with the demands made on her by changing her perspective. With a new orientation program and support groups in place as well as consistent offerings of required courses at convenient sites off campus, the payoffs for Mary would be a smoother moving in, increased options, and fewer difficulties in "hanging in there."

Art ("Mastering new skills") was intent on pursuing his education to improve his competency after he retired from the army. He felt torn by pressures from his wife as a result of the decrease in their economic status. In our new institution Art could be helped to enfranchise himself as a competent person, to gain an understanding that his drive for competency is a natural one. And perhaps his wife could be helped to appreciate his struggle through family therapy sessions at the personal counseling center. Learning often becomes the vehicle for adults to gain what White (1976b) calls the sense of competence. Thus, the payoffs for Art would include not only the new knowledge and skills acquired through more education but also a strong sense of competence that would give him increased confidence in his ability to accomplish whatever he tackles.

Janice ("A need for involvement") had a good first semester in the returning student program. She stuck it out for two years and then left because she did not feel a part of the college community. In our improved institution, she could be connected with several communities. She could be part of a support group for returning women with children. She would be able to find a carpool to get her children to their activities. In our new kind of institution, publicity about different peer support groups would help. Janice could get involved in the adult learner association, where her efforts would be appreciated and she would develop some form of a social life. The loneliness of being a single parent, together with the responsibility for all the decisions about children, home, work, and school, can be overwhelming. When a sense of community is built among adult learners, they have added reasons for continuing their education; and when there is an adult support center, adult learners have a place to meet friends as well as to study and receive messages. Janice would also benefit greatly by knowing about the learning resource center, where she could be helped to organize her work and her time and learn how to learn. When information about such services as the adult learner association and the adult support center is available at registration, adult learners are far more likely to take advantage of them. The biggest payoff for Janice would be enhancement of her sense of connectedness and community, which would help her stay in college and gain better skills and more confidence. We hope that when Janice does decide to give college another chance, she will find an institution and community more responsive to adult learners.

Moving On

Carlo ("I'm changing, and my needs are changing") returned to the university after floundering around and dropping out several times. He shifted from engineering to liberal arts and is now committed to going to law school. In our new kind of institution, Carlo, who "needs a different kind of adviser now," would be connected with a developmental mentor who would provide culminating education. In fact, Carlo's mentor would have been with him since he entered and would know how Carlo should prepare for the law school tests, including taking the LSAT workshop. In addition, his mentor or adviser would refer him to the career planning center to arrange a career encounter with a local attorney for some firsthand feedback about the field of law. With the institution's new focus on adults as learners, Carlo would have more opportunities for access to information that would help him in long-range planning. Carlo could become involved in the "So You're Considering Graduate School" support group. Through these services Carlo would feel affirmed in his ability to complete the process of applying to law school. He would recognize his own competence. His ability to persevere would be encouraged by his mentor. The payoffs for Carlo would be an increased sense of self-determination and a clarity of purpose.

For Virginia ("I'm too old to get the job I want"), her fears of the job market and of how she would be perceived in the work world are her greatest obstacles. Her assets are her excitement, her skills and knowledge, her dependability, and her determination to succeed. In our new institution, Virginia would work with a marital and family counselor to resolve her bitterness regarding the divorce. In her last semester, she would enroll in the culminating education course and spend time with her mentor or adviser evaluating her college experience. As part of the culminating course, she would be involved in a group for older women on assertiveness in the workplace. The facilitator, an advocate for the group, would present examples of situations to handle in the initial and final job interviews. Virginia would also learn ways to handle ageist and sexist comments on the job. Through these opportunities, she would increase her capacity to understand others and to relate to and work with them effectively. Payoffs for Virginia would be increased tolerance for ambiguity, and affirmation that she is competent and can be successful.

Bruce ("I wonder if I made a big mistake") said that it never occurred to him to ask for help in pursuing his teaching certification as he approached graduation. His lack of entitlement contributed to his powerlessness and sense of loss. With our new system, Bruce would have been asked by his mentor or adviser what his plans were long before graduation. The mentor would have suggested ways that Bruce could be more active in planning a career in art photography or related areas. Perhaps the mentor would also have connected Bruce with the teacher certification counselor and even explored the possibility of a job as a provisional art teacher while he worked toward his certification. The culminating education center would help Bruce find the exiting services he needed. The support group "Coping with Graduation and After" could be the vehicle for Bruce to deal with his losses on leaving the university. By talking about his sense of loss and his depression and by coming to recognize that learning can continue thoughout life, Bruce could cope with his loss and realize that he is beginning another important transition. This kind of experience would help Bruce integrate his learning and reach a higher level of intellectual and ethical development. The payoffs for Bruce would be identifying strengths, learning to cope with losses, and moving ahead in achieving a new self-awareness and sense of his own agency.

Amanda ("I need to reevaluate my possibilities") needed help in reappraisal and in job placement. We took Amanda through a model placement service for adult learners in Chapter Eight. After talking with her mentor about integrating her learning from college work, she found that placement services included an orientation program and workshops on job search, résumé writing, and interviewing, as well as employment counseling and interviews with appropriate representatives. She also benefited from the "Making the Plunge into the Professional World" transition group. Through this support group, she could increase her capacity to understand and relate to others and cope with her husband's illness. When Amanda takes a job as a writer for the educational department of the large hospital, she will feel that she has made a reflective choice relating to her major and one that will give her experience to fulfill her dream to influence others through her writing. For now, she appreciates the help she has received in obtaining this position, and she recognizes that through her own efforts and the support of her mentor, her minister, and the transition group, she can reach a higher level of functioning and face the problems ahead. The wellness model helps her balance the different spheres of her life so that she can feel she is on the road to high-level wellness. The payoff for Amanda could be a clearer and more realistic perception of herself, her roles, and her environment. She could also achieve an added appreciation for her spiritual growth and its significance.

Mattering

What payoffs will there be for adult learners when they matter to the institution as they move in, move through, and move on? How important is mattering to them?

We recall Rosenberg and McCullough's (1981, p. 165) definition of mattering as "a motive—a feeling that others depend upon us, are interested in us, are concerned about our fate, or experience us as an ego-extension." A look at the components of mattering—attention, importance, ego-extension, and dependence—helps clarify its importance for adult learners, as well as its payoffs in our new institutions.

Attention. "The most elementary form of mattering is the feeling that one commands interest or notice of another person" (Rosenberg and McCullough, 1981, p. 164). As adults enter our institutions, we will help them feel they matter by giving them attention. Recruitment brochures showing adult learners of various ages in positive surroundings will demonstrate the institution's attention and sensitivity to the concerns of adult learners about feeling included as valuable members of the college or university community. An adult learner association that takes a prominent role in registration, an orientation program designed for adult learners that offers a life, career, and education planning course, and an empathic mentor will give adult learners positive attention. An adult support center that provides opportunities for adult learners to connect with each other and form bonds of friendship will also help adult learners feel they matter. Payoffs for Janice, for example, would be that the attention she receives from her mentor and support group will make her feel she matters and give her a sense of community—thus helping her decide to continue her education despite the many competing demands of being a single parent. In addition, receiving attention may have a halo effect for adult learners and generalize to more positive feelings about self and the institutional environment.

Importance. "To believe that the other person cares about what we want, think, and do, or is concerned with our fate, is to matter" (Rosenberg and McCullough, 1981, p. 164). In our new institution, a developmental mentor or adviser will be the first person to whom an adult learner can turn. The adult learner will know that the mentor or adviser cares, is concerned about his or her fate. Such mentors and advisers, selected for their compassion and concern for adult learners, will make learners feel connected, feel important, feel that they matter—which will also help the institution since, as the next chapter points out, retention is directly related to feelings of being connected, or mattering. When the basic policies of our institution say, "Adult learners are important," when the student handbook features pictures of adult learners as well as traditional-age students, when an adult support center gives visible evidence of the acceptance of adult learners as a vital part of the institution, adult learners know they are important, that they matter. Among the payoffs for adult learners will be increases in self-esteem and self-confidence and better interpersonal relationships.

Ego-Extension. People's perceptions that others are proud of their accomplishments or saddened by their failures are a part of mattering. For adult learners, their families are often the most help with this aspect of mattering. The new institution would reinforce the pride that family members take in their adults enrolled in college by acknowledging the important role families play in supporting the adult learner. Through special orientation programs involving family members, the institution would assist adult learners in feeling they matter to their families and to the institution. Mentors and faculty members would also have an impact on adult learners by showing pride in the accomplishments of their adult mentees and students. A payoff for Walter would be a much easier time in serving as a role model and in encouraging his sons to continue their education after high school. For Gwen, payoffs would include increased understanding and support from her boyfriend, less sabotage from her mother, and greater self-esteem.

Dependence. When others depend on us, we feel we matter to them. When adult learners in a transition support group let the others know they are depending on them to be there and to contribute, it makes the learners feel they matter. Payoffs can be a greater sense of confidence and increased interpersonal competence, as they are for Art and his Thursday night dinner group. The officers of the adult learner association can often help members feel they matter by giving them responsibilities and depending on them to fulfill their commitments. Faculty members can help adult learners feel they matter by counting on them to be in class and by letting them know their contributions are missed when they are absent. Small work groups within classes and group projects help adult learners feel they matter to others.

Sometimes the dependency part of mattering can have a dark side, as for the adult learner with teenage children and elderly parents needing care. She is a member of the "sandwich generation," with too many people depending on her. A family care center established by the institution would help keep this adult learner from "mattering too much."

We believe that mattering is important to all adult learners. For some it may be the single element that makes the difference in their completing their degrees and developing a feeling of satisfaction and a sense of belonging.

Mental Health and Adult Development

As we consider the mental health payoffs for adult learners in our new and improved institutions, we need to keep in mind that each adult learner is a part of many different systems: a family system, a social system, an employment system, an educational system, and a community system. General systems theory proposes that whenever one part of the system is affected, other parts are as well, and the whole is changed. Thus, as we have an impact on the adult learners in our educational systems, the ripples can be felt in their families, their workplaces, the institution, and the larger community.

We also need to ask what makes for a mentally healthy adult, given the current emphasis on wellness and physical health. If we can identify the characteristics of a mentally healthy or well-developed adult, we can ask whether these qualities are among the payoffs for adults in our new and improved institutions.

Getting a handle on what it means to be a mentally healthy adult is not easy: The literature is replete with various concepts of adequate or full functioning, mental health, high self-esteem, maturity, and self-actualization. However, some general characteristics indicative of mental health seem to cut across these concepts:

- Self-acceptance, valuing of self
- Sense of self-determination
- Clear and realistic perception of self and environment
- Openness to emotions and ability to manage them
- Capacity to understand, relate to, and work with others

Grasping some developmental aspects is easier: Theorists such as Perry (1968), Loevinger (1976), and Kohlberg (1973) tell us that development progresses from simple to complex, from external to inner orientation, from absolutism and dogmatism to tolerance for ambiguity and uncertainty, from stereotypic relating to awareness of individual differences and greater empathy for others. A well-developed adult demonstrates such progress. (See Weathersby and Tarule, 1980, for theories of adult development.)

These concepts of mental health and adult development enrich our understanding of adult learners. In addition, Chickering's (1969) vectors—achieving competence, managing emotions, becoming interdependent, establishing identity, freeing interpersonal relationships, clarifying purposes, developing integrity—can be useful to the practitioner who is attempting to provide payoffs for the adult learner.

Adult learners have generally mastered some of these vectors in earlier life phases; however, when they enter or return to higher education, they confront these issues at different levels. Perhaps the most obvious issue is achieving competence in new areas. Adult learners need to prove to themselves and others that they can learn and that they have the intellectual capacity to complete college-level work. After an initial period of feeling somewhat shaky academically, many adult learners gain a sense of competence and often excel because the payoffs for achieving are intrinsic. Most must also learn to manage their emotions and the demands placed on them within a new educational milieu at the same time that their family, social, and work environments are changing. Part of any adult learner's reason for returning to higher education is usually to develop a sense of autonomy, whether that is evidenced in instrumental independence through better career opportunities or in intrinsic independence through a sense of self-improvement.

Although most adult learners feel that they have established their identities earlier in life, creating an identity is a continuing process, often subject to challenges and self-doubts provoked by college and university experiences. With a new identity that includes being an adult learner, they are in a position to seek freer interpersonal relationships. They can move from dependence to independence and recognize their interdependence with others.

With an evolving identity and a sense of competence, adult learners must continuously clarify their purposes. Most have set goals of becoming better educated and of fulfilling a lifelong ambition to have a college degree. In addition, many have specific career goals that help pull them toward graduation. These career goals may involve improving their present work situation or may lead in an entirely new direction. General self-improvement and having a sense of direction will enhance the adult learner's motivation to continue with lifelong learning.

In developing integrity, the adult learner humanizes values by shifting from an absolutist to a more relative view, where connections are made between the rules and the purposes they serve. The adult learner also personalizes values to make them fit and integrates them into the self. Finally, the adult learner develops congruence, in which all behavior becomes consistent with the personal values held. Thus, the adult learner refines his or her sense of integrity. Chickering's vectors help us understand that adult learners are pursuing these competencies and values at different levels, which requires increasing attention to the complexities of these challenges.

Learning How to Learn

An important strategy that can be a beneficial payoff for all adult learners is learning how to learn. The content of the learning that takes place in colleges and universities often fades once the midterm or final exam is behind, and little can be recalled the following semester or year. By the time a student graduates, the material learned in the first years has been forgotten or stored away in the memory banks only to be called forth for games like Trivial Pursuit. The technical skills learned by engineers, if used on a daily basis, will become sharper, but the details of mathematical formulas will need to be retrieved from textbooks. So, too, the liberal arts major may recall the plot of an eighteenth-century novel but forget the names of the chief protagonists. A business major may be able to talk about the differences between macroeconomics and microeconomics but be unable to recall the formulas applied to determine the national debt.

What is important about a college or university education? Is it the details and facts? Certainly some disciplines rely heavily on facts and the recall of details as the foundation of learning. Other disciplines, however, require more abstract and global syntheses in the processing of fundamental information. Critical thinking is the variable ability that tends to differentiate adult learning from adolescent learning. It needs to be encouraged in the context of a complex intellectual environment.

Many institutions are attacking the problem of outcomes assessment, of accountability to legislators and the public, through standardized testing. The tests appear to assess fundamental knowledge about a variety of disciplines. None, however, appears to assess how well the student has learned how to learn, or metalearning.

If students can be exposed to concepts of how to learn, rather than just the content of learning, they will gain more from a college education than just facts. They will develop cognitive capacities that can never be taken away from them. As the proverb says, "Teach people to fish, and they will feed themselves." Teaching learners how to learn empowers those learners.

Brookfield (1986) identifies critical reflection as one of the major principles of facilitative learning. His point is that "education is centrally conceived with the development of a critically aware frame of mind, not with the uncritical assimilation of previously defined skills or bodies of knowledge" (p. 17). His contention is that when educators inculcate a sense of the culturally constructed nature of knowledge, beliefs, values, and behaviors, learning is being effectively facilitated. Learners must become aware of underlying assumptions, norms, and uncritically accepted practices and must be encouraged to imagine alternative structures and practices.

> This process centers on the need for educational activity to engage the learner in a continuous and alternating process of investigation and exploration, followed by reflection on this action, followed by further investigation and exploration, followed by further action, and so on. This notion of praxis as alternating and continuous engagements by teachers and learners in exploration, action and reflection is central to adult learning. It means that exploration of new ideas, skills, or bodies of knowledge does not take place in a vacuum but is set within the context of learners' past, current and future experiences" [Brookfield, 1986, p. 15].

The cycle of exploration, action, and reflection is an essential ingredient of the practica, internships, co-op learning, and field experiences that can constitute some of the most meaningful learning for adults. This same cycle can be applied in classes and other cocurricular experiences of adult learners—if they learn the process. Brookfield reminds us that adult learners do not acquire and internalize ideas, skills, knowledge, and insights in a vacuum. Instead, they first interpret such information through their own mediatory mechanisms. They assign meaning to it, codify it according to categories they have evolved, and test it in real-life situations. When adult learners can become aware of underlying norms, policies, and objectives and view them as relative and determined by context, they can become proactive in advocating change and innovation, can become advocates for their own learning process. This proactive process is a cutting-edge concept for higher education. In fact, self-empowerment of adult learners through metalearning could revolutionize higher education.

In addition, when adult learners understand their own learning styles, psychological types, and learning preferences as well as their underlying assumptions, values, and beliefs, they will have an appreciation for their best ways to learn. They will be able to adapt to other modes of learning as needed, know how to tackle a reading assignment, an essay, a new language, a field experience, a new career. They will have confidence in their abilities to learn new subjects, appreciate their talents in discovering new modes of learning, and be able to participate actively in their advocacy.

As Cross (1986, p. 10) has explained, "In this era of knowledge explosion, what students know when they leave college will not be nearly as important as what they are capable of learning." When institutions teach learning how to learn, they are instilling the lifelong value of learning. As empowered, self-directed adult learners search for knowledge and wisdom, they find that learning itself becomes a positive process.

In Conclusion

The payoffs for adult learners in our new and improved institutions are legion: They will gain in mental health, function more fully, increase self-esteem, and reach new levels of maturity and self-actualization. They will value themselves and others more because they feel they matter to the institution. They will clarify their purposes and increase their determination to fulfill their goals. With opportunities for feedback from mentors, advisers, and faculty, our adult learners will gain clearer and more realistic perceptions of themselves and their environments. They will feel empowered.

Adult learners enter colleges and universities if they believe their needs will be met. They stay away if they believe otherwise. Part of their need has to do with the kind of support they receive from the institution. If they feel they matter, they are more likely to remain. Because our adult learners will feel that they belong to a group that accepts them, that supports them, they will be likely to get involved and stay. Because they will feel they matter, they will tell their friends, and more adults will enter our colleges and universities.

Adult learners in our new and improved institutions will be empowered by learning how to learn. They will feel they are getting full value from their higher education. Their consciousness of their preferences for learning styles and their confidence in their ability to tackle new areas will stay with them throughout their lifetimes. Once an individual catches fire with learning, his or her desire for knowledge will be unquenchable.

As Gibran's "Prophet" said to the Teacher (1973, p. 56):

> No man can reveal to you ought but that which already lies half asleep in the dawning of your knowledge.
>
> The teacher who walks in the shadow of the temple, among his followers, gives not of his wisdom but rather of his faith and his lovingness.
>
> If he is indeed wise he does not bid you enter the house of his wisdom, but rather leads you to the threshold of your own mind.

The leadership of our country rests with the graduates of our higher education institutions. As professionals we need to recognize the important role we play in the mental health of the country by raising the standards of self-esteem, confidence, and maturity for adult learners—and all learners. We can do this most effectively by leading our learners to the thresholds of their own minds and by providing a place to matter in our new institutions.

How Institutions Benefit from Supporting Adult Learners

Program changes that help adult learners move into our colleges and universities more effectively can significantly improve learners' chances for successful and productive experiences. Maggie ("I need to find out who I am") and Gwen ("I want to move forward, to accomplish and achieve"), for example, will benefit greatly from our entry education center in terms of greater clarity of purpose, sense of competence, sense of identity, and autonomy. When our entry education programs serve persons like John ("Just show me the way!") and Walter ("Do I have to start at the beginning?"), they are much more likely to stay with us and profit from the experiences and resources we have to offer.

When adult learners such as Valerie ("Look at me as a person, not as a middle-aged woman"), Mary ("Hang in there!"), Janice ("A need for involvement"), and Art ("Mastering new skills")—and the "bag lady"—have access to our adult support center, they will find the support they need to succeed as they move through. When, for example, our culminating services help Virginia ("I'm too old to get the job I want") and Bruce ("I wonder if I made a big mistake") reflect on what they have accomplished during their college years, sharpen their sense of the knowledge and competence they have acquired, and clarify their immediate occupational plans in the context of long-range aspirations, personal values, and life-style dreams, such learners are much better prepared to move on.

When institutions treat adult learners as though they matter, when we create educational programs to help students move in, move through, and move on, the payoffs for adult learners will be impressive, as noted in the last chapter. But many colleges and universities find it difficult to make the investments required to institute those changes. Programs for entering, supporting, and culminating services for adult learners often get short shrift. They are at the bottom of the totem pole for executive attention, for funding, and for finding and retaining top-quality personnel. Business as usual is presumed to be adequate to provide the services required, and if enough ill-served adult learners gripe, some patching and tinkering here and there will suffice. An underlying assumption seems to be that the main mission of the institution will continue to be to provide student services for traditional-age students who come directly from high school, study full time, live on campus, are totally involved in the institution, and have no areas of significant responsibility. Another underlying assumption seems to be that there is little payoff in making significant investments to serve adult learners well.

A Necessary Change

We see these underlying assumptions as unsound and archaic for all colleges and universities, except, perhaps, for a few highly selective public and private institutions. A fundamental reason is the post-World War II baby boom. Like the proverbial pig in the boa constrictor, that population bulge is moving inexorably through our social corpus. During the 1980s, for example, the thirty to forty-nine age group will increase almost 36 percent, as Table 1 shows.

One outcome of this unprecedented demographic bulge has been the increase in numbers of adult learners seeking higher education in both the 1970s and 1980s. Increases in adult learners in the 1970s were also caused by such major social phe-

Table 1. Population Changes in Age Groups, 1970–2000.

Period	Age Groups		
	15 to 29	30 to 49	50 to 69
1970–1980	+26.7%	+16.4%	+15.0%
1980–1990	−6.3	+35.9	−0.3
1990–2000	−2.5	+13.9	+16.1

Source: Masnick and Pitkin, 1982. Used by permission.

nomena as changes in roles and increased opportunities for women, changing patterns of marital relationships, rapid growth in the number of two-career marriages and single parents, increased speed of obsolescence, and creation of new jobs. These social forces seem unlikely to diminish during the final years of the 1980s and during the 1990s. In fact, most will probably grow in strength. The proportion of baby boomers seeking higher education seems sure to become even larger.

The demographic bulge will also create waves in the age distribution of the nation's workforce. Table 2 shares some of those projections. The fifteen to twenty-nine age group drops

Table 2. Percent Share of Working-Age Adult Population.

Year	Age Groups		
	15 to 29	30 to 49	50 to 69
1980	39.12%	34.25%	26.63%
2000	29.89	44.32	25.79

Source: Masnick and Pitkin, 1982. Used by permission.

nearly 10 percent (from 39 to 30 percent), the thirty to forty-nine age group increases 10 percent (from 34 to 44 percent), and the fifty to sixty-nine age group remains essentially stable at about 26 percent. This means that the actual number of young persons available for entry-level jobs will decrease by 25 percent. The natural marketplace consequence of this sharp drop will be to increase the hourly wages and salaries associated with entry-level work. Thus, the costs in forgone income for young persons choosing college on a full-time basis will increase, and the incentives for enrolling intermittently or only part time will similarly grow.

The 36 percent increase in the thirty to forty-nine age group will mean increased competition for promotion and increased constraints on lateral mobility. For every three people today, there will be four competing for supervisory or middle-management positions, seeking increased responsibilities and higher wages, reaching for more complex, fulfilling, challenging work. A key to success in this increasingly competitive workplace will be the knowledge and competence, the degrees and certificates available from higher education. Thus, the marketplace pressures on young people to become both workers and part-time students will combine with the greater marketplace competition among the baby boomers to sharply increase the numbers of adults seeking services from institutions of higher education.

Yet another force will increase those numbers. Young people are maturing earlier these days. The average age of menarche has dropped about a year in the last fifty years, to about twelve and one-half. Other aspects of physical maturation have dropped correspondingly. But even more powerful in their implications for educational policies and practices are the sharp changes in social and psychological maturation. The age of "social emancipation" of young people, in self-determination, interpersonal relationships, sexual behavior, and other areas of life, has moved steadily downward, from post-high school, through high school, and into the junior high school years.

Well over a decade ago, a presidential commission (Coleman and others, 1974) criticized traditional policies and practices that continue full-time schooling beyond the age of physical and social maturation. Alternative patterns that integrate work and study were recommended as much more compatible with the psychological and social maturity of adolescents. A more recent article recommends a year of national service after high school graduation and a reduction of time in formal, full-time school settings (Woodward and Kornaber, 1985). Today new patterns are in evidence: As of 1984, "one in three of our freshmen has delayed entry into college after high school, more than two in five undergraduates attend college part time, and over half of the bachelor's degree recipients take more than the traditional four years to complete the degree" (Study Group on the Conditions of Excellence in American Higher Education, 1984, p. 7). More recently, when the Carnegie Foundation for the Advancement of Teaching (1986) surveyed a large sample of undergraduates, 30 percent indicated they had taken at least one semester off since starting. These trends contribute to changing age distributions in undergraduate enrollments. Table 3 gives the figures for 1972 and 1982 and projects the picture for 1992.

Table 3. Distribution of Undergraduate Enrollment by Age and Status.

Age and Status	1972	1982	1992 (est.)
24 and under	69%	61%	51%
25 and over	31	39	49
Full-time	66	58	52
Part-time	34	42	48

Source: U.S. Department of Education, 1985.

So we do not have to guess who's coming to college. We know, for sure, that there will be steadily increasing numbers of adult learners pursuing higher education. Only a few selective public and private colleges and universities, defined by very high traditional test scores, high entrance standards, or special mission, will be able to insulate themselves from this social phenomenon. Most institutions, whether they like it or not, will be pushed to respond in some fashion. The payoffs they experience from responding effectively will depend on their orientation and on the ways in which they redefine their mission in relation to these changes.

For adult learners the best sort of institution sees itself in close educational and service relationships with its local, regional, national, and international communities. John Warfield, a professor at George Mason University, makes a nice distinction between the "classical" and the "interactive" university:

Two distinct models of the university come to mind. One is the classical image of the ivory tower, divorced from surrounding events, indifferent to materialistic values, immersed in activities of the mind, detached from all worlds but its own. The other is the interactive university, alert to trends in the society, be they international, national, regional, or local, and sensitive to the potential symmetry in the relation between the university and its many constituencies; oriented to service in the broadest sense, which includes teaching and research; rubbing shoulders with potential consumers of the university's human and intellectual products; immersed in the turbulent environment; and honoring multiple faculty roles inside and outside the institution, with regard to influencing the future [Johnson, 1986].

George Johnson, George Mason's president, who used Warfield's comments in his 1986 State of the University address, commented further on the changes required to become an "interactive university":

We have to approach that kind of need with all due humility, of course, fully conscious that universities themselves must in all probability reorganize and restructure themselves. After all, much of the structure and organization of a modern American university bears the marks of the industrial era, of the factory system. Indeed, it was that great gulping expansion when industrial America capitalized the machine amplification of human muscle that the undergraduate college, the academic department, the graduate school, and professional training formats were all invented. Indeed even the semester credit hour was an invention of that period, and perhaps a significant one, since a moment's review reveals the factory model: quality stan-

dards for input materials; a process which is syn-
chronous, serial, and uniform; output which is
standarized and graded. While other institutions of
our society, including our current factories, have
customized their services and products, universities remain locked in an organization which is an
artifact of an age now gone. . . .

In the face of change I like to say that there
are two basic responses, the bureaucratic and the
entrepreneurial. Bureaucratic planning, which characterizes not simply government agencies but failing businesses and too many universities, rests on
the basis of continuity, assuming that change, if it
occurs, can be kept at the margins of the enterprise and that the central work will go on without
deflection. Entrepreneurial planning rests on an
assumption of discontinuity. Not only is change
anticipated but it is anticipated to be unpredict-
able. The basis for planning is therefore one of
positioning the organization. The bureaucrat builds
higher sea walls; the entrepreneur looks for a better surfboard. It is a matter of stance, of attitude.
Attitudes that today can be predicted to fail are
those which are centered in the individual private
interest; those that succeed are those aligned with a
public interest.

In order to contribute and grow we must
participate in the agenda of others rather than pre-
serving our own.

If an institution shares Johnson's views, if it aims to become highly interactive with its local, regional, national, and
international communities, then admitting and learning to work
effectively with a wide array of adult learners will generate two
kinds of payoffs. One set of payoffs will strengthen the institution's relationships with and support from its "external" constituencies; the other set will strengthen its "internal" capacity
for continued self-renewal and for creating educationally powerful environments.

External Payoffs

There are a significant number of success stories in which institutions have achieved major gains in external support and internal revitalization as a consequence of taking adult learners seriously. These institutions have, through thoughtful investments in planned change, increased their accessibility and their internal responsiveness to diverse adult populations. Several are profiled in a fine book that is must reading for educational leaders interested in helping their institutions move out of nineteenth-century ways of doing things into those appropriate for the twentieth and twenty-first centuries. It is called *Searching for Academic Excellence* (Gilley, Fulmer, and Reithlingshoefer, 1986). Using case histories of twenty colleges "on the move," the authors describe the institutional qualities, motivating forces, leadership qualities, and administrative practices that characterize these institutions and that have sharply increased enrollments, achieved major curricular reforms, reshaped institutional structures, improved educational quality, and augmented financial support.

At the suggestion of one of the authors, Sally Reithlingshoefer, we called Billy Wireman (1987), the president of Queens College, one of the institutions profiled. We asked him about the mix of ingredients and payoffs that worked for his institution in Charlotte, North Carolina. Here are some of his comments:

> The main thing is that adult [learner] programs add *weight* to the institution in the eyes of the community. These programs have increased our attractiveness throughout the Charlotte area through the numerous connections they have generated with businesses, cultural activities, and the church. Before, we were seen as an isolated, good quality, liberal arts college; now we're seen as an integral part of the community, providing useful services, playing significant roles in creating the Charlotte future.
> We have added a whole new network of sup-

port and friends. It is not that they disliked us or did not respect us before. But there was not that regular strong emotional, psychological, and physical interaction so they could really get to know what we had to offer. The key conceptual change is from having been perceived as an isolated enclave to being perceived now as a cultural and academic resource for the whole community.

In a given year we will engage 10,000 Charlotte citizens in ways they have not been engaged before. Multiply those direct engagements by word of mouth, and that's what I mean by increased *weight*. Our Friends of Art, Friends of Music, Friends of the Library all have boards of community representatives and bring outstanding, nationally recognized persons to campus. Those organizations have become an organic part of the community.

Our changes in student services have been substantial. First we had to acknowledge a different time frame. Now there is much activity between 5:30 and 9:00 each evening and also on weekends. We had to develop a whole response system geared to that time frame, from the bookstore and snack bars to counseling and support services. It took some time to sensitize our staff to the differences brought by adult students and to help the staff change their thought patterns and behaviors. We are still working at that but have made good progress.

There have been dramatic consequences for fund raising, public relations, recruiting, and church relations. We have record enrollment and record giving. Our endowment has tripled, with six years of a balanced budget and record surpluses each year. The community now sees us as a key part of the future. They anticipate service and see us as a significant resource rather than as a needy charity and source of problems. We are now seen as part of the aura of the community, as part of the dynamic contributing to its development. We are now seen, not only by the community but by ourselves and our alumni, as having a significant future, as contributing to the future of Charlotte and the region, as serving and not just surviving [personal communication, Oct. 5, 1987].

Note the key payoffs in Wireman's report. A whole array of community relationships now exist. Relationships like these not only boost recruitment, they also provide opportunities for internships, practica, apprenticeships, and field observations. They provide a pool of human resources for active contribution to boards that help plan and carry out a variety of institutional programs and functions. They give the college administrators, faculty members, and student educational services professionals a significantly strengthened sense of their own purpose, their own value, and the importance of their contributions to the community in which they live, love, work, play, and raise their children. These college folk walk the streets, stroll the supermarket aisles, and chat in the checkout lines with a new sense of connectedness and relevance. Record enrollments, budget surpluses, and a fast-growing endowment give the institution and its members running room for continued program development and expanded service.

Once that dynamic gets rolling, everyone benefits, even the alumni who graduated in years long past. Their sense of self-esteem, pride in the institution, and identification with it grows. Their readiness to help in capital campaigns and in annual appeals is bolstered by the clear evidence and certain knowledge that the college has a significant future and is making lasting contributions. Deferred-giving programs are much more attractive when it is clear that the institution will still be alive and flourishing many years hence. This increased enthusiasm is communicated to potential students and to potential donors. Both psychological and material support flourish.

Note also that as adult learners become a significant proportion of our new graduates, they augment the number of alumni who are more likely to be better established financially, since they are occupying or moving into better paying and more secure employment, than the typical twenty-three- to twenty-five-year-old graduates. Older graduates are more likely to have discretionary income as well as discretionary energy to contribute. When a highly positive experience with an institution is vivid in relatively recent memory, they may be more likely to remember the institution in their wills, to include it in deferred-giving plans. For older graduates with the resources and inclination to recognize worthy causes in their wills, it is less likely that other competing worthy beneficiaries will intervene. The number of such alumni is always small, but a steady flow of enthusiastically supportive adult learners can increase the probability that an institution will receive monetary rewards for its efforts to serve adult learners.

For publicly supported institutions there is another key external payoff: political support. Research evidence and our own personal experiences document the degree to which adult learners are better educated, more upwardly mobile, and more frequently community leaders and active participants in community affairs. Students and alumni like these, when they have a positive experience with an institution, become an immediate source of political support at the state and local levels. They are a source of personal contacts. They know the value of political action and know how to use political leverage in their businesses, social agencies, cultural programs.

One publicly supported state college, for example, as part of its early efforts to meet the needs of adult learners, created a labor college for shop stewards, workers, and labor leaders through programs tailored to their backgrounds and educational needs. The program was conducted in cooperation with a group of local unions, and administrators, counselors, and faculty members had offices in a building owned by one of the unions. Orientation programs, classes, and meetings between students and their faculty mentors all were held in this building, which was some distance from the main administrative offices of the college. At the end of the labor college's first year, students were enthusiastic about their experiences and had formed a strong student association. When the governor's budget came out, the college administration was surprised and dismayed to learn that the funding for the labor college had been moved to a large, politically powerful university. The administrators immediately called the leaders of the student association, and that same day some of those leaders were in the offices of the governor and of key legislators in the capitol. By the next morning, the funds for the labor college were back in the budget of the original institution.

Of course, few institutions will face such arbitrary intervention, and few will be able to mobilize such an influential constituency so quickly and to such good effect. But most institutions, once they have served a reasonable number of adult learners with programs that recognize and respect the persons, their backgrounds, their motives, their difficult living realities, will find they have acquired broad-based and effective political supporters throughout their local and regional communities.

Internal Payoffs

At least four kinds of internal payoffs result from creating supportive environments for adult learners: increased retention of students, program improvements for traditional-age young adults, a sustained force for continued institutional growth, and increased enthusiasm and energy from faculty members, administrators, and staff.

We will have a community of satisfied and supportive alumni only if students stay with us long enough to achieve significant intellectual or personal development, to realize value added by our institution to their employability and their capacity for a rich and satisfying life. In many institutions, increased access in the name of equity has simply accelerated the speed of the revolving door and increased the numbers of persons moving in and out of higher education. Given the lost dollars it represents, this revolving door could be made of solid gold. If you take the costs of the admission officers, support staff, mailings, correspondence, travel, and space and divide that by the size of each entering class, you will have the institutional costs for each person admitted. If you multiply that figure by the number of students who leave after the first, second, or third year, you will have a baseline figure for the admission dollars down the drain as a function of the institutional retention rate. Add to that figure the estimated costs of setting up records, maintaining files, and sending out transcripts for those short-term students, and you will have a rough idea of the wastage being incurred. If you use a 50 percent retention rate, which is close to the modal figure for institutions across the country, you are sure to be shocked by the dollar costs associated with that waste.

Even more significant than the dollars wasted is the human effort wasted. Adult learners, especially, make heavy emotional and financial investments in coming to our institutions. They struggle with situational, personal, and institutional barriers at considerable self-sacrifice. Often our institution is the only alternative available to improve their chances for a better life. When we bounce adult learners around from pillar to post, let them wander into inappropriate curricula, pursue unrealistic aspirations, or set their sights well below what they might achieve, we contribute to life-damaging consequences that do not evaporate simply because the adult learners throw in the sponge and go back from whence they came.

We are not arguing that every student should be bound to the institution with bands of steel or even, like Gulliver, tied down with myriad finely woven threads. We are not saying that somehow every student should be enticed to stay enrolled as long as possible. And we certainly are not saying that educational services, curricula, or academic standards should be bent totally out of shape in the interests of retention. Indeed, the best educational service for many students will be to help them become clearer about other institutional or noninstitutional alternatives that are more appropriate for their prior background and for their life, career, and educational aspirations.

Our basic point is that all students should be treated as though they matter. They should be helped to create and sustain the best fit possible with the institution and make the best use possible of its resources. When that fit does not seem appropriate, or when after some experience it clearly is not working well, the institution should care enough about those persons to help them find a better alternative elsewhere.

The research on retention is unequivocally clear that the key variable is caring. Beal and Noel (1980) summarize their wide-ranging project in *What Works in Student Retention* by saying, "Retention research today emphasizes the importance of the interaction between students and the institution. The degree of 'fit' may determine the likelihood of students staying or leaving. Another term, which may describe it better, is 'belonging.' A student develops a sense of belonging as the result of many and varied interactions with the college and student environment. Such a feeling will enhance retention..." (p. 5). A caring attitude of faculty and staff was considered most important by all four types of institutions these researchers studied.

Tables 4 and 5 summarize the key findings from Beal and Noel's multi-institutional project. Note in Table 4 that four of

Table 4. Most Important Factors in Student Retention
(in Rank Order).

Campus/Student Characteristic Rating	Average[a]
Negative	
Inadequate academic advising	3.03
Inadequate curricular offerings	2.81
Conflict between class schedule and job	2.80
Inadequate financial aid	2.63
Inadequate extracurricular offerings	2.61
Inadequate counseling/support system	2.59
Positive	
Caring attitude of faculty and staff	4.29
High quality of teaching	3.90
Adequate financial aid	3.69
Student involvement in campus life	3.30
High quality of advising	3.23
Dropout prone	
Low academic achievement	4.45
Limited educational aspirations	4.09
Indecision about major/career goal	3.93
Inadequate financial resources	3.65

[a]On a scale of 1 (low) to 5 (high).

Source: Beal and Noel, 1980, p. 43. © The American College Testing Program. Used by permission.

Table 5. Action Programs Checked by Type of Institution (in Percentages).

	Two-Year Public	Two-Year Private	Four-Year Public	Four-Year Private	Total
N =	294	55	221	377	947
Improvement of academic advising	48	53	56	54	53
Special orientation activities	49	47	55	49	49
Exit interviews	28	36	36	52	40
Special counseling programs	32	36	43	34	36
Early-warning system	27	35	26	43	33
New academic support/learning services	29	35	39	30	32
Students as peer advisers and counselors	24	20	34	33	30
Curricular innovations for credit	28	27	31	30	29
Expanded placement services	20	13	24	29	24
New extracurricular activities	14	22	16	26	20
Undeclared-major services	13	0	31	18	18
Faculty/instructional development	21	16	15	18	18
Admissions for student-institution fit	15	11	17	17	16
Use of students in institutional decisions	14	13	17	18	16
New noncredit course offerings	22	18	17	10	16
Job-related training programs	15	7	14	15	14
New administrative structures	11	9	20	14	14
Adult student services	18	7	17	10	14
Advising in promotion and tenure	3	4	10	8	7
No special action programs	21	18	13	16	17

Source: Beal and Noel, 1980, p. 50. © The American College Testing Program. Used by permission.

the six most important negative characteristics are directly related to the educational responsibilities of student development professionals: inadequate academic advising, inadequate extracurricular offerings, inadequate financial aid, and inadequate counseling and support systems. Conversely, three of the five positive characteristics can be directly influenced by professional activities: caring attitude of faculty and staff, student involvement in campus life, and high quality of advising. In Table 5, which describes the action programs that made a difference in improving retention, ten of the first eleven activities are typically carried out by student development professionals: improvement of academic advising, special orientation activities, exit interviews, special counseling programs, early-warning system, new academic support/learning services, students as peer advisers and counselors, expanded placement services, new extracurricular activities, and undeclared-major services.

The caring attitude and these action areas are precisely what we address through the program changes we suggest. An entry education center that successfully integrates orientation, advising, financial aid, and life, career, and educational planning as well as the assessment of prior learning will directly improve the quality of orientation, advising, counseling, and access to financial aid. The modifications of the support services we propose, with developmental mentors and a developmental transcript, academic support and learning services, activities programs appropriate for adult learners, a warmline for peer counseling, and an adult student association and lounge, all incorporate those action programs that increase involvement and improve retention.

Beal and Noel strike a responsive note when they say, "If *interaction* is the key to improved retention, specific opportunities . . . need to be not only available but emphasized, fostered, and made visible to students as they proceed through college. The passive offering of student services, programs, and opportunities is not enough, in most cases, to meet the needs of students. An active, dynamic approach is necessary to reach the students who might otherwise leave without ever bothering to consult a college faculty member or official, without finding the answer that could have made a difference" (p. 94). Reaching out to students, taking their needs seriously, actively seeking ways to be more educationally effective with them through our varied student development programs—these are precisely what is needed.

These actions not only will improve retention, they will also improve recruitment. A report from the Southern Regional Education Board (1981, p. 3) puts it well:

> It takes no special insight to know that the best re-cruiters (and the cheapest) are enrolled students. As with a good movie, word-of-mouth news spreads rapidly as students return to their hometowns either to praise or to damn the food service, social life, or faculty. Yet, student services and student life are often the first casualties in a retrenchment climate. The major thrust of several successful strategies to combat decline emphasized the qual-ity of student life.

Throughout this book we have been emphasizing the need for changes to create a supportive environment for adult learners. It is important to recognize that all the changes we recommend will also improve our educational effectiveness with our traditional-age, on-campus students who are pursuing full-time study without the constraints and distractions of adult roles and responsibilities. It is easier for these students to find their way through our fragmented services and programs, to become familiar with our varied prides and prejudices, to find out about and take advantage of special program opportunities. Most traditional-age students are well covered by the flourishing grape-vine that quickly spreads the news, both good and bad, through-out the campus. Indeed, like the trees and bushes under the runaway kudzu in the South, most on-campus students cannot escape that vine even if they wish. But the fundamental shift from a service to an educational orientation, to seeing ourselves as reflective practitioners—and the differences in the nature of the relationships among student development professionals and adult learners that orientation implies—can dramatically strengthen our educational effectiveness with these traditional-age students. The concrete changes we suggest in entering, supporting, and culminating educational activities will substantially increase the accessibility, usefulness, and power of these activities. By adopting the posture and undertaking the changes we have recommended, professionals will not simply increase their effectiveness with a subgroup of students (significant as that group is) but increase their effectiveness with the rest of the students as well.

When adult learners are helped to connect more effectively with an institution and to stay with it through time, a continuing force for institutional growth and change is being introduced. In long-range terms, this may be one of the most significant payoffs of all. The relationships encouraged with diverse businesses, social agencies, and community organizations are constant sources of stimulation and pressure to keep curricula relevant and teaching practices effective. They help the institution continue to develop organizational entities and administrative structures that respond to changing demographic, economic, and political realities. They provide continued opportunities to become and to remain an interactive institution rather than an ivory tower, increasingly isolated from the day-to-day interactions that keep it in tune with local, regional, national, and international developments. Thus, adult learners, their pragmatic orientations, and the community relationships they bring keep an institution vital and growing. They provide continued challenges that can provoke our own self-extension and lifelong learning as reflective practitioners.

Being part of a vital and growing institution, where our professional contributions clearly make a difference and where our knowledge and competence are challenged and stretched, is exhilarating and rewarding. Being part of one or more teams creating improved programs that better meet real needs makes our work life meaningful and strengthens our own sense of competence and contribution. In creating a place where adult learners matter, we create an environment where we and our colleagues matter as well. The days and weeks may be full and demanding. Pressures and frustrations are there in good measure. Accumulated vacation days creep toward the maximum because we can't seem to find the right time to be away. Sick leave days pile up because the challenging and interesting activities of the job are more important than yielding to illness or disease. If this kind of challenging environment would make you look forward to going to work in the morning, then creating a place to matter for adult learners should be a major goal.

In Conclusion

The changes required to achieve both external and internal institutional payoffs do not come easy. They involve reallocating resources, disrupting current organizational patterns, undertaking significant professional development activities, and reorienting our personal and professional postures toward our clients. But the dollars saved through reduced attrition will more than compensate for the costs of making these changes and of the required investments in professional development necessary to make them work. The human savings we experience in our day-to-day contacts with students will sustain us through the risks and hard work that are a necessary part of significant change. And the long-term payoffs in word-of-mouth recruitment, in dollar contributions, and in political support can help sustain a vital institution that is meeting a significant social need.

Changing the Educational Environment for Adults: Advice to Academic Leaders

Suppose we want to create an institution that shares the orientation expressed by President Johnson at George Mason and that might realize some of the benefits described by President Wireman at Queens. How do we get there from where we are now? Four basic elements must be addressed more or less concurrently: (1) recognizing the obstacles to change, (2) undertaking systematic assessment, (3) understanding and acting consistently with basic principles of change processes and planned change, and (4) carrying out appropriate professional development activities with student educational services staff, administrators, and faculty.

Obstacles to Change

Inertia, traditional socialization, inadequate information, traditional structures and rewards, and fear of the unknown are the five major obstacles to change (Lindquist, 1978). Those of us who have tried to make a dent in any given area of institutional policy or practice recognize them well.

Inertia is the first obstacle. Each of our student educational services programs has a momentum and a trajectory of its own, particularly if it is working well with traditional-age

227

students. Student development professionals have acquired a great deal of expertise in dealing with young students and their interests. But we are tempted to agree with Bert Bach (1982, p. 5), vice chancellor for academic affairs of the State University and Community College System of Tennessee, when he says, "In my judgment, colleges do not abhor older students—but they do ignore them. An immediate step that should be taken is for each president to announce an obvious truism—that older students are students. Student affairs offices should be asked to address those students' needs with enthusiasm equivalent to that expressed for sock hops, rock concerts, initial job placement for the twenty-two-year-old, sex education for the eighteen-year-old, fraternities, and intramural athletics." Our staffing patterns, scheduling arrangements, annual cycles of activity, and areas of professional expertise are all established for traditional-age, full-time, mostly on-campus students. And most student development professionals are kept running hard just to meet the needs of these students. This focus makes it very difficult for professionals to find the time, energy, and resources to assess and test an adult learner population and to create new alternatives for them, especially when they are predominantly part-time students living off campus and not nearly as visible or noisy as traditional-age students.

Traditional socialization, built into the norms and expectations of the profession, is the second obstacle. Wherever we look—at the graduate programs preparing student development professionals, at the presentations and associated activities of our professional associations, at the journals that report pertinent research and promising practices—everyone is sharing experiences, reporting new programs and research, talking about traditional-age students. Only in a special commission, in an occasional program or journal article, are adult learners discussed. But they are now part of the mainstream of higher education and their interests need to be brought into the mainstream in our professional preparation, professional meetings, and professional publications. Until they are, the barriers inherent in our traditional professional socialization will remain.

Inadequate information about adult learners and about

appropriate programs to serve them is the third obstacle and a natural consequence of traditional socialization practices. Because we are habituated to our traditional clientele, few of us are geared toward getting useful information about our own students and their changing characteristics. Furthermore, our professional networks are not themselves typically involved with adult learners. And if we are inclined to tackle the problem, we seldom know how to get connected with others who share our concerns.

The traditional organizational structure and reward systems of student personnel services divisions—built on a history of working with full-time, on-campus, eighteen- to twenty-five-year-olds—create the fourth obstacle. Take our recommendation to establish an entry education center that would integrate orientation, admissions, financial aid and planning, and life, career, and educational planning, as well as academic advising and developmental assessment. The current compartmentalizations and hierarchies that characterize most student services divisions would not yield easily to the reorganization required if such a center were to be created. Student development professionals chafe at the ways traditional structures and rewards separate them from important interactions with the academic program and the faculty, leaving them out of important decisions concerning educational policies and practices. This separation is a historical artifact resulting from the fact that student services are relative newcomers to the higher education scene. Strong political interests have crystallized around these bureaucratic structures. Just changing this crystalline structure within our own division can be a daunting task.

Fear of the unknown is the fifth obstacle. All of us are affected by this basic human characteristic in varying degrees. We are skeptical about our own ability to tackle a complex problem successfully when the outcome, with regard to changed expectations for our own performance, is uncertain. We are unsure about our ability to develop the new knowledge, perspectives, or skills that may be required. We wonder whether we might be left out in the cold when reorganization or changed staffing patterns are called for. So, all things considered, it is easy for us to feel like sticking with the current arrangements, with what we already know and can do, with our current job security and status.

These five obstacles can be significant impediments to change. The important thing is to recognize them when they appear and not to minimize their importance. They should be examined for what they are and dealt with as constructively as possible.

Especially helpful in dealing with these obstacles—and the resistance they represent—is distinguishing among conceptual issues, political issues, and feasibility issues. We all know that discussions of change possibilities can generate great clouds of smoke and steam, obscuring the real issues. Elegant theoretical arguments will be brought forth when the basic interest is saving limited dollars for other commitments. Or ideas will be shot down on the claim that resources are limited, when the basic motive is political self-protection. But if we can focus on the three basic sets of issues that need to be addressed in order to implement any kind of planned change, we have the best chance of cutting through the fog and making progress toward our goal.

The first set of issues is conceptual. Does the idea make sense? Is it consistent with our best knowledge concerning educational theory, human development, characteristics of adult learners, and research and theory on adult development? If these questions cannot be satisfactorily answered, modification should be made or other alternatives explored that satisfy basic canons of conceptual validity.

When we are satisfied that our choice is conceptually sound, the next set of questions must focus on the political issues involved in the change. Whose interests are going to be threatened and whose interests will be strengthened? Which institutional values are consistent with this recommendation and which does it challenge? Keep in mind that political interests and institutional values are entirely legitimate factors. After all, vested political interests often boil down to real human concerns, to real efforts to protect people from harm and preserve their dignity and well-being. So vested interests should be recognized and addressed as effectively as possible.

When we have a proposal that is conceptually sound and that accommodates diverse political interests as best it can, we can focus on the final set of issues, which involve feasibility. Are the resources required too far out of line with existing institutional realities? Would the proposed staffing and competency requirements call for massive infusions of either professional development time and energy or new persons? Would the demands for physical space and equipment require major renovations? Is there enough discretionary money available to support an initial pilot effort?

Because these three sets of issues—conceptual, political, and feasibility—need to be dealt with before significant change can occur, we need to keep them distinct during the hot and lengthy discussions, recognize who is speaking to which and why, and keep lists of the key points made in each of these areas. We also need to undertake systematic assessment.

Assessment: Establishing the Basis for Change

Self-awareness is the hallmark of Schön's (1983) reflective practitioner. Organizational self-awareness is a hallmark of America's best-run companies and best-run programs. According to Peters and Waterman (1982, pp. 13–15, 294), such organizations have a "bias for action." They are analytical but not "hung up" on analyses. "Do it, fix it, try it" is the operating procedure. They stay "close to the customer," learning from the people they serve, getting some of their best ideas from their clients. They listen "intently and regularly." Autonomy and entrepreneurship are key ingredients. "They encourage practical risk taking and supporting good tries." "Productivity through people" is fundamental. They recognize that the rank and file are the basic source of productivity and high quality. Respect for each individual is a cornerstone tenet. They are "hands on and value driven" and "stick to the knitting," building on their central strengths and competence. We need to adapt these principles to our own practices if programs responsive to the needs of adult learners are to be created, improved, and sustained.

In our chapters on moving in, moving through, and moving on, we called attention to items from the *ACE Adult Learner Assessment and Planning Guide*. Accompanying the *Guide* is *Improving Institutional Service to Adult Learners* (W. H. Warren, 1986), a manual that helps us understand how to use self-assessment—not simply as a self-justifying ritual but as the starting point for useful improvement.

Program assessment is likely to show us how well many of our policies and practices serve adult learners. But if self-validation were our only purpose, our time and energy could be better used elsewhere. Our basic motive should be increased understanding of our particular adult learners and how we can best serve them. The kind of assessment we are talking about is often called *action research*. For Buhl and Lindquist (1981), action research catalyzes and informs action. It also provides a solid foundation of knowledge to individuals, groups, organizations, or communities as they work to decide whether their methods should be changed. Action research is more a problem-solving process than a theory-based, hypothesis-testing, classical approach to research. It typically addresses four questions: What are our goals? How well are we achieving them? What is keeping us from doing better? How can we reduce problems and improve performance? Action research means that decisions about the data to be collected, the data-gathering process itself, and data analysis and interpretation, should all be shared widely among concerned parties, not decided on and carried out by a small group of specialists. "Ownership" of the process, the findings, and the interpretations is required if concerned parties are going to act on the results.

The action researchers—those with primary responsibility for carrying out the assessment—have two key roles. One is to facilitate decisions concerning the types of data to be collected, the methods to be used, and the analyses to be undertaken. The other is to facilitate the problem-solving process itself, involving appropriate persons in interpreting data, thinking through the implications, considering possible constructive responses, looking at alternatives that seem to work elsewhere, and creating and testing new alternatives. In both these roles they will encounter plenty of debate and conflict. But dealing with these issues and reactions up front helps smooth the way for later implementation.

Three fundamental areas must be assessed: the need for change, potential solutions or improvements, and the climate for change. The first two areas are usually approached in reasonably systematic fashion; the third is often neglected.

Is change needed? Here we must ask questions concerning objectives, outcomes, characteristics of the clients, and strengths and weaknesses of programs as experienced by the clients.

What are potential solutions or improvements? Here we must ask such questions as: What alternative approaches seem to work well elsewhere? How do the clients at these institutions compare with ours? What are the similarities and differences in available resources? Are there key differences in institutional context or mission? What approaches are consistent with the basic principles of student development—or adult development and learning—that undergird our own approach? What are the local institutional norms and values, organizational styles, typical patterns of authority and responsibility?

What is the climate for change? We may hear grumbles about resistance, apathy, and the like, but seldom do we see systematic attempts to size up the situation in this area. Here are some of the questions for focusing our assessment of the climate for change: Is there support at the top? What kind of interest, commitment, resources, or active intervention can we expect from the president, vice-president, dean, director? What is the nature of our relationships with the persons who will need to be involved in assessing the need for change, in assessing alternative solutions, and in final implementation? What are some of the dysfunctional or prickly points that have developed in our close working relationships? How open are we, and other key actors, to new ideas? Are we and others ready to reach out for new policies and practices if they are required? How much risk taking is generally encouraged or tolerated? What is the likelihood that we can create a sense of strong collaboration and ownership that will sustain this process through time? What are the critical elements of our current reward systems, and how will these efforts be seen in the light of those systems? Are there additional extrinsic or intrinsic rewards that can be identified and made available?

This third area should really be addressed first. Assessing the climate for change establishes the basis for getting started—that is, for deciding on the appropriate unit (or units) for assessment and for creating the working group. Deciding which units to address and in what sequence rests on two criteria: impact and numbers. Perhaps the first and most obvious units to be assessed are those having the greatest impact on adult learners. Thus, we may choose those serving large numbers of adult learners, or we may choose those with the greatest potential for good or ill. Orientation, advising, and program planning, for example, might meet both criteria. For better or worse, they serve most adult learners, and the quality of that service may have important consequences for the future relationships between a particular adult learner and the institution. Only a small proportion of adult learners may make use of personal counseling, but the consequences may be devastating or dramatically life enhancing. So impact and numbers are important criteria. But openness to change and readiness to undertake self-study must also be taken into account, which is what climate assessment helps us do. It is almost always better to begin with a unit or two in which there is openness and readiness for change, even though the unit might fall further down the list in terms of the number of adult learners served or the importance of the service. One or two successful change efforts that demonstrably improve performance, that achieve local, regional, or national recognition, and that provide other rewards for staff members and clients can create models and strengthen motivation for other, more reluctant units. This is why assessing the climate for change early in the process can be so helpful.

Selecting the members of the working group that will carry forward the assessment and planned change effort is crucial. Yet such groups are often put together with little thought, typically by a chief executive or division head who sits down and lists a few people who seem to be obvious choices because of their formal positions or prior interest. Selections can be made far better with the benefit of the information and reflection that flow from climate assessment. W. H. Warren (1986, p. 14) describes the characteristics of working groups that have been effective in assessment and planned change for adult learners:

- They respect local patterns of inquiry and decision making.
- They operate with public sanction and commitment from as high in the organizational hierarchy as possible.
- They engage faculty and administrators who have nothing to gain or lose from the results (and even those who may oppose changes) jointly with those who are involved in the programs and services being examined.
- They seek the broadest possible perspective on the units being examined by involving those who will be affected by the outcomes.
- They include adult learners themselves.

Putting together a working group that conforms to these characteristics and that reflects the climate assessment takes time and thought. But this extra effort will pay off handsomely in the soundness of the assessment effort and in institutional readiness for acting on the implications.

Noteworthy principles about assessment include the following:

- Use multiple methods and gather different types of information.
- Obtain qualitative as well as quantitative data. Remember that three or four powerful flesh-and-blood vignettes are more persuasive than mountains of statistics.
- Combine hard numbers and human interest to increase the chances of significant followthrough.
- Be alert to "unobtrusive measures."
- Find out what kinds of data are already available in the files and consider what kinds of analyses of existing information might yield insights. For example, looking at differences in the age distributions associated with different types of student activities and how they are managed might yield clues about content, scheduling, or leadership styles. Information

about occupation, income, and prior education, available from admissions records, examined in relation to participation in and profiting from orientation, advising, and peer counseling services might suggest interactions between socio-economic status and such programs. These interactions might in turn suggest some useful changes in staffing patterns, accessibility, and the like.

A final important principle is to use standardized instruments that have been field tested and debugged, rather than homegrown alternatives. We have repeatedly referred to the *ACE Adult Learner Assessment and Planning Guide* created by the Commission on Higher Education and the Adult Learner and available from the American Council on Education. It is the best single instrument currently available. It does not need to be used in toto; appropriate portions can be selected. It can also be adapted to the specific institution. Consultants can help local professionals create adaptations in light of experiences accumulated elsewhere. Another instrument that provides useful basic data concerning adult learners and has space for local options is the Adult Learner Needs Assessment Survey marketed by the American College Testing Program. There are others, but these two have received the greatest amount of testing and are known to be useful.

Planned Change

By now it is clear that increased self-awareness through program assessment is the starting point for planned changes to improve performance for adult learners. This is the purpose of assessment, not accountability to some higher authority, self-validation, or self-congratulation. Even institutions and programs with long histories of effective services to adult learners continue to find significant ways to improve programs and individual performance. Providing useful services that are educationally and developmentally productive for adult learners is a challenging and complex task.

One reason so little productive change occurs in colleges and universities is that most of us are totally naive about change strategies and the change process. Fortunately, there is a growing body of literature about and practical experience with change in higher education. It builds on the longer traditions of research and theory originally rooted in studies of the dissemination and adoption of new agricultural practices, supplemented by more recent findings on corporate, industrial, and military research dissemination and diffusion. The most pertinent publication related to higher education is Jack Lindquist's *Strategies for Change* (1978). He also has an excellent section in *Developing the College Curriculum* with chapters by Chickering, Halliburton, Bergquist, and Lindquist (1977).

Experience with several multi-institutional planned change efforts suggests that we should have in mind some key principles concerning the change process. Lindquist's FLOOR model lays out some important fundamentals. FLOOR stands for *f*orce, *l*inkages, *o*penness, *o*wnership, and *r*ewards. Lindquist developed these basic elements out of his experiences as a leader of and contributor to several multi-institutional change projects. In the descriptions that follow, we draw especially from reports of two projects carried out through the Center for the Study of Higher Education at Memphis State University (Lindquist and Marienau, 1981; Lynch, Doyle, and Chickering, 1984).

The main *force* in effecting change at institutions is the change team itself. Teams can be especially effective because of critical mass, team leader status, personality mix, leadership skills, knowledge about adult learners, strong motivation, and political savvy about the change process at the institution. A second force is administrative support, in which top priority is given to the work of the team, team efforts are publicly endorsed, and both financial and psychological support are provided.

Linkages to people and to outside information are both important. Successful teams make good connections within the institution to obtain information, to recruit political advocates, and to respond to critics. Team members develop their own internal support systems as they work at developing networks among faculty, staff, and students through direct contact, newsletters, publicity, and other media and through on-campus workshops. Teams that extend themselves beyond immediate team members and help local faculty, administrators, and student development staff connect with people and practices outside the institution make important contributions. Many institutions have little information about adult learning, adult learners, and successful alternatives elsewhere. Helping key decision makers visit institutions with especially interesting programs or meet representatives from such programs can help increase legitimacy, reduce anxiety, and strengthen motivation.

Openness is demonstrated in many ways at many levels. Do team members listen to each other and try to appreciate diverse points of view? Are outside consultants welcomed and used energetically and effectively? Will team members and other concerned parties take time to read pertinent literature or reports? Can team members gain access to top administrators when they need it? Will top administrators hear out diverse points of view? Teams in which openness is the norm and that encourage openness in others are more successful than those characterized by hidden agendas, conspiracies of silence, superficial cordiality, passive resistance, and caucuses around the water cooler.

Ownership means that those who are to be involved in and affected by the changes feel part of the assessment, change strategies, and final decisions. Ideally the changes respond to needs these people feel, conditions they want to address, strengths they have or want to develop, values they hold. Often the change process bogs down with implementation and institutionalization. The processes of assessing the need for change, identifying possibilities, and deciding on appropriate modifications seem to go smoothly. Everyone apparently agrees. Wonderful new language is adopted to describe the changes to be made. Sometimes fancy public announcements are made and promotional literature is produced. But then nothing much seeems to happen. Business continues pretty much as usual. Why? Professionals usually have a high degree of self-determination: Unless they feel ownership and commitment to the changes, they may not really work on starting the new alternatives and may quickly revert to old practices once the spotlight is turned off.

Rewards in the early stages are usually intrinsic. "I'm learning. It's challenging. I enjoy working with these folks on an important problem. My views are heard. We're making progress.

I really believe in what we're trying to do." But the road is long and hard. Intrinsic rewards are seldom sufficient to sustain the energy, to fight through one more political battle, to put together one more draft staffing pattern and budget revision. Release time from regular job duties, adequate secretarial help and support staff, and travel monies to visit other locations and attend or make presentations at professional meetings are needed to sustain efforts through initial testing and early implementation. Even a few dollars for social amenities to ease long meetings and hard work can make a big difference.

If the basic elements for planned change efforts are all present in good measure, how long will it take from initial assessment through experimental modifications to solid implementation and institutionalization? The typical time period is seldom less than three years, and it often stretches to five. For example, in the two multi-institutional projects that involved change efforts at more than twenty different institutions, none was fully institutionalized in less than three years. At the end of the four-year project period, some were still in early solution-finding or experimentation stages. Thus, for the self-renewing organization, as for the self-renewing person, planned change is a continuing process, never a final product. Adapting student educational services to the needs of adult learners, becoming reflective practitioners in dialogue with our adult learner clients, and confronting our meanings for adult learners and their meanings for us will require continued efforts to learn and to change.

Lindquist's FLOOR model applies to almost any kind of planned change in colleges and universities. Specific principles that can help us tackle changes particularly oriented toward adult learners—adapted from a more extensive set in *Turning Colleges Toward Adults* (Lindquist and Marienau, 1981, pp. 107–111)—are as follows:

Principles for Adults as Learners and Innovators

- Recognize that *you* are an adult learner; within yourself are significant clues to understanding adult learners.
- Adopt the belief that personal development is a legitimate outcome of education.

- Recognize the value of diversity and the potential of individual differences.
- Recognize the powerful role of experience in adult lives.
- Accept your responsibility to experience what you want others to encounter.
- Acknowledge that life realities of adult learners take priority over institutional convenience.
- Accept your responsibility to be theoretically informed about adult development and learning.

Principles for Group Processes

- Build improvement teams that have strong administrative support, a clear sense of mission, a well-defined identity, and time to meet intensely.
- Select your change team members for their interest, knowledge, political clout, and skill.
- Attend to the well-being and dynamics of your team.
- Learn to ask for timely help.
- Pace yourself so you have the stamina and inclination to stay with it over time.
- Maintain a sense of humor; take time away from daily confines when needed.

Principles for Change Processes

- Launch programs with modest expectations about what can be accomplished.
- Approach your task with informed intentionality, then be open and flexible to new learnings.
- Plan in recognition of the mutual dependency of the traditional and nontraditional.
- Reach beyond the familiar core group to enable others to share your efforts.
- Communicate, in nickel words, your actions and intentions to your colleagues.
- Use criticism as an avenue for educating the nonbelievers.
- Provide rewards, at whatever level you control, for the efforts of your constituents.

Principles for the Nature of Change

- Maintain the perspective that gains are small in the context of the total institution but significant in enlarging the circle of the influenced.
- Understand that change comes about slowly.
- Understand that change is a process, not a conclusion.
- Acknowledge that some factors are beyond your control.
- Keep this in mind: "The future is not a predetermined place to which we are going. It is rather a destiny that you and I can build together."

Understanding the basic concepts of the change process and following the concrete suggestions listed here can significantly increase the probability that program improvement will be made and that new alternatives can be introduced. That probability becomes even more likely if those change processes are associated with a sound assessment to identify the areas in which change is needed, to discover possible solutions, and to size up the climate for change. But lasting results depend on the professional development of those already at work and on some significant modification in our graduate preparation programs.

Professional Preparation and Development

Our modern conception of the roles and responsibilities of student educational services and student development professionals includes the following four components:

1. We should see ourselves as educators, not as service providers.
2. We should see ourselves as reflective practitioners rather than in traditional professional-client terms.
3. We should be well informed and up-to-date on research and theory pertinent to our students and our practices and able to apply that information to our own professional behaviors.
4. We should sustain ongoing efforts at self-evaluation, program evaluation and improving practice.

These fundamentals have powerful implications for both the content and processes that characterize graduate preparation of professionals and for the content and processes used in ongoing professional development activities. Perhaps the best way to speak to both these arenas is to recognize that our graduate education and our professional development activities should conform to our best knowledge concerning adult development and learning. This means that the instructional units we create for graduate education, and the workshops and professional development seminars we create for our own individual development and program improvement, should satisfy the following criteria:

- The content should be pertinent to pragmatic problem areas of direct concern to the professionals for whom they are intended.
- The outcomes should be described in terms of desired competencies and concepts.
- The educational processes and instructional strategies should recognize individual differences in prior learning and in learning styles.
- The educational activities should include appropriate combinations of theory and practice, concrete experiences and abstract concepts, observation, reflection, and active application.
- Pre- and post-assessment should be used to guide planning and to evaluate gains in the desired competencies and concepts.
- Educational strategies and materials should be created suitable for both on-site and remote delivery.

None of us will be able to satisfy these criteria the first time around. Some of us have been trying to educate in these ways for more than twenty years and still have much to learn. These criteria will be a major challenge for those whose teaching is mainly by lecture, textbook, and multiple-choice exam, occasionally supplemented by student discussion and term papers. Those who create national conferences and local professional development programs that are basically speech panels and paper presentations will be significantly challenged as well.

We can already suggest some of the major areas of knowledge competence and concepts that need to characterize graduate preparation and professional development programs if our ambitious aspirations are to be realized. Priorities will vary according to the backgrounds and biases of the faculty members or professional practitioners involved. For us they comprise core areas that should be part of any sound program.

Individual Differences. In accordance with our own particular prejudices, we assign the greatest significance to research, theory, and practices concerning individual differences. Higher education has moved from an aristocratic through a meritocratic to an egalitarian orientation. During the 1960s national and state policies shifted toward a commitment to equal educational opportunity, to providing higher education not only for bright, well-prepared, middle- and upper-class, mostly white students but also to working-class students, regardless of race, ethnicity, or disabilities. This policy shift applied not only to traditional-age students but also to adult learners of all ages and backgrounds. Higher education is no longer limited to socializing the elite; it now aims to educate and train the masses.

This basic change to equal opportunity in the service of an egalitarian system has resulted in sharply increased student diversity, especially in publicly supported institutions. The change has also been accompanied by increased pressure for accountability in providing effective education for these diverse students. State-mandated assessment programs are becoming widespread. Throughout its history, higher education has enjoyed the luxury of being able to choose students to fit the college programs; now we must give up that luxury and learn how to design programs to fit the students. The range of individual differences among students seeking the knowledge and competence offered by student educational services and student development professionals has exploded.

Individuals differ on a variety of significant dimensions. The problem is to select those dimensions that are most important for practice. This selection in turn will determine major curricular segments and major arenas for more extensive learning and application. One dimension we are used to taking into account is differences in basic skills and academic preparation. At the graduate level and in our professional development programs, this dimension should not present critical problems, but we note it because on occasion there may be surprising gaps for some persons.

One significant dimension in which individuals differ is addressed in research and theory concerning cognitive styles and learning styles. The work of Herman Witkin and his followers concerning field dependence and field independence has powerful implications for a variety of student educational services programs. Other conceptual frameworks that have received attention include breadth of categorization, cognitive complexity versus cognitive simplicity, leveling versus sharpening, reflection versus impulsivity, risk taking versus cautiousness, and converging versus diverging (see *Individuality in Learning*, Messick and Associates, 1976, for a good review of this area). Kolb's (1984) model of learning style preference has received a great deal of attention. It arises from Kolb's experiential learning theory and postulates four types: divergers, assimilators, convergers, and accommodators. The linkage between these learning style preferences and his experiential learning theory makes Kolb's conceptual combination especially applicable to educational services in higher education and the corporate world.

The Myers-Briggs Type Indicator is another framework for understanding individual differences that is proving to be useful to practitioners not only in education but in corporate human resources development as well. This instrument generates sixteen different types, depending on scores for four dimensions: introversion-extraversion, sensing-intuition, thinking-feeling, and judging-perceiving.

Our object here is not to be exhaustive but suggestive. Each faculty or group of professional practitioners will want to select the particular conceptual framework of cognitive and learning styles that seems most consistent with their own thinking and most useful for their own applications.

Another significant dimension of individual differences is to be found in research and theory concerning adult life phases and transitions. This book is anchored heavily in that area. Not surprisingly, we find Schlossberg's work especially useful. Additional frameworks are described in the conceptual chapters earlier in the book. In addition, the work of Neugarten, Fiske, and others remains pertinent. As our baby boom bulge moves through various life phases, the research spotlight will in turn follow those moves or anticipate them. There is already a burgeoning literature concerning the elderly. Current demographic and social changes suggest that more and more persons age sixty and beyond will be coming to our colleges and universities. Age distributions, with adult students now heavily concentrated in the late twenties, the thirties, and the early forties, will surely flatten out, with increasing proportions in their fifties, sixties, and seventies. By 1995 the seventy-five-year-old graduate will no longer be unusual. He or she will simply move through the diploma line with plenty of peers. To understand the motives, educational interests, activity preferences, personal dilemmas, and life-style constraints of such students, we will need to keep ourselves well informed about the growing literature in this area and well in touch with changing practices that recognize differences.

A third dimension significant in understanding individual differences concerns developmental stage theories. Contributions in this area include Perry's (1968) positions of intellectual and ethical development, Loevinger's (1976) stages of ego development, and Kegan's (1982) "constitutions of the self." Chickering's seven vectors might fall into this category, though strictly speaking that conceptual framework does not have the hierarchy and sequentiality typical of stage theories. Developmental theories, particularly those of Loevinger and Kegan, provide the most comprehensive framework for understanding and acting on individual differences in personality structure. Stage differences include complex interactions among cognitive styles, impulse control, interpersonal relationships, and the ways in which values and beliefs are held. The comprehensiveness and complexity of these theories makes them difficult to grasp and to apply. But if we can build such perspectives into our working knowledge, we can dramatically enrich our ability to hear more perceptively the diverse meanings underneath the motives and aspirations, words and deeds, that adult learners bring to our diverse areas of professional practice.

A final significant dimension of individual differences is gender. Research and theory underscore the differences within each gender while looking at the differences between the two. The work of Gilligan, of Belenky and others, and of Josselson adds in important ways to our understanding of women. Gilligan (1982) demonstrates that women's voices are different from men's and that developmental theories have been based on men's voices alone. Belenky, Clinchy, Goldberger, and Tarule (1987) build on the work of Gilligan and Perry and add useful information to our understanding of the human condition. Through interviews with 135 women, they ascertained that women have at least five different ways of thinking about truth or the meaning of life. One group of women experiences the world in silence, feeling "deaf and dumb" (p. 24); another group receives knowledge of the world by listening carefully to others; a third group knows by intuition; a fourth group knows by developing rational procedures for uncovering the truth; and a fifth group constructs knowledge by integrating the subjective and rational. These categories, in some respects similar to Perry's, provide a clue to various ways in which different individuals process information and understand the world in which they live.

In a longitudinal study of thirty-four women, Josselson (1987) concluded that the different pathways women follow in their identity development tell more about women than looking at roles. In other words, what is relevant is not whether a woman is a mother, a worker, a single parent, or childless but rather the way in which the woman separates and anchors or commits in the adult world. Although there is no pure type, Josselson identifies four general categories of women, based on the 1966 work of Marcia: *foreclosures*—those women who "remain securely embedded in their family network and bypass exploration of identity" (p. 34); *identity achievements*—those who have tested new waters, are forging their own identities, and keep focusing on the future; *moratoriums*—those who continue "testing and searching" and are "struggling to make commitments but have not yet found the right ones" (p. 30); and *identity diffusions*—those who are "drifting, avoiding the identity-formation task" (p. 30). Josselson's major finding corroborates Gilligan's work: that women of all types find meaning in relationships. For some, it is still with the family of origin; for others, it is with husbands and children; for still others it is work or friends. "Anchoring is a way of attaching to aspects of the adult world. . . . this attachment . . . involves connection to other people, even in the world of work" (p. 178).

Each of the major dimensions of individual differences is also an area of human development. In addressing each of these dimensions, therefore, we need to focus not only on the varied categories of individual differences but on the developmental sequences and processes as well. The diverse adult learners seeking our educational services will be tackling life span developmental tasks and transition problems. They will need to achieve better balance, to be helped to become more aware of their own development through the perspectives provided by theories of adult development so as to make more intentional decisions about the kind of person they want to be and to become.

Faculty Roles. We are increasingly convinced that faculty are the first line "interventionists" for adult learners. How they respond and relate to adult learners will be critical in how learners perceive themselves and the institution.

Throughout this book we have alluded to different roles that faculty might take to further the development of adult learners. For faculty to take on these new roles, they need a program of professional development that pays specific attention to adult development and focuses on appropriate instructional strategies for enhancing each adult learner's purposes and development.

The mentor/adviser role, which may use such strategies as contract learning, experiential learning, and cooperative education, is particularly important in our conceptualization. Within the mentor/adviser role, faculty can help adult learners clarify their purposes, set goals, identify learning activities, and make judgments about the methods and criteria for evaluation. In contract learning, for example, discussion of long-range goals and specific contract purposes can raise larger questions about meaning and direction and require the adult learner to confront implications for his or her current life-style, personal relationships, and future plans and aspirations.

Closely allied to the mentor/adviser role is the broker/negotiator role. Within this role, faculty members negotiate with adult learners regarding various learning experiences and opportunities within the institution and in the larger community. In this new—and potentially difficult—area, faculty may need assistance in giving up their reliance on grading on a curve (norm-referenced evaluation) and learn to create explicit criteria for awarding grades (criterion-referenced evaluation). Subtle and sometimes hard-nosed negotiations will be needed to reach agreement between adult learner and faculty member, between adult learner and faculty committee, between adult learner and degree program. Because faculty have a responsibility for assuring the quality of adult-learner performance, they must be clear about institutional requirements and their own expectations. This area can be the soft spot in educational programs for enhancing individual development. The quality of adult-learner education frequently rests on the degree to which faculty manage this broker/negotiator role.

The traditional faculty role of instructor/tutor can take on different dimensions in facilitating adult learning. With this perspective, faculty are more often asking key questions, drawing together insights from diverse sources, and suggesting particular strategies for learning difficult subject matter or for strengthening weak areas. In facilitating adult learning, faculty recognize the reality and variety of experiences that adult learners can contribute to class discussions. Teachers using the strategy of collaborative learning seize opportunities for group projects and small-group exercises. Clear agreements regarding desired outcomes, methods, and criteria ensure effective evaluation.

Most college and university faculty members are not well prepared for—and may not feel comfortable with—these roles.

Thus, the lack of readiness on the part of faculty is a major obstacle to the widespread development of such educational alternatives as contract learning, experiential learning, and the use of developmental transcripts. We need to make significant investments in professional development to overcome faculty discomfort and make these new roles and approaches part of our new educational endeavor to provide payoffs for adult learners and their institutions.

Professional Development Programs. Serving as a model for setting up professional development programs for faculty, as well as administrators and student development professionals, was the Higher Education for Adult Mental Health Project at Memphis State University. In this project, sponsored by the National Institute of Mental Health through the College of Education's Center for the Study of Higher Education, teams of administrators, faculty, and student development professionals from eighteen colleges and universities around the country participated in training activities over a three-year period. Objectives of the training program, carried out with the interdisciplinary teams from the diverse institutions, were to help the teams and their members as follows:

1. Use theory, research, and applications to develop and institute model programs and practices responsive to the needs of their growing adult-learner constituencies.
2. Understand the implications for curriculum, teaching, and evaluation; learning resources and educational environments; admissions and orientation; advising, counseling, and mental health services; and cocurricular programming.
3. Increase working knowledge of research, theory, and practices concerning life span, ego development (with special attention to intellectual, moral, and ethical development), learning styles, preventive mental health, and planned institutional change.

The interdisciplinary teams served as the major vehicle for local professional development activities and for creating the model programs. At each institution, the team leader, who served as the intermediary between the team and the project staff, was assured of sufficient time and support to develop the team and the model program. Team leaders were generally middle management administrators or faculty members designated for the position. Some were primarily involved with adult learners, some included responsibilities for adult learners among their other duties, and a few had no assignment in relation to adult learners other than that of team leader. Team members were generally faculty members or student development professionals and came from every part of the institution. Most team leaders committed from 20 to 25 percent of their time to the project, team members from 5 to 25 percent.

The training, which included six residential workshops in addition to activities at each institution, was planned so as to integrate adult development, preventive mental health, and planned institutional change theory and practice. Adult development theory got the team members to see themselves as adult learners; prevention concepts helped teams assess their institutions; planned change theory was integrated into the workshops as team members became comfortable with their new roles. *The Modern American College* (Chickering and Associates, 1981) served as the major text. The workshops sequentially emphasized direct experience, theory, application, implementation, evaluation, and dissemination.

The workshops, planned by project staff in consultation with team members, assumed a context of ongoing learning and required substantial preparation in the form of reading, exercises, and team discussions. Resource persons, including project staff, stimulated thinking and action. Teams worked hard to develop plans that were based on the assessed needs of adult learners at their institutions and the particular skills and knowledge of the team members.

Follow-up activities on each campus helped maintain the momentum of the action and provided a framework for testing theories in practice; they included institutional assessments, consultation visits by project staff, adult learner surveys, faculty interviews, and evaluation.

Team building was a crucial ingredient of the project. At each institution the teams were the effective force for the innovation process, for successful planned change. Activities and exercises at workshops away from campus as well as regular meetings on campus to work on and implement action plans helped to develop the sense of being a team. Team members became important sources of support to one another during crucial moments as the teams worked toward project goals.

Networking, which emphasized and capitalized on the expertise of the participants, was another important ingredient. Team members were encouraged to meet and work with other members of their own faculty and staff to increase awareness of the needs of adult learners. Team members also became resource persons to project teams at other institutions, forming a network for personal and professional encouragement as well as for sharing information on problems, obstacles, and effective practices. Team members shared their knowledge, skills, and programs with institutions outside the project through professional organizations, state conferences, and individual contacts.

As we noted earlier, assessment establishes the basis for change. In the project, team members found that faculty interviews were particularly helpful in assessing faculty perceptions and in assessing the climate for adult learners at the institutions. Each team member conducted interviews with five faculty who were involved with adult learners in order to find out about faculty educational philosophy, practices, opinions, and attitudes toward adult learners. The interviews were also useful in assessing faculty needs for knowledge and professional development activities regarding adult development and preventive mental health, in setting the stage for planned change, and in increasing faculty awareness of adult-learner concerns.

Team members reported that the faculty they interviewed were in general receptive to and aware of the growing numbers and special needs of adult learners, and they had a clear sense of the need to support adult learners by helping reduce anxieties and increase self-confidence. Most did not perceive a need to employ different teaching methods with adult students, but they said they would like to attend workshops and seminars on adult development and adult learners and would like to read more literature and become more knowledgeable on these subjects.

What the project demonstrates is that someone has to take the lead in changing the climate for adult learners, in implementing the changes suggested in this book, in determining a curriculum and a process for educating faculty, administrators, and student development professionals about adult learners and their needs. The project also demonstrates that using a team to take the lead has important advantages. Members of a team may be the most effective assessors of institutional climate and of readiness for professional development programs on adult development and adult learners. Members of a team may be the most perceptive arrangers for ongoing workshops—first for receptive faculty and staff, later for skeptics—and for professional development programs on adult learners that will serve as a stimulus for faculty and staff renewal. (For more information about the project, see Lynch, Doyle, and Chickering, 1984.)

In Conclusion

In conclusion, then, there needs to be a combination of committed leadership at the top and sophisticated teamwork that includes key implementors. This leadership and program development team needs to recognize the obstacles to change, undertake systematic assessment of current strengths and weaknesses, operate in ways consistent with basic principles concerning planned change, and establish an ongoing series of professional development activities. This kind of effort pursued over time will help current student development professionals become increasingly effective reflective practitioners. The result will be institutions truly responsive to adult learners.

A New Strategy
for Supporting
Adult Learners
in Higher Education

We have looked at adult learners as they move in, move through, and move on and have tied their needs to the sequencing of educational programs. Figure 3 displays this relationship. (Although the table lists institutional responses in a linear fashion, these responses are, of course, continuous and overlapping.) We hope such a graphic presentation will push educators to see adult learner needs and educational programs in a developmental fashion.

In some instances, all that an institution may need in order to implement this approach is an amplification of an existing program. In other instances, the institution may need to create a separate program to make it more visible and attractive. We suggest no hard and fast rules. Rather, each institution must assess its own needs and design its own approach. It is for this reason that we earlier suggested quality circles made up of reflective practitioners and adult learners—to design educational programs that will reach adult learners.

Our varied student educational services, and the knowledge and competence we have and will acquire, have much to offer adult learners. Modifying policies and practices in ways

Figure 3. A Model for Educating Adult Learners: The Sequence of Student Educational Services.

	Moving In *"Learning the ropes"*	Moving Through *"Hanging in there"*	Moving On *"Planning next steps"*
Learner needs		Variability Individuality	
Institutional responses	*Entry Education Center* Preadmissions Recruitment Financial aid and planning Admissions Entry/orientation course Student employment Academic advising/educational planning Registration Assessment of prior learning Developmental assessment	*Supporting Educational Services* Academic support services Career development Life and personal counseling; support groups Educational programming Recreational, athletic, and cultural activities Health services and wellness programs Student government Adult support center Residential life Child care/family care Adult learner association Developmental mentoring	*Culminating Education Center* Culminating course Practica, internships, and co-op learning Academic review and integration Placement services; job search, résumé writing, and interviewing Transition groups Developmental transcript review
Payoffs for learners	Help with identifying resources for more effective coping with self, situation, supports, and strategies Mattering Involvement Developmental needs being met with regard to acquiring sense of competence, managing emotions, developing interdependence, establishing identity, maintaining freer interpersonal relationships, developing purpose, establishing integrity		
Payoffs for institutions	Retention of learners Involvement of learners Alumni support Community involvement Strengthened internal sense of community and renewal		

that position us to be truly helpful will be a significant challenge. As Figure 3 illustrates, the range of educational programs to be addressed and the organizational changes implied are substantial. Developing our own knowledge and competence as reflective practitioners, so that we can carry forward these new alternatives in an educationally powerful fashion, will require that all of us become no less than lifelong learners ourselves. We will need to become more aware of our own learning and cognitive styles, more aware of our own transitions, more aware of and thoughtful about our own developmental stage, more sensitive to our own particular blend of masculinity and femininity. It will certainly be hard and challenging work. But taking care of our own love, work, and personal development from this perspective can make for a wonderfully fulfilling and satisfying existence. By creating a place where adult learners matter we will be doing both them and ourselves a great service.

References

Adams, W. W. *Research Summaries on the Educational Development of Adults: Making the Commitment to Return to School and Managing Learning.* Charleston, W. Va.: Appalachia Educational Laboratory, 1986.

Albee, G. "A Competency Model Must Replace the Defect Model." In L. A. Bond and J. C. Rosen (eds.), *Competence and Coping During Adulthood.* Hanover, N.H.: University Press of New England, 1980.

The American College Testing Program. *The Adult Learner Needs Assessment Survey.* Iowa City, Iowa: The American College Testing Program, 1982.

American Council on Education, Commission on Higher Education and the Adult Learner. *Postsecondary Institutions and the Adult Learner: A Self-Study Assessment and Planning Guide.* Washington, D.C.: American Council on Education, 1984.

Anderson, R. B. *Job Search Handbook.* Hattiesburg: Career Development Center, University of Southern Mississippi, 1983.

Ardell, D. *High Level Wellness: An Alternative to Doctors, Drugs, and Disease.* Emmaus, Pa.: Rodale Press, 1977.

Arp, R. S., Holmberg, K. S., and Littrell, J. M. "Launching Adult Students into the Job Market: A Support Group Approach." *Journal of Counseling and Development,* 1986, *65* (3), 166–167.

Aslanian, C. B., and Brickell, H. M. *Americans in Transition: Life Changes as Reasons for Adult Learning.* New York: College Entrance Examination Board, 1980.

Astin, A. W. *Four Critical Years: Effects of College on Beliefs, Attitudes and Knowledge.* San Francisco: Jossey-Bass, 1977.

Astin, A. W. "Student Involvement: A Developmental Theory for Higher Education." *Journal of College Student Personnel,* 1984, *25* (4), 297–308.

Astin, A. W. "The Importance of Student Involvement." *Journal of Counseling and Development,* 1986, *65,* 92–95.

Bach, B. *Higher Education for Adult Mental Health: The Role of the Large State System.* Memphis, Tenn.: Center for the Study of Higher Education, Memphis State University, 1982.

Baltes, P. B., and Reese, H. W. "The Life-Span Perspective in Developmental Psychology." In M. H. Bernstein and M. E. Lamb (eds.), *Developmental Psychology: An Advanced Textbook.* Hillsdale, N.J.: Erlbaum, 1984.

Baltes, P. B., and Willis, S. L. "Plasticity and Enhancement of Intellectual Functioning in Old Age: Penn State's Adult Development and Enrichment Project (ADEPT)." In F.I.M. Craik and S. E. Trehub (eds.), *Acting and Cognitive Processes.* New York: Plenum, 1982.

Barger, B., and Lynch, A. Q. "University Housing: A Healthy Learning Laboratory." In J. Katz (ed.), *Services for Students.* New Directions for Higher Education, no. 3. San Francisco: Jossey-Bass, 1973.

Barra, R. J. *Putting Quality Circles to Work: A Practical Strategy for Boosting Productivity and Profits.* New York: McGraw-Hill, 1983.

Barton, P. *Worklife Transitions: The Adult Learning Connection.* New York: McGraw-Hill, 1982.

Baruch, G. K., Biener, P., and Barnett, R. C. "Women and Gender in Research on Work and Family Stress." *American Psychologist,* 1987, *42* (2), 130–136.

Beal, P. E., and Noel, L. *What Works in Student Retention.* Boulder, Colo.: American College Testing Program and National Center for Higher Education Management Systems, 1980.

Belenky, M., Clinchy, B., Goldberger, N., and Tarule, J. *Women's Ways of Knowing.* New York: Basic Books, 1987.

Bernard, J. S. *The Female World.* New York: Free Press, 1981.

Bertaux, D. "The Life Course Approach as a Challenge to the Social Sciences." In T. K. Hareven and K. J. Adams (eds.), *Aging and Life Course Transitions: An Interdisciplinary Perspective.* New York: Guilford Press, 1982.

Boorstin, D. Comment on "MacNeil-Lehrer News Hour." Sept. 9, 1987.

Bowlsbey, J. "DISCOVER Recreated in 1987." *ACT Discover News.* Hunt Valley, Md.: American College Testing Co., 1987.

Bridges, W. *Transitions: Making Sense of Life's Changes.* Reading, Mass.: Addison-Wesley, 1980.

Brookfield, S. D. *Understanding and Facilitating Adult Learning.* San Francisco: Jossey-Bass, 1986.

Brown, R. D., and DeCoster, D. A. (eds.). *Mentoring-Transcript Systems for Promoting Student Growth.* New Directions for Higher Education, no. 19. San Francisco: Jossey-Bass, 1982.

Buhl, L. C., and Lindquist, J. "Academic Improvement Through Action Research." In *New Directions for Institutional Research: Increasing the Use of Institutional Research.* San Francisco: Jossey-Bass, 1981.

Campbell, A., Converse, P., and Rodgers, W. *The Quality of American Life.* New York: Russell Sage Foundation, 1976.

Campbell, J. (ed.). *The Portable Jung.* New York: Viking Press, 1971.

Campbell, M. D., Wilson, L. G., and Hanson, G. R. *The Invisible Minority: A Study of Adult University Students.* Final report submitted to the Hogg Foundation for Mental Health. Austin: Office of the Dean of Students, University of Texas, 1980.

Carnegie Foundation for the Advancement of Teaching. *Carnegie Survey of Undergraduates.* Washington, D.C.: Carnegie Foundation for the Advancement of Teaching, 1986.

Carnevale, A. P. "The Future of Higher Education, Part II." *CAEL NEWS,* 1987, *11* (2), 3-4.

Cattell, R. B. "Theory of Fluid and Crystallized Intelligence: A

Critical Experiment." *Journal of Educational Psychology,* 1983, *54,* 1–22.

Charner, I., and Schlossberg, N. K. "Variations by Theme: The Life Transitions of Clerical Workers." *Vocational Guidance Quarterly,* 1986, *34* (4), 212–224.

Chickering, A. W. *Education and Identity.* San Francisco: Jossey-Bass, 1969.

Chickering, A. W. "College Advising for the 1970s." In J. Katz (ed.), *Services for Students.* New Directions for Higher Education, no. 3. San Francisco: Jossey-Bass, 1973.

Chickering, A. W. *Commuting versus Resident Students: Overcoming the Educational Inequities of Living Off Campus.* San Francisco: Jossey-Bass, 1974.

Chickering, A. W. "Education, Work, and Human Development." In T. C. Little (ed.), *Making Sponsored Experiential Learning Standard Practice.* New Directions in Experiential Learning, no. 20. San Francisco: Jossey-Bass, 1983.

Chickering, A. W., and Associates. *The Modern American College: Responding to the New Realities of Diverse Students and a Changing Society.* San Francisco: Jossey-Bass, 1981.

Chickering, J. N., and Clement, J. *Warmline Training Manual.* Memphis, Tenn.: Center for Student Development, Memphis State University, 1987.

Coleman, J., and others. *Youth: Transition to Adulthood.* Chicago: University of Chicago Press, 1974.

Commission on Higher Education and the Adult Learner. *Postsecondary Institutions and the Adult Learner: A Self-study Assessment and Planning Guide.* Washington, D.C.: American Council on Education, 1984.

Cross, K. P. *Adults as Learners: Increasing Participation and Facilitating Learning.* San Francisco: Jossey-Bass, 1981.

Cross, K. P. "A Proposal to Improve Teaching or What 'Taking Teaching Seriously' Should Mean." AAHE *Bulletin,* 1986, *39* (1), 9–14.

Cullinane, M., and Williams, D. *Life, Career, Educational Planning: A Facilitator's Manual.* Suffern, N.Y.: Rockland Community College, 1983.

Daloz, L. A. *Effective Teaching and Mentoring: Realizing the*

Transformational Power in Adult Learning Experiences. San Francisco: Jossey-Bass, 1986.

Dalton, C. W., Thompson, P. H., and Price, R. L. "The Four Stages of Professional Careers: A New Look at Performance by Professionals." *Organizational Dynamics,* 1977, *6* (1), 19–42.

DeCoster, D. A., and Mable, P. M. (eds.). *Understanding Today's Students.* New Directions for Student Services, no. 16. San Francisco: Jossey-Bass, 1981.

Durcholz, P., and O'Connor, G. "Why Women Go Back to College. Women on Campus: The Unfinished Liberation." *Change Magazine,* 1975.

Erikson, E. H. "Identity in the Life Cycle." *Psychological Issues,* 1959, *1,* 18–164.

Fiske, M. "Changing Hierarchies of Commitment in Adulthood." In N. J. Smelser and E. H. Erickson (eds.), *Themes of Work and Love in Adulthood.* Cambridge, Mass.: Harvard University Press, 1980.

Gallagher, D., Thompson, L. W., and Levy, S. M. "Clinical Psychological Assessment of Older Adults." In L. W. Poon (ed.), *Aging in the 1980s: Psychological Issues.* Washington, D.C.: American Psychological Association, 1980.

Gibran, K. *The Prophet.* New York: Knopf, 1973.

Giesen, C. B., and Datan, N. "The Competent Older Woman." In N. Datan and N. Lohman (eds.), *Transitions in Aging.* Orlando, Fla.: Academic Press, 1980.

Gilley, J. W., Fulmer, K., and Reithlingshoefer, S. *Searching for Academic Excellence.* Washington, D.C.: American Council on Education, 1986.

Gilligan, C. *In a Different Voice.* Cambridge, Mass.: Harvard University Press, 1982.

Gould, R. *Transformations: Growth and Change in Adult Life.* New York: Simon & Schuster, 1978.

Gould, R. "Discussion of Schlossberg-Brammer-Abrego Papers." *The Counseling Psychologist,* 1981, *9* (2), 44–46.

Griffin-Pierson, S. "A New Look at Achievement Motivation in Women." *Journal of College Student Personnel,* July 1986, 313–317.

Gruebel, J. "Adults Learning by Television, a Reappraisal." *The College Board Review,* 1983, *128,* 11–15.

Gutman, D. C. "The Cross-Cultural Perspective: Notes Toward a Comparative Psychology of Aging." In J. E. Birren and K. W. Schaie (eds.), *Handbook of the Psychology of Aging.* New York: Van Nostrand Reinhold, 1977.

Hagestad, G. O. "The Changing World for Adults." Paper presented at the New Options for Adult Counselors Conference, College Park, Md., May 20, 1986.

Hammer, A. L. and Marting, M. S. *Manual for Coping Resources Inventory.* Palo Alto, Calif.: Consulting Psychologists Press, 1988.

Heath, D. *Growing Up in College.* San Francisco: Jossey-Bass, 1968.

Heilman, M. E. "Sometimes Beauty Can Be Beastly." *New York Times,* Sunday, June 22, 1980, p. E16.

Heitzmann, D., Schmidt, A. K., and Hurley, F. W. "Career Encounter: Career Decision Making Through On-Site Visits." *Journal of Counseling and Development,* 1986, *65* (4), 209–210.

Helmreich, R. L., and Spence, J. T. "Achievement-Related Motives and Behavior." In J. T. Spence (ed.), *Achievement and Achievement Motives: Psychological and Sociological Approaches.* New York: Freeman, 1983.

Hettler, B. "Strategies for Wellness and Recreation Program Development." In F. Leafgren (ed.), *Developing Campus Recreation and Wellness Programs.* New Directions for Student Services, no. 34. San Francisco: Jossey-Bass, 1986.

Hodgkinson, H. *Guess Who's Coming to College: Your Students in 1990.* Research Report, State-National Informational Network for Independent Higher Education. Washington, D.C.: National Institute for Independent Colleges and Universities, 1983.

Johnson, C. "New Perspectives on Career Counseling for Adults." In J. Miller (ed.), *Issues in Adult Career Counseling.* New Directions for Continuing Education, no. 32. San Francisco: Jossey-Bass, 1986.

Johnson, G. State of the University Address. George Mason University, Fairfax, Va., 1986.

Josselson, R. *Finding Herself: Pathways to Identity Development in Women.* San Francisco: Jossey-Bass, 1987.

Jung, C. G. *The Collected Works of C. G. Jung.* New York: Bollingen Foundation, 1953.

Kegan, R. *The Evolving Self: Problem and Process in Human Development.* Cambridge, Mass.: Harvard University Press, 1982.

Kelly, G. M. "A Factor Analytic Investigation of the Needs of Older Adults Enrolled in College." Ed.D. diss., Memphis State University, 1984. *Dissertation Abstracts International,* 1985, *46* (4), 873A.

Knefelkamp, L. L., and Moore, W. S. *The Measures of Intellectual Development: A Brief Review.* Farmville, Va.: Center for the Applications of Developmental Instruction, 1982.

Kohlberg, L. "Continuities in Childhood and Adult Moral Development Revisited." In P. B. Baltes and K. W. Schaie (eds.), *Life-Span Developmental Psychology: Personality and Socialization.* Orlando, Fla.: Academic Press, 1973.

Kohn, M. L. "Job Complexity and Adult Personality." In N. J. Smelser and E. H. Erickson (eds.), *Themes of Work and Love in Adulthood.* Cambridge, Mass.: Harvard University Press, 1980.

Kolb, D. A. "Learning Styles and Disciplinary Differences." In A. W. Chickering and Associates, *The Modern American College.* San Francisco: Jossey-Bass, 1981.

Kolb, D. A. *Experiential Learning: Experience as the Source of Learning and Development.* Englewood Cliffs, N.J.: Prentice-Hall, 1984.

Kuhlen, R. G. "Motivational Changes During the Adult Years." In R. G. Kuhlen (ed.), *Psychological Backgrounds for Adult Education.* Chicago: Center for the Study of Liberal Education for Adults, 1963.

Labouvie-Vief, G. "Individual Time, Social Time, and Intellectual Aging." In T. K. Hareven and K. J. Adams (eds.), *Aging and Life Course Transitions: An Interdisciplinary Perspective.* New York: Guilford Press, 1982.

Lazarus, R. S., and Folkman, S. *Stress, Appraisal, and Coping.* New York: Springer, 1984.

Levinson, D. J., and others. *The Seasons of a Man's Life.* New York: Ballantine Books, 1978.

Lindquist, J. "Curricular Implementation." In G. H. Quehl (ed.),

Developing the College Curriculum. Washington, D.C.: Council for Independent Colleges, 1977.

Lindquist, J. *Strategies for Change.* Washington, D.C.: Pacific Soundings Press, Council for Independent Colleges, 1978.

Lindquist, J., and Marienau, C. *Turning Colleges Toward Adults.* Memphis, Tenn.: Center for the Study of Higher Education, Memphis State University, 1981.

Lipman-Blumen, J. and Leavitt, H. S. "Vicarious and Direct Achievement Patterns in Adulthood." In N. K. Schlossberg, and A. D. Entine (eds.), *Counseling Adults.* Monterey, Calif.: Brooks/Cole, 1976.

Loevinger, J. *Ego Development: Conceptions and Theories.* San Francisco: Jossey-Bass, 1976.

Louis, M. R. "Surprise and Sense Making: What Newcomers Experience in Entering Unfamiliar Organizational Settings." *Administrative Science Quarterly,* June 1980, *25,* 226–251.

Lowenthal, M. F., and Pierce, R. "The Pretransitional Stance." In M. F. Lowenthal, M. Thurnher, and D. Chiriboga, (eds.), *Four Stages of Life: A Comparative Study of Men and Women Facing Transitions.* San Francisco: Jossey-Bass, 1975.

Lowenthal, M. F., Thurnher, M., and Chiriboga, D., (eds.). *Four Stages of Life: A Comparative Study of Men and Women Facing Transitions.* San Francisco: Jossey-Bass, 1975.

Lynch, A. Q. "Type Development and Student Development." In J. A. Provost and S. Anchors (eds.), *Applications of the Myers-Briggs Type Indicator in Higher Education.* Palo Alto, Calif.: Consulting Psychologists Press, 1987.

Lynch, A. Q., and Chickering, A. W. "Comprehensive Counseling and Support Programs for Adult Learners: Challenge to Higher Education." G. W. Walz and L. Benjamin (eds.), *New Perspectives on Counseling Adult Learners.* Ann Arbor, Mich.: ERIC/CAPS, 1984.

Lynch, A. Q., Doyle, R., and Chickering, A. W. *Higher Education for Adult Mental Health: Model Programs, Professional Development and Institutional Change to Serve Adult Learners.* Memphis, Tenn.: Center for the Study of Higher Education, Memphis State University, 1984.

Maccoby, E. E., and Jacklin, C. N. *The Psychology of Sex Differences.* Stanford, Calif.: Stanford University Press, 1974.

Maccoby, M. "Work and Human Development." *Professional Psychology,* 1980, *11* (3), 509–519.

Manske, D. H. *Report on Retention Strategies.* Memphis, Tenn.: Educational Support Program, Memphis State University, 1987.

Marris, P. *Loss and Change.* New York: Pantheon Books, 1974.

Maryland Public Television, Ohio University, and Maddux/Boldt Productions (producers). *Rites of Renewal.* Columbia, Md.: International University Consortium, 1985. [Videotape.]

Masnick, G., and Pitkin, J. *The Changing Population of States and Regions.* Cambridge, Mass.: MIT/Harvard Joint Center for Urban Studies, 1982.

Merton, R. K. *Social Theory and Social Structure.* Glencoe: Force Press, 1957a.

Merton, R. K. *The Student-Physician: Introductory Studies in the Sociology of Medical Education.* Cambridge, Mass.: Harvard University Press, 1957b.

Messick, S., and Associates. *Individuality in Learning.* San Francisco: Jossey-Bass, 1976.

Miller, J., Schooler, C., Kohn, M. L., and Miller, K. A. "Women and Work: The Psychological Effects of Occupational Conditions." *American Journal of Sociology,* 1979, *85* (1), 66–94.

Mohney, C., and Anderson, W. "The Effect of Life Events and Relationships on Adult Women's Decisions to Enroll in College." *Journal of Counseling and Development,* 1988, *66* (6), 271–274.

Moody, H. R. "Education in an Aging Society." *Daedalus,* 1986, *115* (1), 191–210.

Moos, R. H. *Evaluating Educational Environments.* San Francisco: Jossey-Bass, 1979.

Morris, E. R. "Description and Preliminary Analysis of the Effectiveness of the Child Care Voucher Program at the University of Washington." *NASPA Journal,* 1984, *22* (2), 59–63.

Morse, S. "Private Lives: Divorce at an Older Age." *Washington Post,* Mar. 20, 1984, p. B5.

Myerhoff, B. *Number Our Days.* New York: Dutton, 1978.

Myerhoff, B. "Rites and Signs of Ripening: The Intertwining of Ritual, Time, and Growing Older." In D. I. Kertzer and

J. Keith (eds.), *Age and Anthropological Theory.* Ithaca, N.Y.: Cornell University Press, 1984.

Myers, I. B. *Gifts Differing.* Palo Alto, Calif.: Consulting Psychologists Press, 1980.

Myers, I. B., and McCaulley, M. H. *Manual: A Guide to the Development and Use of the Myers-Briggs Type Indicator.* Palo Alto, Calif.: Consulting Psychologists Press, 1985.

National Institute of Education. *Involvement in Learning: Realizing the Potential of American Higher Education.* Study Group on the Conditions of Excellence in American Higher Education. Washington, D.C.: National Institute of Education, 1984.

Neugarten, B. L. (ed.). *Middle Age and Aging.* Chicago: University of Chicago Press, 1968.

Neugarten, B. L. "Time, Age, and the Life Cycle." *American Journal of Psychiatry,* 1979, *136* (7), 887–894.

Neugarten, B. L. *Successful Aging.* Paper presented to the annual meeting of the American Psychological Association, Washington, D.C., Aug. 1982.

Neugarten, B. L., and Neugarten, D. A. "The Changing Meanings of Age." *Psychology Today,* 1982, *21* (5), 29–33.

Pearlin, L. I. *Aging and Life Course Transitions: An Interdisciplinary Perspective.* New York: Guilford Press, 1982.

Pearlin, L. I., and Schooler, C. "The Structure of Coping." *Journal of Health and Social Behavior,* 1978, *19,* 2–21.

Perry, W. G. *Forms of Intellectual and Ethical Development in the College Years: A Scheme.* New York: Holt, Rinehart & Winston, 1968.

Perry, W. G. "Cognitive and Ethical Growth: The Making of Meaning." In A. W. Chickering and Associates, *The Modern American College.* San Francisco: Jossey-Bass, 1981.

Peters, T. J., and Waterman, R. H., Jr. *In Search of Excellence: Lessons from America's Best-Run Companies.* New York: Harper & Row, 1982.

Peterson, C., and Seligman, M. E. P. "Causal Explanations as a Risk Factor for Depression: Theory and Evidence." *Psychological Review,* 1984, *91* (3), 347–374.

Pleck, J. H. *The Myth of Masculinity.* Cambridge, Mass.: MIT Press, 1981.

Provost, J. A., and Anchors, S. *Applications of the Myers-Briggs Type Indicator in Higher Education.* Palo Alto, Calif.: Consulting Psychologists Press, 1987.

Quehl, G. N. (ed.). *Developing the College Curriculum.* Washington, D.C.: Council for Independent Colleges, 1977.

Rest, J. R. *Development in Judging Moral Issues.* Minneapolis, Minn.: University of Minnesota Press, 1979.

Riker, H. C. "Residential Learning." In A. W. Chickering and Associates, *The Modern American College.* San Francisco: Jossey-Bass, 1981.

Ritter, B. *Career Check-up Workshops.* College Park, Md.: Career Counseling Center, University of Maryland, 1987.

Rosen, B., and Jerdee, T. H. "Too Old or Not Too Old." *Harvard Business Review,* Nov./Dec. 1977, pp. 97–106.

Rosenberg, M., and McCullough, B. C. "Mattering: Inferred Significance and Mental Health Among Adolescents." In R. Simmons (ed.), *Research in Community and Mental Health,* vol. 2. Greenwich, Conn.: JAI Press, 1981.

Sandler, B. R., and Hall, R. M. "The Classroom Climate: A Chilly One for Women?" *Project on the Status and Education of Women.* Washington, D.C.: Association of American Colleges, 1982.

Sanford, N. *Self and Society: Social Change and Individual Development.* Hawthorne, N.Y.: Aldine, 1966.

Schlossberg, N. K. *Counseling Adults in Transition.* New York: Springer, 1984.

Schlossberg, N. K. "Taking the Mystery out of Change." *Psychology Today,* 1987, *21* (5), 74–75.

Schlossberg, N. K., Lassalle, A., and Golec, R. *The Mattering Scale for Adults in Higher Education* (6th ed.). College Park, Md.: University of Maryland, 1988.

Schlossberg, N. K., Troll, L. E., and Leibowitz, Z. *Perspectives on Counseling Adults: Issues and Skills.* Monterey, Calif.: Brooks/Cole, 1978.

Schlossberg, N. K., and Warren, B. *Growing up Adult: Reactions to Nontraditional Learning Experiences.* Columbia, Md.: Council for Advancement of Experiential Learning, 1985.

Schön, D. A. *The Reflective Practitioner: How Professionals Think in Action.* New York: Basic Books, 1983.

Siegel, J. S., and Taeuber, C. M. "Demographic Perspectives on the Long-Lived Society." *Daedalus*, 1986, *115* (1), 77–118.

Southern Regional Education Board. "Colleges Respond to Decline: Resistance Versus Adaptation." *Issues in Higher Education*, Nov. 17, 1981.

Spence, J. T. "Achievement American Style: The Rewards and Costs of Individualism." *American Psychologist*, 1985, *40* (12), 1285–1295.

Steele, B. H., Rue, P., Clement, L., and Zamostry, K. "Quality Circles: A Corporate Strategy Applied in a Student Services Setting." *Journal of College Student Personnel*, 1987, *28* (2), 146–151.

Steltenpohl, E., and Shipton, J. "Facilitating a Successful Transition to College for Adults." *Journal of Higher Education*, 1986, *57* (6), 637–658.

Study Group on the Conditions of Excellence in American Higher Education. *Involvement in Learning: Realizing the Potential of American Higher Education*. Washington, D.C.: National Institute of Education, 1984.

Super, D. E. "A Life Span, Life-Space Approach to Career Development." *Journal of Vocational Behavior*, 1980, *16*, 282–298.

Super, D. E., and others. *A Career Development Inventory*. Palo Alto, Calif.: Consulting Psychologists Press, 1981.

Sussman, M. B. "An Analytic Model for the Sociological Study of Retirement." In F. M. Carp (ed.), *Retirement*. New York: Human Sciences Press, 1972.

Sutton, R. I., and Kahn, R. L. "Prediction, Understanding, and Control as Antidotes to Organizational Stress." In F. M. Andrews (ed.), *Research on the Quality of Life*. Ann Arbor: Survey Research Center, Institute for Social Research, University of Michigan, 1986.

Task Panel on Prevention of the President's Commission on Mental Health. (G. W. Albee, Chmn.). In D. G. Forgays (ed.), *Environmental Influences and Strategies in Primary Prevention*. Hanover, N.H.: University Press of New England, 1978.

Thomas, R., and Chickering, A. W. "Education and Identity Revisited." *Journal of College Student Personnel*, 1984, *25*, 392–399.

Thomas, R., Murrell, P., and Chickering, A. W. "Theoretical Bases and Feasibility Issues for Mentoring and Developmental Transcripts." In R. D. Brown and D. A. DeCoster (eds.), *Mentoring-Transcript Systems for Promoting Student Growth*. San Francisco: Jossey-Bass, 1982.

Troll, L. *Continuations: Adult Development and Aging*. Monterey, Calif.: Brooks/Cole, 1982.

Troll, L., and Hagestad, G. O. "Horizontal Bonds: Marriage and Friendship." In Schlossberg and others, *The Adult Years: Continuity and Change*. Columbia, Md.: International University Consortium and Ohio State University, 1985.

Troll, L., and Nowak, C. "How Old Are You? The Question of Age Bias in the Counseling of Adults." *The Counseling Psychologist*, 1976, *6* (1), 41–43.

Trotter, R. J. "Stop Blaming Yourself." *Psychology Today*, 1987, *21* (2), 31–39.

Turner, V. *The Ritual Process*. Hawthorne, N.Y.: Aldine, 1969.

U.S. Department of Education. *Trends in Adult Student Enrollment*. Washington, D.C.: U.S. Department of Education, National Center for Educational Statistics, 1985.

Vaillant, G. E. *Adaptation to Life*. Boston: Little, Brown, 1977.

Viniar, B. "Adult Development Theory: The Medium and the Message." *Insight—An Annual Collection of Articles on Teaching and Learning by Faculty of the Community Colleges and State Universities of New York, 1983–1984*. Albany, N.Y.: New York State Board of Regents, 1984.

Warren, D. A. (ed.). *Improving Institutional Services to Adult Learners*. Washington, D.C.: Commission on Higher Education and the Adult Learner, American Council on Education, 1986.

Warren, W. H. (ed.). *Adult Learners: Impetus for Change*. Washington, D.C.: Commission on Higher Education and the Adult Learner, American Council on Higher Education, 1986.

Warren, W. S., and Madden, E. S. *Placement Services for Graduate Students*. Memphis, Tenn.: Placement Services, Memphis State University, 1986.

Weathersby, R. P., and Tarule, J. M. *Adult Development: Implications for Higher Education*. AAHE/ERIC/Higher Education

Research Report, no. 4. Washington, D.C.: American Association for Higher Education, 1980.

White, R. "Strategies of Adaptation: An Attempt at Systematic Description." In R. Moos (ed.), *Human Adaptation: Coping With Life Crises.* Lexington, Mass.: Heath, 1976a.

White, R. W. *The Enterprise of Living: A View of Personal Growth* (2d ed.) New York: Holt, Rinehart & Winston, 1976b.

White, R. W. "Humanitarian Concern." In A. W. Chickering and Associates, *The Modern American College.* San Francisco: Jossey-Bass, 1981.

Willis, S. L., and Baltes, P. B. "Intelligence in Adulthood and Aging: Contemporary Issues." In L. W. Poon (ed.), *Aging in the 1980s: Psychological Issues.* Washington, D.C.: American Psychological Association, 1980.

Winston, R. B., Miller, T. K., Enders, S. C., Grites, T. J., and Associates. *Developmental Academic Advising: Addressing Student Educational, Career and Personal Needs.* San Francisco: Jossey-Bass, 1984.

Witkin, H. A. "Cognitive Styles in Learning and Teaching." In F. Messick (ed.), *Individuality in Learning.* San Francisco: Jossey-Bass, 1976.

Woodward, K. L., and Kornaber, A. "Youth Is Maturing Later." *New York Times,* May 10, 1985, p. A31.

Index

A

Academic advisers: culminating reviews with, 173–174, 176–177; in support services, 124–126

ACE Adult Learner Assessment and Planning Guide: on academic advising, 125–126; on academic support services, 129–130; on admissions, 73–75; on assessment of prior learning, 85–86; on career development, 134; on commitment to adult learners, 118–119, 144; on culminating education, 188–189; on financial aid and planning, 78–79; on orientation, 82; on recruitment, 69–70; on residential life, 140; and self-assessment, 232, 236

Achievement: need for, at moving in stage, 41–42

Action research, and assessment for change, 232–233

Adams, W. W., 60–61, 63n, 64, 66–67, 170, 192, 193

Admissions: application questions for, 72–73; and entry programs, 71–75; institutional barriers to, 71–72; model of process for, 60–63; reading level of materials for, 66–67

Admissions Management Information Tracking System (ADMITS), 71

Adult development: change in, at moving on stage, 148–150, 163; and mental health, 201–203; principles of, 202–203; professional awareness of stages in, 245–246; and social clock, 93–94; stages of, 121

Adult Learner Needs Assessment Survey, 83, 131, 143, 236

Adult learners: and age, 2–3; agendas of, 18–20; applying new perspectives to, 1–12; barriers to, 28; benefits to, 191–207; competing demands on, 88, 109; conceptualizing, 13–20; conclusions on, 12, 206–207; culminating programs for, 168–190; as dependent, 7; differentiating qualities of, 20; entry programs for, 56–87; environmental changes for, 227–252; environmental fit with, 24–26; environments for, 23–32; and faculty interaction, 32, 223–224; goals for, 175; implications at moving in stage for, 39, 42–43, 44–45, 52–53; implications of moving on stage for, 150, 152–153, 157,